portuguese

Manuela Cook

TEACH YOURSELF BOOKS

For UK order queries: please contact Bookpoint Ltd, 130 Milton Park, Abingdon, Oxon OX14 4SB. Telephone: (44) 01235 827720. Fax: (44) 01235 400454. Lines are open from 9.00–18.00, Monday to Saturday, with a 24-hour message answering service. Email address: orders@bookpoint.co.uk

For U.S.A. order queries: please contact McGraw-Hill Customer Services, P.O. Box 545, Blacklick, OH 43004-0545, U.S.A. Telephone: 1-800-722-4726. Fax: 1-614-755-5645.

For Canada order queries: please contact McGraw-Hill Ryerson Ltd., 300 Water St, Whitby, Ontario L1N 9B6, Canada. Telephone: 905 430 5000. Fax: 905 430 5020.

Long renowned as the authoritative source for self-guided learning – with more than 30 million copies sold worldwide – the *Teach Yourself* series includes over 300 titles in the fields of languages, crafts, hobbies, business and education.

British Library Cataloguing in Publication Data

Library of Congress Catalog Card Number: on file.

First published in UK 1987 by Hodder Headline Plc, 338 Euston Road, London, NW1 3BH.

First published in US 1993 by NTC/Contemporary Publishing, 4255 West Touhy Avenue, Lincolnwood (Chicago), Illinois 60646 – 1975 U.S.A. This edition published by Contemporary Books, A Division of The McGraw Hill Companies.

This edition published 2001.

The 'Teach Yourself' name and logo are registered trade marks of Hodder & Stoughton Ltd.

Typeset by Transet Limited, Coventry, England.
Printed in Great Britain for Hodder & Stoughton Educational, a division of Hodder Headline Plc, 338 Euston Road, London NW1 3BH by Cox & Wyman Ltd, Reading, Berkshire.

Impression number   10 9 8 7 6 5 4 3 2 1
Year   2007 2006 2005 2004 2003 2002 2001

CONTENTS

INTRODUCTION

Welcome to *Teach Yourself Portuguese*!

Is this the right course for you?

If you are an adult learner with no previous knowledge of Portuguese and studying on your own, then this is the course for you. Perhaps you are taking up Portuguese again after a break from it, or you are intending to learn with the support of a class? Again, you will find this course very well suited to your purposes.

Developing your skills

The language introduced in this course is centred around realistic everyday situations. The emphasis is first and foremost on **using** Portuguese, but this course also aims to give you an idea of how the language works, so that you can create sentences of your own.

The course covers all four of the basic skills – listening and speaking, reading and writing. If you are working on your own, the audio recordings will be all the more important, as they will provide you with the essential opportunity to listen to Portuguese and to speak it within a controlled framework. You should therefore try to obtain a copy of the recordings if you haven't already got one.

The structure of this course

The course book contains **25 course units**, including an introductory unit, plus a **reference section** at the back of the book. There is also a two-hour

audio recording which you really need to have if you are going to get maximum benefit from the course. A number of icons will signpost the listening material and will help you find your way through the different sections in each unit.

The course units

The course units can be divided roughly into the following categories, although of course there is a certain amount of overlap from one category to another.

Statement of aims

At the beginning of each unit you will be told what you can expect to learn to do in Portuguese by the end of the unit.

Presentation of new language

In most units this is in the form of two or more initial dialogues ▓. These are recorded ▓ and also printed in the book. They introduce the main **topic area and language features** dealt with in the unit. Assistance with new vocabulary is given ▓. The language is presented in manageable chunks, building carefully on what you have learned in earlier units.

Practice of the new language

Under the rubric **Exercícios** (*Exercises*) ▓, practice is graded, so that activities which require mainly **recognition** come first. As you grow in confidence in manipulating the language forms, you will be encouraged to **produce** both in writing and in speech. Some of these activities also involve your response to audio recorded material ▓. At the end of the book you will find a **Key to the exercises** so that you can check your answers.

Pronunciation and intonation

The best way to acquire a good pronunciation and intonation is to listen to native speakers and to try to imitate them. But most people do not actually notice that certain sounds in Portuguese are pronounced differently from their English counterparts, until this is pointed out to them. For this reason specific advice and practice are included under **Como se pronuncia** (*How to pronounce it*) ▓ within the course units. There is also a **Pronunciation** guide at the end of the book which includes a table of Portuguese sounds. You will also find it at the end of the recording.

Key phrases and expressions

With the heading **Expressões-chave** (*Key phrases*) 🔑 you are given new vocabulary and groups of words that you can use in different situations related to the aims of the unit. At the end of the book there is a cross-section index of the several **Topics** covered in the different units, so that you can locate quickly key phrases and vocabulary of particular interest to you in each topic.

Description of language forms and grammar

In the section **Como funciona** (*How it works*) 🔧 you learn about the forms of the language, thus enabling you to construct your own sentences correctly. For those who are daunted by grammar, assistance is given in various ways. This includes the following, at the end of the book: a **Glossary of grammatical terms**; additional information on verbs and **Verb tables**; and a cross-section **Index to grammar and problem words**.

Vocabulary

New vocabulary is generally presented as it occurs. There is also a Portuguese–English and an English–Portuguese reference **Vocabulary list** at the end of the book, and you will be given practice on how to look up Portuguese verbs and other words as you would do in a dictionary.

Information on Portuguese-speaking countries

Throughout this course, you will find relevant information about aspects of the Portuguese-speaking world. This ranges from how to use the language for politeness, formality and informality, to material on cuisine, traditions and historical sights. Cultural notes appear in a variety of ways including dialogues, specific information items and 'real' texts from different sources.

Revision practice and self-assessment tests

To help you monitor your progress, exercises are provided at the end of each unit for you to check whether you have mastered the main points. Units 5, 10 and 15 are for consolidation and revision of what you have learned so far. There you will find plenty of additional opportunities to check your progress. The same applies to the last four units in the course, which contain material for overall revision of structures and for vocabulary expansion. Throughout you can see how well you have done by comparing your results with the **Key to the exercises** at the end of the book.

How to use this course

Make sure at the beginning of each course unit that you are clear about what you can expect to learn.

Read any background information that is provided. Then either read the initial dialogues or listen to them on the audio recording. With audio recordings try to get the gist of what is being said before you look at the printed text in the book. Then refer to the printed text and the boxed-in key words in order to study the dialogues in more detail. Listen to the dialogues again and try to imitate the speakers. First listen to and repeat each short set of words; then listen to and repeat each full sentence.

Don't fall into the trap of thinking you have 'done that' when you have listened to the audio a couple of times and worked through the dialogues in the book. You may **recognise** what you hear and read, but you almost certainly still have some way to go before you can **produce** the language of the dialogues correctly and fluently. This is why you are recommended to keep listening to the audio at every opportunity – sitting on the tube or bus, waiting at the dentist's or stuck in a traffic jam in the car, using what would otherwise be 'dead' time. Of course, you must also be internalising what you hear and making sense of it – just playing it in the background without really paying attention is not enough!

Move on to the **Certo ou errado?** (*Right or wrong?*) and the **Perguntas e respostas** (*Questions and answers*) exercises. These are mainly recognition activities which will further help you internalise the contents of the initial dialogues. Always check your results against the **Key to the exercises** at the end of the book before moving on.

Next read the English sound-alikes and other tips in the section **Como se pronuncia**. Listen to your cassettes/CDs and try to imitate the speakers. For extra help, refer to the **Pronunciation** guide in the back of the book.

Study the contents of the **Expressões-chave** section. Don't rush through, but make sure you take in all the new information. Imagine yourself in a situation in which you would use any Portuguese expressions you see in this section and say them aloud even if they are the same or close to what you met in the initial dialogues.

You can now study the **Como funciona** section. Grammar explanations have been made as user-friendly as possible. It is up to you just how much time you spend on studying and sorting out the points in this section. Some people find that they can do better by getting an ear for what sounds right, others need to know in detail how the language is put together. At this stage you may want to look up the relevant names in the **Glossary of grammatical terms** as well as the extra information on **Verbs** at the end of the book, where applicable.

You will then be ready to move on to the final set of **Exercícios** and work through the exercises following the instructions that precede them. Do not forget to check your answers carefully in the back of the book. It is easy to overlook your own mistakes. If you have a **study buddy** it's a good idea to check each other's answers.

Portuguese in the modern world

Portuguese is spoken by around 200 million people. It is the sixth most spoken language in the world and the third most spoken European language in the world, after English and Spanish. Portuguese is the official language of seven countries, in three continents, namely Angola, Brazil, Cape Verde, Guinea-Bissau, Mozambique, Portugal and São Tomé and Príncipe. There are also significant Portuguese-speaking communities in Canada and the United States of America; in South American countries such as Venezuela and Argentina; in France, Germany, Spain, other countries in continental Europe and in the British Isles; in South Africa and other African countries; in Australia; and in Macao and East Timor. Portuguese speakers across the world share a common language, and the different accents and local words are no obstacle to communication.

What kind of Portuguese am I learning?

The language chosen for your *Teach Yourself Portuguese* course is standard Portuguese, which will allow you to communicate with speakers anywhere in the Portuguese-speaking world. The audio recordings have been done by speakers from Portugal and from Brazil so that you become familiar with both accents.

Differences between Peninsular and South American Portuguese are explained throughout the course and highlighted with the abbreviation **Br.**

for Brazilian and **Eur.** for European which will also apply to Africa unless stated otherwise. Lexical and other alternatives, however, are not always mutually exclusive. For example, **comboio** (Eur.) / **trem** (Br.), for *train*, will mean that you should use the former east of the Atlantic Ocean and the latter in Brazil; but **vermelho / encarnado** (Eur.), for the colour *red*, will mean that the former circulates anywhere in the Portuguese-speaking world and you can also use the latter east of the Atlantic.

Where can I find real Portuguese?

Don't expect to be able to understand everything you hear or read straight away. If you watch Portuguese-speaking programmes on TV or buy newspapers or magazines written in Portuguese, you should not get discouraged when you realise how quickly native-speakers speak and how much vocabulary there is still to be learned. Just concentrate on a **small** extract – either a video/audio clip or a short article – and work through it till you have mastered it. In this way, you'll find that your command of Portuguese increases steadily.

When you visit a Portuguese-speaking country, make the most of any notices and advertisements directed at the general public. They can be good examples of everyday language presented in small chunks. You will find some 'real' texts in this volume which have been used with the kind permission of the respective organisations. The author is grateful for their cooperation.

But you don't have to leave home to keep in touch with authentic material. Television and radio options include the following:

– TV channel RTPI via satellite (Hotbird 2/13° East/11727.48 mhz/transponder 50/vertical polarization). Website: http://rtpi.rtp.pt/
– Radio station TSF over the Internet at http://www.tsf.pt

On-line LusoNEWS publishes news from across the Portuguese-speaking world in Portuguese, English and other languages. It usually includes a number of short information and publicity items which a beginner learner of Portuguese should be able to understand. It can be found at http://www.LusoNEWS.org

After having completed Unit 15, also try the following: http://www.aeiou.pt and http://achei.com.br. The former is specifically for Portugal and the latter for Brazil, but material on other Portuguese-speaking countries is also included.

Newspapers and magazines are a good source of topical and up-to-date reading as you progress through the course units. After having mastered Unit 20, you may wish to try some of the easiest pages of Expresso and Brasil Europa.

We hope you enjoy working your way through *Teach Yourself Portuguese*. Try not to let yourself get discouraged. Mastering a new language does take time and perseverance, and sometimes it can seem just too difficult. But then you'll come back to it another day and things will begin to make more sense again.

MUITO PRAZER
Delighted to meet you

In this introductory unit you will learn how to:

- greet people
- ask someone's name and give your name
- say goodbye

🎧 A) Greeting people

You will hear a number of people greeting each other. The first exchange is printed for you.

1 Look at the drawings and listen to the different greetings on your cassette/CD.

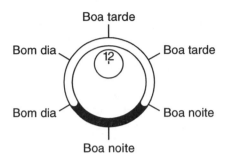

Boa tarde

Bom dia — Boa tarde

Bom dia — Boa noite

Boa noite

Bom dia   *Good morning*   **Boa noite**   *Good evening / night*
Boa tarde   *Good afternoon /*
   evening

---

2   Read the greetings above. Listen to the cassette/CD again and say each
    greeting, trying to imitate the speaker.

O dia means *the day*; **a tarde** is the part of the day between noon and
sunset; **a noite** is *the night*. Say **bom dia** from daybreak to midday. Say
boa tarde from midday until dark. Then switch over to **boa noite** until
daybreak. Note that you will find a translation for *good evening* in both
boa tarde and **boa noite**, depending on whether it is light or dark.

3   (*a*) Someone will meet you at the airport to take you to your hotel.
         You arrive at 11 pm. Greet the person.
    (*b*) At about 10 am you go into a bank to exchange currency. Greet the
         bank clerk.
    (*c*) It's 1 pm and you go into a restaurant. Greet the waiter.

4   You will hear some more people greeting each other. Listen to what
    they say and look at their mini-dialogues which are printed for you,
    below.

    – Boa noite, Sr. José.
    – Boa noite, D. Laura.

– Olá, boa noite.   – Oi! (Br.)
– Olá!   – Oi!

– Tudo bem?
– Tudo bem.

You can add words to make your greeting more formal. This is the case when you address a woman as **dona** or a man as **senhor**, usually abbreviated in writing as **D.** or **d.** and **Sr.** or **sr.** respectively. It will be even more formal if you address José by his surname as **Sr. Santos** (*Mr. Santos*).

For a very informal greeting, you can use **Olá!**, (*Hello!, Hi!*). **Oi!**, (*Hi!*), is a very informal greeting in Brazil.

Tudo bem is used both as a question and as a statement. When given a rising asking intonation, it corresponds to *How is it going? How are things?* (*literally, (Is) everything well?*). As a reply it means *Fine (All (is) well)*.

5 Listen to the formal and informal greetings again and repeat them after the speaker.

6 (*a*) Laura has greeted you formally. Reciprocate in the same manner. (It's 3 pm.)

  (*b*) Joana has greeted you very informally. Respond in the same way.

B) Asking someone's name and saying your name

1 You will hear some people who are meeting for the first time. They exchange names and shake hands. Listen to the recording and look at what they say, printed below.

– César Oliveira. Qual é seu nome?
– Fátima Rocha.
– Muito prazer.
– Muito prazer.

– Qual é o seu nome?
– Marcelo Ribeiro. E o seu?
– Cristina Silva.
– Muito prazer.
– Igualmente.

Qual é o seu nome? (Eur.)
   Qual é seu nome? (Br.)
 What is your name?
 O meu nome é .... (Eur.)
 Meu nome é .... (Br.)
 My name is ....
	E o seu? *And yours?*
	 Muito prazer *Delighted, Very*
	   pleased (to meet you)
	 Igualmente *Likewise*

2 Listen again several times to the people who are meeting for the first time.

3 When you feel confident, act out each one of the parts in the dialogues substituting your name.

C) *Saying goodbye*

1 You will hear four people saying goodbye. Look at the drawings and listen to what they say.

2 Now you will hear more goodbyes. Listen and tick the box(es) in the table below for each person. The first one is done for you.

Parting words	1	2	3	4
(a) bom dia				
(b) boa tarde	✔			
(c) boa noite				
(d) até logo				
(e) até breve				
(f) adeus				
(g) tchau				

Bom dia, **boa tarde** and **boa noite** are both greetings and parting words. Rather than formal, these expressions are neutral in tone. As with greetings, adding for example **dona Laura** or **senhor José** will add formality.

With people you know and friends, you may wish to use **adeus** in Portugal, where Brazilian **tchau** has also become popular. These can be used on their own or in conjunction with the other expressions: **Adeus, bom dia, até a próxima/até à próxima!** (Eur.); **Até logo, bom dia, tchau!**

Até breve corresponds to *See you / talk to you soon*. Expressions such as **até logo** and **até a próxima/até à próxima** (Eur.) also express the notion of '*see you again*'. In Portugal, the former may convey the meaning of '*see you again later today*'.

3 Listen again to the different parting words and repeat each goodbye after the speaker.

4 (*a*) It's mid-morning. You want to buy something and go to a shop. Say goodbye to the shop assistant when you leave.

   (*b*) You go to a restaurant for a meal in the early afternoon. Say goodbye to the waiter when you leave.

   (*c*) Say goodbye to your Portuguese colleague (you are having a business meeting later the same day).

   (*d*) Say bye to your Brazilian friend.

1 | ONDE É A SAÍDA?
Where is the exit?

This unit aims to help you find your way when you first arrive in a Portuguese-speaking country.

You will learn how to:

- ask the way
- understand simple directions
- seek clarification and help

 Onde é a saída?

 Portuguese Pedro is in the airport terminal. He stops Isabel, another passenger, to ask where the exit is. Listen to what they say and study the printed dialogue with the help of the words in the box below.

Pedro	Por favor, pode me dizer onde é a saída?
Isabel	Em frente, à direita.
Pedro	Como?
Isabel	Em frente, à direita.
Pedro	Obrigado.
Isabel	De nada.

por favor *excuse me, please*
pode me dizer...? *can you tell me...?*
(literally, *can (you) + me + to tell*)
onde *where*
é *is, (it) is*
a saída *the exit, way out*

em frente *straight on*
à direita *on the right*
como? *pardon?*
obrigado *thank you* (said by male)
de nada *not at all*

Onde são os telefones?

Ana wants to make a phone call. She approaches Paulo to ask where the telephones are. Listen to them and study the new words.

Ana   Desculpe, pode me dizer onde são os telefones?

Paulo (*pointing to the steps*) Lá em cima, no correio. O correio é à esquerda, a seguir ao banco e em frente da farmácia.

Ana   Como? Mais devagar, por favor.

Paulo Lá em cima..., no correio... O correio é à esquerda..., a seguir ao banco... e em frente da farmácia...

Ana   Obrigada.

Paulo De nada.

---

desculpe *sorry to trouble you*
são *are, (they) are*
os telefones *the telephones*
lá em cima *upstairs*
no (= **em** + **o**) **correio** *in the post office*
à esquerda *on the left*
a seguir ao (**a** + **o**) **banco** *past the bank* (lit. *past + to + the + bank*)

e *and*
em frente da (**de** + **a**) **farmácia** *opposite the chemist's* (lit. *in front of + the chemist's*)
mais devagar *more slowly*
obrigada *thank you* (said by female)

Exercícios *Exercises*

1.1 Certo ou errado? *Right or wrong?*

Tick the **C** or the **E** box for each statement below according to whether it is correct or not. The first tick has been entered for you.

	C	E
1 A saída é à esquerda.	❑	☑
2 A farmácia é lá em cima.	❑	❑
3 O correio é em frente da farmácia.	❑	❑

1.2 Perguntas e respostas *Questions and answers*

Choose the right answer and write it down.

1 Onde é a saída?
    (*a*) À direita.   (*b*) Em frente, à direita.

2 Onde é a farmácia?
    (*a*) Lá em cima, à direita.   (*b*) Lá em cima, a seguir ao correio.

3 Onde são os telefones?

   (a) No correio, lá em cima, em frente da farmácia e do banco.

   (b) No correio, lá em cima, à esquerda, em frente da farmácia.

🎧 *Como se pronuncia* How to pronounce it

Pronounce the following words trying to imitate the speaker on the cassette/CD. Pay special attention to the part highlighted in bold.

-ão and s**ão**:

   esta**ção** (*station*); perd**ão**!(*sorry!*). Say *ow* in *how*, through your nose.

-ões:

   informa**ções** (*information services/desk*). Say *o* in *note* plus *y* in *yet* but through your nose.

-lh-: reco**lh**a de bagagem (*baggage reclaim*). Say *lli* in *million*.

-nh-: sen**h**ora (*lady*). Say *ni* in *onion*.

For extra help, refer to the Pronunciation guide at the end of the book. There you will find more English sound-alikes and more information.

🔑 Expressões-chave Key phrases

Please and Thank you

Faz favor or **por favor** is literally a request for a favour. The former is used in Portugal. The latter is used on both sides of the Atlantic. Use **por favor** or **faz favor** (or **se faz favor**) when in English you would say *please* and/or *excuse me* to draw someone's attention or to accompany a request.

Por favor/Faz favor (Eur.),	*Excuse me, please, can*
pode me dizer onde é a saída?	*you tell me where the exit is?*

or simply,

Por favor / Faz favor (Eur.),	*Excuse me, please,*
onde é a saída?	*where is the exit?*

Pode me fazer um favor? (literally, *Can you do me a favour?*) is applicable when in English you would say *Can you help me?*

Both **desculpe** and **perdão** are an apology.

- Say **desculpe** instead of **por favor** or **faz favor** to draw someone's attention or to precede a request, when you feel that you are inconveniencing the person.

Desculpe, pode me dizer onde são os telefones?	*Sorry to trouble you, can you please tell me where the telephones are?*

(You have, for example, interrupted someone's conversation to ask your question.)

- Say **perdão** or **desculpe** when in English you would say *sorry* to apologise:

Perdão! or **Desculpe!**	*Sorry!*

(You have, for example, bumped into someone.)

Obrigado or **obrigada**   *thank you*   (literally, *obliged, grateful*) is understood as *I am grateful to you.* (For the different ending **-o/-a**, please see page 19.) **Muito obrigado** or **muito obrigada,** i.e., *much obliged,* corresponds to *Thank you very much.* (**Muito**) **agradecido** or (**Muito**) **agradecida** are alternatives with the same meaning.

Pardon?

Como? is the abridged version of **Como disse?** or **Como é?** (lit. *How did you say?* or *How is it?*). This is what you say when you cannot understand, as *Pardon?* in English.

When someone speaks too fast for you, you can also add **mais devagar, por favor / faz favor** as an easy way of asking the person to speak more slowly.

Directions and locations

Note that **lá em cima** and **lá em baixo** (Eur.) / **embaixo** (Br.) translate both *upstairs / downstairs* and *at the top / at the bottom.*

O banco é lá em cima.	*The bank is upstairs* or *at the top of this slope.*

Also, some words can be used for both direction and location:

em frente	*straight on*	*opposite*
à direita	*to the right*	*on the right*
à esquerda	*to the left*	*on the left*

As lojas são em frente.   *The shops are straight ahead.*
As lojas são em frente da   *The shops are opposite the*
   entrada.   *entrance.*

Como funciona   *How it works*

Gender

In Portuguese nouns are either masculine or feminine.

masculine	*feminine*
o homem (*the man*)	a mulher (*the woman*)
o banco (*the bank*)	a saída (*the exit*)
o câmbio (*the foreign exchange*)	a alfândega (*the customs*)

How can you tell whether a noun is masculine or feminine?

- By the meaning: masculine for male beings, feminine for female beings.

- By the ending: a noun ending in **-o** is likely to be masculine; a noun ending in **-a** is likely to be feminine, as also are nouns ending in **-gem**; **-dade**; **-tude**; **-ão** (when in the translation of the word the ending corresponds to the English *-ion*):

    a viagem (*the journey*); **a verdade** (*the truth*); **a juventude** (*the youth*); **a estação** (*the station*).

There are, however, exceptions – e.g. **o dia** (*the day*), **-a** but masculine – and the only sure way of knowing the gender is to learn each noun with its definite article (its word for *the*) which will be either **o** or **a**:

o before a noun shows that it is masculine.
a before a noun shows that it is feminine.

Always memorise a new noun with the **o** or **a** before it. In the vocabulary lists at the end of the book, (m) after a noun means that it takes an **o**, (f) that it takes an **a**.

Adjectives, and some other words when used as an adjective, are also masculine or feminine. This explains why:

■ you should say b**om** dia (m) for *good morning* (*good day*) but b**oa** noite (f) for *good evening / good night*.

■ for *thank you* you should say **obrigado** if you are a male but **obrigada** if you are a female.

Muito obriga**do** pela sua hospitalidade.	*Thank you very much for your hospitality.*
	(John talking to Janet)

the

The definite article (*the*) agrees with the noun in both gender (masculine or feminine) and number (singular or plural). In English we have only *the* but in Portuguese there is **o** (*m*.), **os** (m. plural) and **a** (*f*.), **as** (f. plural).

o homem, **os** homens	*the man, the men*
a saída, **as** saídas	*the exit, the exits*

Note that Portuguese **a** does not mean the same as English *a/an* but corresponds to *the*.

de

de can often be translated by the English prepositions *of* and *from*:

em frente **do** (=de + o) banco	(lit. *in front of the bank*)
	opposite the bank
longe **do** (=de + o) aeroporto	*far from the airport*

de is often used to link a noun to another word (noun or other) which adds some meaning to the first noun:

a bagagem **de** mão
the baggage of hand

the hand baggage

o depósito **de** bagagem (*left luggage lockers/office*), o bilhete **de** passagem (*travel ticket*), o cartão **de** embarque (Eur.) / a ficha **de** embarque (Br.) (*boarding card*), a porta (Eur.) / o portão (Br.) **de** embarque (*boarding gate*), a carta **de** condução (Eur.) / a carteira **de** motorista (Br.) (*driving licence*)

Contracted words

Some prepositions contract and combine with the definite article:

de + o	→ do	de + a	→ da	*off/from the*
a + o	→ ao	a + a	→ à	*to/at/on the*
em + o	→ no	em + a	→ na	*in/on the*

O hotel é **na** rua a seguir **à** estação   *The hotel is on the road past the*
no centro **da** cidade.   *station, in the town centre.*

Note the following:

– The Portuguese word **no** does not translate English *no*.
– Portuguese **a** as a preposition can translate English *for* and/or *to*, e.g., the Customs sign 'Nada **a** declarar' (lit. *nothing + for + to declare*) for *Nothing to declare*.

Plurals

Nouns, adjectives and some other words, when used as an adjective, follow the same basic rules.

Words ending with a vowel add **-s** in the plural:

telefone (*telephone*); telefone**s** (*telephones*)

But note that some **-ão** endings (often corresponding to *-ion* in English) change to **-ões**:

esta**ção** (*station*); esta**ções** (*stations*)

Words ending in a consonant other than **-m** or **-l** add **-es**:

mulher (*woman*); mulher**es** (*women*)

Words ending in **-m** substitute **-ns**:

home**m** (*man*); home**ns** (*men*)

Words ending in **-al** substitute **-ais**:

hospit**al** (*hospital*); hospit**ais** (*hospitals*)

Exercícios *Exercises*

1.3

You will hear five short dialogues in which the following places are mentioned.

(o) recebimento *or*
(a) recolha de bagagem
  baggage reclaim

(as) informações
information desk

(o) controle de passaporte
passport control

(o) ponto de encontro
meeting point

(os) sanitários
toilets
... para senhoras*
... for ladies
... para homens**
... for men

(o) aluguer de carros
(Eur.) /**(o) aluguel de
carros** (Br.) *car hire*

**(a) praça de táxis /
(o) ponto de táxi** (Br.)
taxi-rank

* signposted **S** (Senhoras) or **D** (Damas)
** signposted **H** (Homens) or **C** (Cavalheiros)

1.3.1 In these dialogues people are asking the way and being given directions. Listen to what they say and look at the pictures below. Tick two boxes that will take each person to the place he or she is looking for. The first one has been done for you.

(i)   A recolha de bagagem:

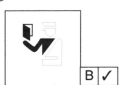

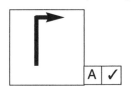

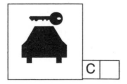

(ii)   As informações:

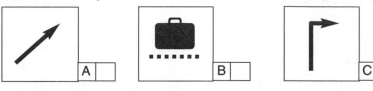

(iii)   Os sanitários para senhoras:

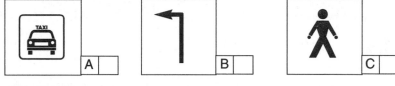

(iv)   O aluguer (Eur.) de carros:

(v)   A praça de táxis:

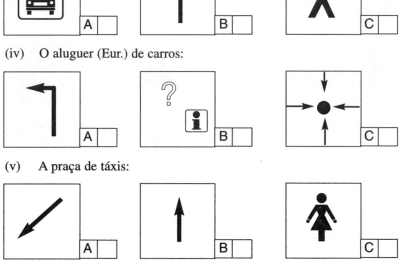

1.3.2   Now listen again to the dialogues and write them down.

1.4

1.4.1   Ask where the following is:

(*a*) the chemist's   (*b*) the bank
(*c*) the information desk   (*d*) the 'gents'

1.4.2   If you didn't quite catch what you were being told, what would you say to seek clarification?

1.4.3   What would you say to thank for the help received?

1.5

It is your turn to help others. You are going to hear some people asking the way. Look at the notices and fill in the boxes with the appropriate directions. But first listen to the example.

Example:

Chegadas	à direita

(i) Partidas Internacionais / International Departures

(ii) Partidas Domésticas / Domestic Departures

Your turn now:

(i) Partidas Internacionais	
(ii) Partidas Domésticas	

Say aloud what you have written down.

1.6

(o) câmbio de divisas	*foreign currency exchange*

A woman is asking for the foreign exchange bureau. Listen to her on your cassette/CD and rearrange the words below so as to match what she is saying.

Por favor, / o câmbio? / onde / pode / é / me / dizer

2 IDA E VOLTA, POR FAVOR
A return ticket, please

In this unit you will learn how to:

- buy travel tickets
- understand simple public notices
- ask for what you need on arrival

Para o Porto

 Clara is in a Portuguese railway station buying a ticket to Porto.

Clara	Queria um bilhete para o Porto.
Empregado	Ida e volta?
Clara	Sim, ida e volta, por favor.

Para São Paulo

Beatriz is in a Brazilian railway station buying a ticket to São Paulo.

Beatriz	Queria uma passagem para São Paulo.
Empregado	Ida e volta?
Beatriz	Não, somente ida, por favor.

queria I would like	**sim** yes
(lit. (*I*) *wanted*)	**uma passagem para** (Br.) *a/one*
um bilhete para (Eur.) *a/one*	fare to
ticket to	**não** no
(**a**) **ida e volta** return	**somente** only
(lit. *way there and back*)	(**a**) **ida** single

Para Coimbra

Alice is in a Portuguese coach station buying tickets to Coimbra.

Alice   Queria dois bilhetes de ida para Coimbra.
Empregado   Como? Quantos?
Alice   Dois, faz favor.

Para o Rio

Rosana is in a Brazilian coach station buying tickets to Rio de Janeiro.

Rosana   Queria duas passagens para o Rio, ida e volta.
Empregado   Como? Para onde?
Rosana   Para o Rio de Janeiro.
Empregado   Para hoje ou reserva?
Rosana   Como? Desculpe. Faça o favor de falar mais devagar.
Empregado   Para hoje... ou... reserva?
Rosana   Para hoje, por favor.

---

dois bilhetes (Eur.) *two tickets*
quantos? *how many?*
duas passagens (Br.) *two fares*
para onde? *where to?*
(lit. *to where*)
para hoje *for today*

ou *or*
(a) reserva *reservation*
faça o favor de falar *would you please speak* (more lit. *would (you) do the favour of + to speak*)

Exercícios

2.1 Certo ou errado?

           C   E

1 Para o Porto é ida e volta. ❏ ❏
2 Para Coimbra são dois bilhetes. ❏ ❏
3 Para São Paulo são duas passagens. ❏ ❏

2.2 Perguntas e respostas

1 Quantos são os bilhetes para o Porto?
   (a) Um.   *(b)* Dois.

2 Como são os bilhetes para Coimbra?
   (a) De ida.   *(b)* De ida e volta.

3 Quantas e como são as passagens para o Rio?
   (a) Uma de ida e volta.   *(b)* Duas de ida.
   (c) Duas de ida e volta.

🎧 Como se pronuncia

Say the English word *anchor* and see how you use the back of your mouth to obtain the *an* sound. Then practise these sounds with your cassette/CD.

vowel + -n:

   ba**n**co; ce**n**tro; fre**n**te; ci**n**co (*five*); ci**n**to (*belt*); o**n**de; lo**n**ge; po**n**to; e**n**co**n**tro.

vowel + -m:

   be**m**; se**m** (*without*); viage**m**; bagage**m**; passage**m**; si**m**; fi**m** (*end*); si**m**ples (*simple, single*); bo**m**; co**m** (*with*); u**m**.

🔑 Expressões-chave

Queria

By adding different words to **Queria** (*I would like*), you can ask for whatever you may first need, be it a train ticket or a cup of coffee.

Queria um bilhete para o Porto.	*I would like a ticket to Oporto.*
Queria uma passagem para São Paulo.	*I would like a fare to São Paulo.*
Queria um café.	*I would like a coffee.*

An even easier way of asking for something, when you expect it to be available, is just to say **Um** _____ or **Uma** _____ , accompanied by **por favor / faz favor** (Eur.).

Um bilhete para o Porto, faz favor.	*Please, ... a ticket to Oporto.*
Por favor, uma passagem para São Paulo.	*a fare to São Paulo.*
Um café, faz favor.	*a coffee.*

Similarly, when you take a taxi, you can tell the driver **Queria ir para** (*...to go to*) _____ , or simply **Para** _____ , adding where you want to go to.

Para o Hotel Sol-Mar, por favor. *Please, ... to the Hotel Sol-Mar.*

O bilhete de passagem

When purchasing **um bilhete de passagem**, *a travel ticket* the Portuguese prefer asking for a ticket (**um bilhete**) and the Brazilians for a fare (**uma passagem**). In both cases, the word for ticket or fare can be omitted and often the whole sentence is shortened.

	Please ...
Um de ida para o Porto, faz favor.	*one return to Oporto.*
Um, ida, para o Porto, faz favor.	*one return to Oporto.*
Por favor três, ida e volta, para o Rio.	*three returns to Rio.*

In some areas the word **simples** is also used for a single ticket.

	Please ...
Faz favor, um, simples, para Cascais.	*one single to Cascais.*

For practical purposes, in this course the ticket clerk and other individuals in the services sector are referred to as (**o**) **empregado**. Where a state-owned company is implied, the term (**o**) **funcionário** is also applicable, i.e., '(**o**) empregado do Estado'. The respective feminine forms are (**a**) **empregada** and (**a**) **funcionária**.

Favor

In addition to **por favor** and **faz favor** (Eur.), there are **faça favor** and **faça o favor de**. Common to all is the word '**favor**' (*favour*). Except for **por favor**, they also all share a form of 'fazer' (*to do*).

Faça favor is an elegant alternative version of **faz favor**.

Faz favor/faça favor, pode me dizer onde são os telefones?	*Excuse me, please, can you tell me where the telephones are?*

Faça o favor de... is another polite way of making a request.

Faça o favor de falar mais devagar	*Would you please speak more slowly?* or, more freely translated, *Could you please speak more slowly?*
Faça o favor de me dar um mapa.	*Could you please give me a map?*
Faça o favor de chamar um táxi para mim. / Faça o favor de me chamar um táxi (Eur.).	*Could you please send for a taxi for me?*
Faça o favor de me levar para o Hotel Sol-Mar.	*Could you please take me to the Hotel Sol-Mar?*

Faça o favor de... can also be used in public notices. A more impersonal but still courteous alternative is **É favor...** (lit. *it is (a) favour...*).

É favor esperar aqui.   for   *Please wait here.*

🗝 Como funciona

Oporto and Rio de Janeiro

English *Oporto* is, in fact, the Portuguese definite article – **o** – and the name of the Portuguese city – **Porto** – put together into one word. Indeed, the definite article is used with the name of a number of cities.

Queria um bilhete para o Porto.   *I would like a ticket to Oporto.*
Queria duas passagens para o Rio. *I would like two fares to Rio.*

This tendency applies to the name of countries and place-names where the name (or part of it) is recognisable as a common noun with an existence of its own.

Queria três para a Madeira.   *I would like three (tickets) to Madeira.*

a / an

For the indefinite article, in English we have *a* (or *an*), but in Portuguese we have **um** (m.) or **uma** (f.), as it agrees with the noun in both gender (masculine or feminine) and number (singular or plural).

um homem *(a man)*   **uma** saída *(an exit)*

Also **uns** or **umas**, which translates *some/any* in the sense of *a certain number* or *a certain quantity*, and *a certain* (= *specific*).

uns amigos, **umas** amigas   (*some/a few friends*)

Numbers 1 to 10

1 um / uma	3 três	5 cinco	7 sete	9 nove
2 dois / duas	4 quatro	6 seis	8 oito	10 dez

Note the following:

- there is a masculine and a feminine form for *one* and *two:* **um** / **uma** and **dois** / **duas.**

     um bilhete *(one ticket)*   **duas** passagens *(two fares)*

- **um** / **uma** can translate both the indefinite article (*a* or *an*) and the numeral *one*.

     um bilhete (*a ticket*)   **um** bilhete (*one ticket*)

Plurals

A few words (nouns and adjectives) end in **-s** in the singular and sound like a plural. They do not change.

     cais; cais (*quay*)   simples; simples (*simple, single*)

In the sequence noun + **de** + noun or other word, only the first element takes a plural ending.

     bilhete de passagem; bilhetes de passagem (*travel ticket, travel tickets*)
     fim de semana; fins de semana (*weekend; weekends*)

Verbs: the three conjugations

-ar, -er, -ir

All Portuguese verbs have one of the three infinitive endings above, with the exception of the verb **pôr** (*to put*) and its compounds, e.g., **compor** (*to compose*), **supor** (*to assume*). You do not need to use the accent (^) with the compounds.

Some verbs have anomalous forms, but most fall into one of three conjugation patterns according to their infinitive endings. Below are three regular verbs which will give you the model endings for the three conjugations throughout this course:

Infinitive

compr**ar** (*to buy*)   vend**er** (*to sell*)   part**ir** (*to leave*)

Past participle

compr**ado** (*bought*)   vend**ido** (*sold*)   part**ido** (*left*)

e.g. | **Vendido** | for a | *Sold* | notice

For verbs with anomalous forms see the Verb Guide at the back of the book. Always check a new verb against these notes.

Infinitives are often used in public notices and instructions as well as in a variety of other messages directed at the general public.

Some examples

> On a door: **Empurrar** (lit. *to push*) for *Push* or **Puxar** (lit. *to pull*) for *Pull*

> On a machine dispensing tickets, chocolates or drinks: **Introduzir as moedas** (lit. *to introduce + the coins*) for *Insert the coins.*

> On a food packet: **Consumir antes de** (lit. *to consume + before + of*) meaning *Use by* followed by a date.

> In a telephone booth, depending on the country you are in:

>> **Introduzir o cartão** *Insert the telephone credit card* or

>> **Depositar uma ou mais fichas** (lit. *to deposit...*) for *Insert one or more phone tokens.*

On a mobile phone: **Ler** (lit. *to read*), **Enviar** (lit. *to send*), for, respectively, *Read* and *Send* a text message.

Facing your aircraft seat: **Não fumar** (lit. *not to smoke*) and **Apertar cintos** (lit. *to fasten belts*), for, respectively, *No smoking* and *Fasten your belt.*

Note that there are two ways of wording, say, a *No smoking* sign: **Não fumar**, presented as an instruction, and **É proibido fumar**, presented as a prohibition. Past participles are also often used, as, e.g., **proibido** in **É proibido fumar**.

Exercícios

2.3

Work out what the following public notices and signs mean. You saw 1–3 on different doors; 4–5 at the railway station; 6–7 as you were travelling along the road; 8 in a restaurant; and 9 above a litter-bin in a public park.

In order to best work out their meaning, convert the past participles into their infinitives (e.g., **fechado** → **fechar**). When you have done so, look up the obtained word in the vocabulary at the end of the book.

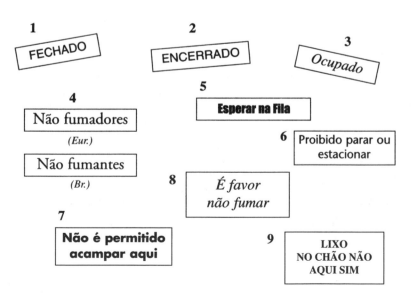

1 FECHADO

2 ENCERRADO

3 Ocupado

4 Não fumadores *(Eur.)*

Não fumantes *(Br.)*

5 Esperar na Fila

6 Proibido parar ou estacionar

7 Não é permitido acampar aqui

8 É favor não fumar

9 LIXO NO CHÃO NÃO AQUI SIM

2.4

You will hear a number of people asking for various things.

2.4.1   Number the boxes in the order of what you hear. The first one you hear has been done for you.

(i) um mapa *a map*	
(ii) dois cafés *two coffees*	*1*
(iii) quatro sandes (Eur.) / sanduíches *four sandwiches*	
(iv) papel de carta e uma caneta *writing paper and a pen*	
(v) um penso adesivo (Eur.)/ esparadrapo (Br.) *a sticking plaster*	
(vi) alguma coisa para dor de cabeça *something for a headache*	
(vii) alguma coisa para indigestão *something for indigestion*	
(viii) alguma coisa para queimadura de sol *something for sunburn*	

2.4.2   Listen again to the different requests and write them down. Then take these people's place and ask for the same things as they did.

2.5

You will hear different people buying train, coach, ferry and air tickets.

2.5.1   Complete and tick the boxes according to how many tickets they want and whether these are single or return fares. The first line has been done for you.

	Quantos bilhetes? (Eur.) / Quantas passagens? (Br.)	Para onde?	Ida / Simples	Ida e volta
(i)	*três*	Faro	✓	
(ii)		Porto		
(iii)		Cacilhas		
(iv)		Estoril		
(v)		Manaus		
(vi)		Belo Horizonte		
(vii)		Rio		
(viii)		Salvador		

2.5.2   Listen again to the recording and repeat what you hear.

2.5.3   Now buy these tickets:

(i)   In Brazil, going by train
      to Belo Horizonte

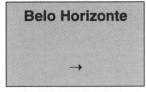

x 2

(ii) In Portugal, going by coach
      to Faro

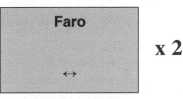

x 2

(iii) In Brazil, flying
      to Manaus

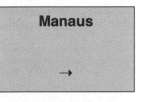

x 4

(iv) In Portugal, crossing the Tagus
      in Lisbon

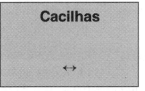

x 8

2.6

2.6.1   Rearrange the words below so as to ask whether:

(i) you can have the telephone directory – (**a**) **lista dos telefones**
    Pode / a lista / me / dos telefones? / dar

(ii) you can be put through – **ligar** – to 'this number'– **este número**
    Pode / para / este número? / me / ligar

2.6.2   Listen to the two voices on your recording and find out:

(i) the telephone booth – (**a**) **cabine** – you are being directed to for
     your call – (**a**) **chamada** – at the post office.

(ii) the cashdesk – (**a**) **caixa** – you are being directed to when cashing
     traveller's cheques – (**os**) **cheques de viagem** – at the bank.

3 | UM QUARTO SIMPLES OU DUPLO?

A single or double room?

In this unit you will learn how to:

- book in at a hotel
- find your way around town
- locate shops and services

 Na estação

 Maria goes to the information desk to look for a hotel.

Maria	Por favor, pode me dizer onde fica o hotel mais próximo?
Empregado	O hotel mais próximo fica na primeira rua à esquerda a seguir à estação. É o Hotel Central.
Maria	É longe?
Empregado	Não, não é. Fica perto, a uns dez minutos a pé.
Maria	Muito obrigada. Bom dia.
Empregado	Não tem de quê. Bom dia.

---

fica *is, (it) is*
(alternative to **é** for location)
o hotel mais próximo *the nearest hotel* (lit. *the hotel most near*)
(a) primeira rua *first street*
é longe? *is (it) far?*

não, não é *no, (it) is not*
perto *near, nearby*
a uns dez minutos *about ten minutes* (lit. *at some ten minutes*)
a pé *on foot, walking*
não tem de quê (alt. to **de nada**)

Na recepção do Hotel Central

Maria is at the reception desk at the Hotel Central asking for a room.

Maria　　　　　Tem quartos vagos? Queria um quarto simples, para uma noite.

Recepcionista　(*checking*) Um momento. Vago somente quarto duplo, com cama dupla.

Maria　　　　　Duplo... Pode me mostrar o quarto?

Recepcionista　Claro! Fica lá em cima no segundo andar. A escada é à direita e o elevador é a seguir. Com licença...
(*stepping in front of Maria to lead the way*).

Maria　　　　　(*after viewing the room*) Está bem. Fico com o quarto. (*back in reception*)

Recepcionista　Tem um documento de identidade? (*Maria produces her passport.*) Faça o favor de assinar. (*Maria signs the registration form.*) Obrigado. Aqui está a chave do quarto.

---

tem...? *have (you), has (it)?*
(o) quarto vago *vacant room*
simples, duplo *single or double*
um momento *just a moment (please)*
(a) cama dupla *double bed*
mostrar *(to) show*
claro *of course*
(o) segundo andar *second floor*
a escada *the stairs, staircase*

o elevador *the lift*
com licença *excuse me*
está bem *it's all right, okay*
fico com *I'll have (lit. (I) have)*
um documento de identidade
　an identification document
assinar *to sign*
aqui está *here (it) is*
a chave *the key*

Exercícios

3.1 Certo ou errado?

		C	E
1	O hotel é longe.	❑	❑
2	O hotel tem um quarto vago.	❑	❑
3	O quarto tem cama dupla.	❑	❑

3.2 Perguntas e respostas

1 Onde fica a rua do hotel?
   (a) Na primeira à direita a seguir à estação.
   (b) Na primeira à esquerda a seguir à estação.
2 Onde fica o quarto duplo?
   (a) Lá em baixo(Eur.)/embaixo(Br.).
   (b) Lá em cima no primeiro andar.
   (c) Lá em cima no segundo andar.
3 Onde é o elevador?
   (a) Longe da escada.   *(b)* Perto da escada.

🎧 Como se pronuncia

Below are some sounds for you to pronounce after the speaker on your cassette/CD. They are diphthongs, in other words, sounds such as in the English word *coin* where you begin with one vowel (*o*) but move towards another (*i*).

-ai-: m**ai**s.   **-au-**: **au**tomóvel.   **-ei-**: dir**ei**ta; chuv**ei**ro.
-eu-: m**eu**; mus**eu**.   **-oi-**: d**oi**s; n**oi**te.   **-ou-**: **ou**.
                      -ui-: m**ui**to.

In 'pr**ai**a' the diphthong -ai- is followed by the usual ending -a.

Note that there are vowel sequences which are not diphthongs. Instead each vowel is pronounced separately. Practise the following:

d**ia** (=di+a); b**oa** (=bo+a); d**ua**s (=du+as); sa**í**da (sa+í+da) (in sa**í**da the accent over the **i** is used to 'undo' the diphthong -ai-).

🗝 Expressões-chave

Somewhere to stay

There is a wide range of options as regards where to stay. These include hotel (**o hotel**), boarding house (**a pensão**), motel (**o motel**), inn (**a pousada** *or* **a estalagem** *or* **a albergaria**), students' hostel (**o albergue da juventude** *or* **o lar de estudantes**), camping / caravanning complex (**o parque de campismo** (Eur.) *or* **a aldeia de campistas** (Eur.) *or* **o camping** (Br.)). Or you may opt for a small holiday house advertised under names such as **a vila** or **o chalé**.

You may wish to have a double room (**um quarto duplo** *or* **um quarto de casal**) with double bed (**com cama dupla** *or* **com cama de casal**) or twin beds (**com duas camas** *or* **com camas individuais**). You may want instead a single room (**um quarto simples** *or* **um quarto individual** *or* **um quarto de solteiro** *or* **um quarto de pessoa só**). Particularly in Brazil, **o quarto** may not be expected to include a private bathroom, but **o apartamento** will. **O apartamento** covers a wide meaning which can range from a small flat to a bedsitter or a hotel room with en-suite bathroom and, in some cases, a kitchenette (**uma pequena cozinha**).

To ask for private bathroom facilities, you can just say **com banho**. If you wish to be more specific, say **com chuveiro** or **com duche** (Eur.) / **ducha** (Br.) to ask for a shower, and **com banheira** to ask for a bathtub. **A casa de banho** (Eur.) / **o banheiro** (Br.) is the bathroom. This name is also used euphemistically as an alternative word to **o sanitário** when referring to the toilet, a term equally used as **o toilete** (Eur.) or **o toalete** (Br.). 'Facilities for the disabled' finds its translation in (**as**) **instalações** or (**as**) **facilidades para deficientes físicos**.

A diária is the daily cost of your stay at a hotel. What you pay for your room usually includes breakfast – **o pequeno almoço** (Eur.) / **o café da manhã** (Br.). In some cases this may be spelt out as 'bed and breakfast' – **dormida e pequeno almoço** (Eur.) / **pernoite e café da manhã** (Br.). Alternatively half-board (**meia pensão**) and full-board (**pensão completa**) may also be available.

Queria... Pode... Faça o favor de...

You have come across these three different approaches to asking for something. Although often they are interchangeable, they also play specific roles. The following guidelines will help you select which to use:

Queria..., (*I would like*) puts the focus on you, the person who is making the request.

    Queria um quarto simples.   *I would like a single room.*

Pode... ? (*Can you... ?*) and **Faça o favor de ...** (*Would you please.../ Would you kindly... / Could you please...*) put the focus on the person who is being asked to help. The former is better reserved for cases when you are enquiring about possibility rather than willingness.

> **Pode me dar um quarto simples?** *May I have a single room?*
> *(Can you give me a single room?)*
> – is better for making an enquiry.
>
> **Faça o favor de me dar um** *May I have a single room?*
> **quarto simples.** *(Would you kindly give me a single room?)* – is better for making a request.

Com licença

Com licença means, literally, *with (your) permission*. Use this expression when in English you would say *Excuse me* to accompany an action, for example, when you need someone to step back for you to get through the door or a line of people or when you are trying to get out of a crowded train or bus.

▣ Como funciona

quarto vago *and* bom dia

Word-order:

Noun + adjective is the usual word-order.

quarto vago
room   vacant

vacant room

This applies both to adjectives and adjective-like words such as past participles used adjectivally, as in the following 'no entry' sign:

entrada proibida *no entry* (lit. *entry prohibited*)

However, adjective + noun is the word-order when the adjective, or adjective-like word, is used in a less literal and/or more emotive sense.

pequeno almoço (Eur.) i.e., *small lunch*, for *breakfast*
bom dia! *good morning!*

The latter word-order also applies for ordinal numbers.

segundo andar *second floor*; **primeira rua** *first road, street*

Agreement:

Adjectives, adjective-like words and ordinals must agree with their noun in both gender (masculine or feminine) and number (singular or plural).

Fem. pl.	entradas proibidas	*Masc. sing.*	pequeno almoço (Eur.)
Fem. sing.	primeira rua		segundo andar
Masc. pl.	quartos vagos		bom dia

not and no

To make the verb negative, i.e., 'not', just say **não** before the verb.

O hotel **não** é longe. *The hotel is not far.*

Note that **não** can translate both *no* and *not*.

Não, o hotel **não** é longe. *No, the hotel is not far.*

More than one element of negation can be present in the same sentence. This is the practice when **nada** (*nothing*), **nenhum** (*none*) or **ninguém** (*no one*) comes after the verb. For example, you use a double negative when you tell the customs officer that you have not got anything to declare: **Não** tenho **nada** a declarar.

é – fica – está

Use **é** (*it*) *is*, for location of non-movables.

O hotel **é** na primeira rua   *The hotel is in the first road*
à esquerda.   *on the left.*

Use **está** (*it*) *is*, for something that can change easily as is the case with the location of movables.

Aqui **está** a chave.   *Here is the key (your key).*

Fica can be used as an alternative to **é** above:

> O hotel **fica** na primeira rua *The hotel is in the first road*
> à esquerda.   *on the left.*

The plural to **é**, **fica** and **está** is, respectively, **são**, **ficam** and **estão**.

> Os hotéis **são / ficam** na primeira *The hotels are in the first*
> rua à direita.   *road on the left.*

Aqui **estão** as chaves. *Here are the keys (your keys).*

Fico com is used to say that you accept something (an object).

> **Fico** com o quarto. *I'll have the room,*
>   *I'll keep the room.*

your

In English we use *your* more often than its Portuguese counterpart **seu** (m.) or **sua** (f.).

> Aqui está a chave. *Here is your key.*

Another difference is that in Portuguese the definite article (**o/a**) can be used with *your* and the other possessives: **o seu – a sua** (*your*); **o meu – a minha** (*my*). However, in Brazil it is often omitted.

> **A sua** mala *or* **Sua** mala

'ping-pong' replies

Sim translates *yes*. However, in a *yes* reply, the main verb of the question tends to be bounced back instead. This is known as the reiterative reply. **Sim** may follow, or precede, the reiteration but is often omitted.

> Question: É longe?   *Is it far?*
> Reply: **É.** *or* **É**, sim. *or* Sim, **é.**   *Yes, it is.*

In a *no* reply, there is a tendency to add the verb, in the negative.

> Question: É longe?   *Is it far?*
> Reply: **Não, não** é.   *No, it isn't.*

🎧 Exercícios

3.3

You will hear some people asking for hotel accommodation.

3.3.1 Listen to what each one would like and tick the row of pictures it matches. The first one you will hear has been entered for you.

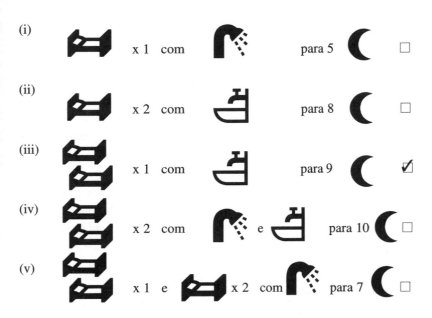

(i) x 1 com para 5 ☐

(ii) x 2 com para 8 ☐

(iii) x 1 com para 9 ☑

(iv) x 2 com e para 10 ☐

(v) x 1 e x 2 com para 7 ☐

3.3.2 Write down what the five people have said, and read aloud what you have written.

3.4

Say that you would like the following:

(*a*) One single room, with shower, for one night.
(*b*) A double room, with bathtub, for two nights.
(*c*) One double room and one single room, with shower and bathtub, for seven nights.
(*d*) A double room, with shower, for five nights. Add that you would like two beds.

3.5 O nome – *Your name*

(o) nome de baptismo (Eur.) / **batismo** (Br.)	*Christian name*	or
(o) nome próprio (Eur.) / **(o) prenome** (Br.)	*first name, given name*	
(o) nome de família	*family name*	or
(o) apelido (Eur.) / **(o) sobrenome** (Br.)	*surname*	

3.5.1 Make a mental note of how a Portuguese full name – **(o) nome completo** – is made up.

As in English, most people have two given names, but, unlike English, they may have a number of surnames. E.g., Ana Isabel Vieira Gama Magalhães – Given names: Ana Isabel. Surnames: Vieira (from her mother), Gama (from her father), Magalhães (from her husband).

3.5.2 Stewart Martin is booking in at a hotel. There is some confusion about his name. How could he explain the following in Portuguese:

Stewart is the first name and Martin is the surname.

 ### 3.6

You will hear people requesting and giving directions in town.

3.6.1 Study the map on the opposite page. Then listen to the different people asking the way on your cassette/CD. Put a number against the place each one wants to go to.

(a) estrada *open road*	**(o) turismo** *tourist office*
(o) supermercado *supermarket*	**(a) paragem de autocarros** (Eur.) /
(a) bomba de gasolina *petrol pump, fuel pump*	**(a) parada de ônibus** *or* **(o) ponto de ônibus** (Br.) *bus stop*
(o) restaurante *restaurant*	**(a) passagem subterrânea** *subway*
(a) igreja *church*	(lit. *underground passage*)
(o) museu *museum*	**(a) praia** *beach*

3.6.2 Listen again, repeating each question after the speaker.

3.6.3 Miguel is equally trying to find his way through town. He is standing where the cross is, facing Rua da República. On page 43 are directions Miguel has been given.

Write Miguel's question for each direction received, starting with **Por favor / Faz favor, pode me dizer onde...** Then read them aloud.

---

atrás (de) *behind* **ao lado (de)** *beside* **no fim (de)** *at the end*

em frente a = em frente de

(i) É a estrada à esquerda, no fim da Rua da República.
(ii) Fica lá em baixo (Eur.) / lá embaixo(Br.), à direita, no fim da Rua da República.
(iii) É à direita, no fim da Rua da República, a seguir à estação.
(iv) Fica em frente do turismo. A entrada é em frente à igreja.
(v) Fica na rua atrás, à esquerda, a seguir ao banco.
(vi) É atrás do correio, ao lado da estação.
(vii) São na Rua da República, à esquerda, a seguir à farmácia e em frente ao restaurante.
(viii) Fica numa rua atrás da igreja.

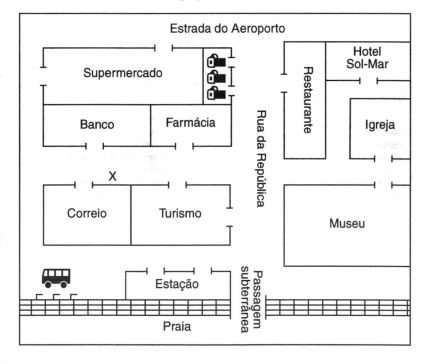

4 | TEM PÃO E LEITE?
Do you stock bread and milk?

In this unit you will learn how to:

- ask for what you want in a shop
- ask whether what you want is available
- book in at a caravan or camping site

  ### Numa loja

 At a convenience store Sandra is asking the sales assistant whether what she is looking for is available.

Sandra   Por favor, tem pão e leite?

Vendedor   O pão e o leite estão à esquerda a seguir às frutas. (*Sandra takes her shopping to the checkout.*)

Vendedor   Uma garrafa de leite, dois pães, meia dúzia de ovos, três maçãs e quatro bananas. Mais alguma coisa?

Sandra   Queria, sim, mas provavelmente não tem. Queria um guarda-chuva.

Vendedor   Não, nesta loja não. Mas pode encontrar guarda-chuvas numa das lojas mais perto da cidade. Não ficam longe.

---

estão *are, (they) are*	**mais alguma coisa?** *anything else?*
(a) fruta *fruit*	(lit. *more + some + thing*)
uma garrafa de leite *a/one bottle of milk*	**mas** *but*
dois pães *two loaves of bread*	**provavelmente** *probably*
meia dúzia *half a dozen*	**(o) guarda-chuva** *umbrella*
(o) ovo *egg*	**nesta** (= **em** + **esta**) *in this*
(a) maçã *apple*	**encontrar** *to find*
(a) banana *banana*	**numa** (= **em** + **uma**) *in one*

No turismo

Mário is finding out whether the campsite he has been recommended has a space for his large caravan and family tent.

Empregada	Este está quase cheio. Não tem vagas para veículos grandes ou barracas, somente para automóveis e tendas. Há outro aqui perto, com vagas, mas não tem piscina.
Mário	Não tem importância. Queria uma reserva. (*before leaving*) Desculpe, pode me fazer o favor de indicar o caminho?
Empregada	Continuando nesta estrada e virando à direita no segundo semáforo, fica à esquerda. Fica a uns dez minutos daqui, de carro, claro.

este *this, this one*	**(a) piscina** *swimming pool*
quase cheio *nearly full*	**não tem importância** *it doesn't matter*
(a) vaga *vacancy*	(lit. *not + has + importance*)
(o) veículo grande *large vehicle*	**indicar o caminho** *to direct*
(a) barraca *tent, frame tent*	**(o) caminho** *way, route*
(o) automóvel *automobile, car*	**continuando** *continuing*
(a) tenda *tent, ridge or bell tent*	**virando** *turning*
há... *there is...*	**(o) semáforo** *traffic lights*
outro *other, another one*	**daqui** (= **de** + **aqui**) *from here*
aqui perto *nearby* (lit. *here + near*)	**de carro** *by car*

Exercícios

4.1 Certo ou errado?

                                                           C   E

1 Na loja há pão. ❑ ❑

2 O primeiro parque de campismo (Eur.) /
   camping (Br.) está cheio ❑ ❑

3 O segundo parque de campismo (Eur.) /
   camping (Br.) tem piscina ❑ ❑

4.2 Perguntas e respostas

1 Loja: Tem pão e leite?
   (*a*) Não, tem somente frutas.   (*b*) Tem, tem pão e leite.

2 Primeiro parque de campismo (Eur.) / camping (Br.): Tem vagas?
   (*a*) Não, não tem vagas.   (*b*) Tem, para automóveis e tendas.

3   Segundo parque de campismo (Eur.) / camping (Br.): Onde fica?
    (a) Fica perto do segundo semáforo.
    (b) Fica nesta estrada, a dez minutos daqui, a pé.

🎧 Como se pronuncia

Below there are some singular-to-plural sound changes for you to practise following the speaker on the cassette/CD. See also the section on Plurals in Unit 1 and later in the present Unit.

-l to **-is**:
   hospital → hospitais; hotel → hotéis; automóvel →
   automóveis; lençol → lençóis.

-o- (say English o in *note*) to **-o-** (say English o in *jolly*):
   ovo → ovos; novo → novos; almoço → almoços.

-ão to **-ões** (revise what you learned about **-ão** and **-ões** in Unit 1):
   estação → estações; informação → informações.

-ão to **-ães** (say *ey* in *they* but through your nose):
   pão → pães.

Note that **-ão**, **-ões** and **-ães** are all nasal diphthongs (revise what you learned about diphthongs in Unit 3).

🔑 Expressões-chave

Tem...

We have been using different ways of asking for something when you can expect it to be available – **queria...**; **faça o favor de me dar...**

If, however, you don't know whether what you want is available, then use one of the following approaches:

   tem...? *have you got?*
   há...? *is / are there...?*

which you can precede with **por favor**, **faz favor** or **desculpe**.

   Por favor, tem pão e leite?   *Excuse me, please, do you stock*
                                        bread and milk?

Similarly,

> **Faz favor, tem vagas?** (*any hotel rooms / any campsite spaces available?*)
>
> **Desculpe, tem sacos de dormir?** (*sleeping bags?*)
>
> **Por favor, tem uma mesa vaga?** (*a table free?*)
>
> **Faz favor, há lojas aqui perto?** or **... perto daqui?** (*any shops nearby?*)
>
> **Por favor, há água potável por aqui?** (*drinking water hereabouts?*)

Although **há...?** / **há...**, (*is there...?* / *there is...*) is used on both sides of the Atlantic, some Brazilians also use **tem...?** for *have you got...?* in the sense of *has one got...?/ is there...?*. Therefore, the question **Tem pão e leite?** may receive the reply **Tenho** (*Yes, (I) have*); or the reply **Temos**, *Yes, (we) have*; or the reply **Tem**, meaning both *Yes, (you) have / one has* and *there is/are*.

Another special use of **tem** can be found, this time on both sides of the Atlantic, where **tem** is used to express a relationship that in English is expressed with *your* when something is being handed over.

Aqui tem o recibo.	*Here is your receipt.*
	(lit. *here (you) have the receipt*)
Aqui tem a chave.	*Here is your key.*
	(lit. *here (you) have the key*)

This is an alternative to

Aqui está o recibo.	*Here is your receipt.*
	(lit. *here is the receipt*)
Aqui está a chave.	*Here is your key.*
	(lit. *here is the key*)

Motor caravans and towed caravans

Um carro de moradia (*caravan*, lit. *a home car*) can be motorised (**motorizado**) or towed by an automobile (**rebocado por automóvel**). Therefore, a motor caravan is **um carro de moradia motorizado**, whilst a towed caravan is **um carro de moradia rebocado**. Anything being towed is known as **um reboque**. You will also come across other names, depending on which side of the Atlantic you are. On the American side, **o trailer**, on the European side, **a caravana** or **a rulote** are synonymous with **o carro de moradia rebocado**. You may also come across **o carro-cama**, a shorter term for **o carro de moradia motorizado**.

Tem vaga para um trailer,   *Have you got a vacancy for*
isto é, carro de moradia   *a 'trailer', that is to say, a*
rebocado, e uma barraca?   *towed caravan, and a tent?*

📇 Como funciona

Verbs: the three conjugations

Present participle / Gerund (the -*ing* form)
compr**ando** (*buying*)   vend**endo** (*selling*)   part**indo** (*leaving*)
Similarly,

Vir**ando** à direita no primeiro   *Turning right on the first set of*
semáforo, o hotel fica à esquerda.   *lights, the hotel is on the left.*

Contracted words

The following prepositions contract and combine with a following
definite article (*the*) or indefinite article (*a/an*):

por + o → pelo	por + a	→ pela	*by/for the*
de + um → dum	de + uma	→ duma	*of/from a*
em + um → num	em + uma	→ numa	*in/on a*

O trânsito é **pela** esquerda   *Does one drive on the left or on*
ou **pela** direita?   *the right?* (lit., *Is the traffic by*
                                   the left or by the right?)

Há lojas **numa** rua aqui perto.   *There are shops in a street nearby.*

Note the following:

■ In **pela esquerda/direita**, the word for *hand* (**a mão**) is omitted but
implied. This is also the case with **à direita/esquerda**:

pela direita = por + a (+ mão) direita
à direita = a + a (+ mão) direita

There is a general preference for **de um / de uma** although the following
form also occurs: **dum/duma** (sometimes spelt **d'um/d'uma**).

A loja fica perto **de uma** igreja.   *The shop is near a church.*

Prepositions can also contract and combine with a number of other words, as, for example:

de + este	→ deste	de + esta	→ desta	*of/from this*
em + este	→ neste	em + esta	→ nesta	*in/on this*
em + outro	→ noutro	em + outra	→ noutra	*in/on other*
de + aqui	→ daqui			*from here*

A loja fica **nesta** estrada, a cinco minutos **daqui**, de carro.
The shop is on this road, five minutes from here, by car.

Plurals

Words (nouns and adjectives) ending:

-el (–)	substitute	-eis	
-el (+)		-éis	
-il (–)		-eis	(+) stressed
-il (+)		-is	(–) unstressed
-ol (–)		-ois	
-ol (+)		-óis	
-ul		-uis	

automóv**el** (*automobile*), automóv**eis** (*automobiles*); hot**el** (*hotel*), hot**éis** (*hotels*); fác**il** (*easy*), fác**eis** (*easy*); gent**il** (*courteous*), gent**is** (*courteous*); álco**ol** (*alcohol*), álco**ois** (*alcohols*); lenç**ol** (*sheet, bed sheet*), lenç**óis** (*sheets, bed sheets*); az**ul** (*blue*), az**uis** (*blue*)

There are three different plural forms for words ending in **-ão**:

Some just add -s	Some change to -ões	Some change to -ães
m**ão** (*hand*) m**ãos** (*hands*)	esta**ção** (*station*) esta**ções** (*stations*)	p**ão** (*bread, loaf*) p**ães** (*loaves*)

Similarly,

cida**dão** → cida**dãos**, (*citizen(s)*); edre**dão** → edre**dões** (Eur.), (*eiderdown(s), bed quilt(s)*); c**ão** → c**ães**, (*dog(s)*).

Words in **-ês** lose the accent in the plural:

m**ês** (*month*); m**eses** (*months*)
portugu**ês** (*Portuguese*); portugu**eses** (*Portuguese*)

A number of masculine words which have a closed -o- in the stressed root syllable open this vowel in the plural in addition to adding -s.

ovo (*egg*), **ovos** (*eggs*); alm**o**ço (*lunch*), alm**o**ços (*lunches*); n**o**vo (*new, young*), n**o**vos (*new, young*); post**o** (*post, service station*), post**o**s (*posts, service stations*); port**o** (*port, harbour*), port**o**s (*ports, harbours*).

In compound words (verb/etc. + noun), only the noun takes a plural ending:

guarda-chuv**a**, guarda-chuv**as** (*umbrella(s)*, from **guardar**, *to guard*); guarda-s**ol**, guarda-s**óis** (*parasol, sunshade*).

But some already end in -s in the singular:

saca-rolh**as**, saca-rolh**as** (*corkscrew*, from **sacar**, *to take/pull out*).

In compound words (adjective/ordinal + noun), both elements take a plural ending:

pequen**o** almoç**o** (Eur.) (*breakfast*), pequen**os** almoç**os** (*breakfasts*) (*); sext**a**-feir**a** (*Friday*), sext**as**-feir**as** (*Fridays*).

Note that the linking hyphen is often omitted, particularly between adjective and noun:

pequen**o(s)**-almoç**o(s)** = pequen**o(s)** almoç**o(s)**.

(*) Lit. *small lunch* – (**o**) **almoço**, *lunch*

☑ Exercícios

4.3

You have entered a food store to look for some provisions.

4.3.1   Bread and milk are items you cannot find. Ask whether they are available, starting with **Desculpe, tem...**

4.3.2   They are available, and there is fruit too. Say you would like the following, starting with **Queria...**

(i)

(iii)

(iv)

(ii)

 4.4

You will hear some people talking about campsites.

4.4.1 Campo-Mar is publicising its facilities. Study their advertisement and listen to its radio version on your cassette/CD. Use the vocabulary at the end of the book for any words you may not know.

Campo-Mar

para um bom fim de semana e para umas boas férias
aberto os doze meses do ano
Inverno, de sexta-feira a domingo, Verão, sete dias por semana

🚿	chuveiro frio e quente	🛒	loja
🍴	restaurante		piscina

praia perto daqui – 10 minutos a pé
a cidade mais próxima fica a 10 minutos de carro

⊙⊙	tomada de corrente *power point*	🍃	gás para campistas *camping gas*
	lavandaria (Eur.) lavanderia (Br.) *launderette*	✳	frigorífico (Eur.) geladeira (Br.) *cold storage*
	secador de cabelo *hairdryer*		sala de televisão *TV room*

Write the answers in Portuguese:

(i) current opening days (it's Winter): _____

(ii) Summer opening days: _____

(iii) distance to the nearest beach: _____

(iv) distance to the nearest town: _____

4.4.2 Ask whether there is a camping/caravanning site near where you are, with the following facilities. Write down your enquiry and then read it out aloud (number (i) has been written for you):

Há um parque de campismo (Eur.) / um camping (Br.) perto daqui com piscina, secador de cabelo e restaurante?

(i) ⟿ + ⟍ + ✕   (ii) ⬛ + ⟍ + ⬜

(iii) ⊙ + ✳ + ⬜   (iv) ⟍ + ⬚ + ⬚

4.4.3 Four people are looking for somewhere to stay. Listen to them and tick what they need a space for. Then write down all they said.

	carro de moradia motorizado	carro de moradia rebocado	reboque pequeno	barraca	tenda
(i)					
(ii)					
(iii)					
(iv)					

4.4.4 Ask whether there is a space for you. Write down your enquiry and then read it out aloud (number (i) has been written for you):

Tem vaga para um carro-cama, isto é, carro de moradia motorizado, e uma barraca?

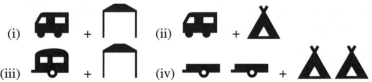

4.5

Study the pictures below, listen to your cassette/CD and complete the speech bubbles. Say them yourself aloud.

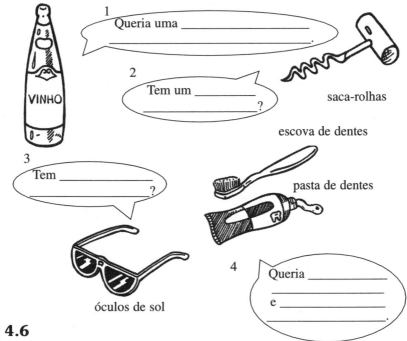

1 Queria uma _____ _____.

2 Tem um _____ _____?

saca-rolhas

escova de dentes

3 Tem _____ _____?

pasta de dentes

óculos de sol

4 Queria _____ _____ e _____ _____.

4.6

You are trying to work out how to pay for making phone calls.

4.6.1 Rearrange the following words so as to say that you would like to make a reversed charge call (**uma chamada a cobrar**) to Canada.

Queria / uma / a cobrar / para o Canadá. / chamada / fazer

4.6.2 Rearrange the words below so as to ask for the following:

A In Portugal
phone cards – **o cartão credifone**
Tem / credifone / cartões / ?

B In Brazil
phone tokens – **a ficha telefônica** (= telefónica (Eur.))
Tem / telefônicas / fichas / ?

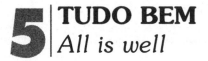

5 TUDO BEM
All is well

In this revision unit there is more practice on how to:

- speak to the people you meet on arrival
- work out your route and use different forms of transport
- get what you need and the accommodation you like

5.1

You have been attending Portuguese classes, and your teacher has given you a language self-help kit that you can use to overcome any communication difficulties you may experience initially.

5.1.1 Study what she has written on the board and listen to the new words being pronounced for you. Tick each word as you hear it.

Faça o favor de	falar repetir *repeat, say it again*		mais devagar mais alto *louder*	
	escrever aqui *write down* (lit., *write* *here*)	quanto é *how much it is* o nome *the name* o endereço *the address* o número do telefone *the telephone number* essa palavra *that word...* essas palavras *those words...* (*... that you have said*)		
	me mostrar *show me*	no dicionário *in the dictionary*	essa(s) palavra(s) *the word(s) you have just said*	
		no mapa *on the map*	onde fica *where it is* onde estou *where I am*	
		as horas *the time (... on your watch)*		

5.1.2 Listen again and say the new words.

5.1.3 Follow the example you already know – **Faça o favor de falar mais devagar** – and combine words from the different columns so as to say the following (write it down):

Could you please / Would you kindly...

   (i) say it again, more slowly.
  (ii) write down how much it is.
 (iii) write down the name, address and telephone number.
  (iv) write down what you have just said.
   (v) show me that word in the dictionary.
  (vi) show me on the map where it is.
 (vii) show me on the map where I am.
(viii) show me the time (... on your watch).

5.1.4 Say aloud what you have written.

5.2

When going through Customs, you want to say that you have nothing to declare, but the words have got jumbled up. Listen to the officer's question and rearrange your words so as to give your reply.

   – Tem alguma coisa a declarar?
   – Não / não / a / tenho / , / declarar / . / nada

5.3

You are producing some personal documents you have been asked for, first at the passport control, then at the car hire.

5.3.1 Fill in the gaps with words from the box, listen to the recording and play your part in the mini-dialogues.

> (o) meu   (a) minha

A In Portugal

(i) <u>No controle de passaporte</u>
   – O seu passaporte, por favor.
   – Aqui está _____ passaporte.

(ii) <u>No aluguer de carros/automóveis</u>
   – A sua carta de condução, por favor.
   – Aqui está _____ carta de condução.

B In Brazil

(iii) <u>No controle de passaporte</u>	(iv) <u>No aluguel de carros/automóveis</u>
– Seu passaporte, por favor.	– Sua carteira de motorista, por favor.
– Aqui está _____ passaporte.	– Aqui está _____ carteira de motorista.

5.3.2 Listen again to what you are being asked. This time reply with **Aqui tem...**

5.4

Study the following words you may need when you hire a car.

(a) lista dos modelos e preços	*model and price list*
pagando por dia	*paying per day*
** por semana**	*per week*
** por quilómetro** (Eur.) /	*per kilometre travelled*
** quilômetro** (Br.) **rodado**	
(o) seguro contra todos os riscos	*comprehensive insurance*
(a) caução	*guarantee deposit*
com / sem motorista	*with / without a driver*
(os) documentos do carro	*car documents*
(o) recibo	*receipt*

5.4.1 Listen how the people on your cassette/CD are going about hiring a car, and tick each new word above as you hear it.

5.4.2 Listen again to what they say, write it down and read aloud what you have written.

5.4.3 It's your turn to choose a car.

Make your enquiry, asking:
- (i) to be shown the model and price table (**Pode...**)
- (ii) how much it is per day (**Quanto...**)
- (iii) how much is the insurance and the guarantee deposit.

Make your decision, saying:
- (iv) you would like this car, paying per day (**Queria...**)
- (v) you would like the car for two days and no driver.

Ask for:
- (vi) a receipt (**Pode...**)
- (vii) the car documents

5.5

Read the signs on the petrol and other fuel pumps, work out their meaning and match each sign with the English version below.

(1) SUPER = AZUL   (2) NORMAL = COMUM

(3) SEM CHUMBO   (4) GASÓLEO   (5) ÁLCOOL

(*a*) regular / two-star   (*b*) premium / four-star
(*c*) unleaded   (*d*) alcohol fuel (in Brazil)   (*e*) diesel fuel

5.6

You are going to help four different people who have got lost in town.

5.6.1 Study the signposted directions.

> **(a) câmara municipal** *town hall* (Eur.) (*) **(a) polícia** *police*
> **(o) centro de saúde** *health centre* **(os) bombeiros** *fire services*

5.6.2 Listen to your cassette/CD
and reply to each question
using a complete sentence.

câmara municipal

bombeiros

polícia

Example:
(1)
A polícia fica
à esquerda

centro de saúde

(*) *town council* (Br.)

5.7

Four people are trying to find out what platform their train leaves from. Two are travelling in Portugal and two are travelling in Brazil.

(o) comboio (Eur.) / **(o) trem** (Br.)	*train*
(o) cais (Eur.) / **(a) plataforma** (Br.)	*platform*

5.7.1 First, look at the destination boards, study the questions and replies below, and fill in the gaps as appropriate.

PORTUGAL

Porto
3

Braga
1

BRASIL

Rio
5

Campinas
2

(i) – De que cais parte o comboio para o Porto?
   – Do cais _____ .

(ii) – De que _____ parte o comboio para Braga?
   – Do cais número _____ .

(iii) – De que _____ parte o trem para o Rio?
   – Da plataforma _____ .

(iv) – De que plataforma parte _____ para Campinas?
   – Da segunda _____ .

5.7.2 Now you are ready to help the four travellers. Listen to their questions on your cassette/CD and give them the right information. Read it aloud.

5.7.3 Finally, take their place and ask the questions yourself (**De que...?**).

5.8

On your cassette/CD, some people are asking for specific features they would like in their hotel accommodation.

5.8.1 Number each feature being asked for as you hear it.

(i)	(a) varanda *balcony*	
(ii)	(a) vista para o mar *sea view (view on to the sea)*	
(iii)	(o) ar condicionado *air conditioning*	
(iv)	(o) aparelho de televisão *television set*	
(v)	(o) barulho *noise*	

5.8.2 Write down everything each person says and read it aloud.

5.8.3 Check that the accommodation you are being offered has got the following: (**Tem...**)

    (i) air conditioning; (ii) television set; (iii) balcony and sea view.

5.8.4 Say you would like (**Queria...**) a room with no noise.

5.9

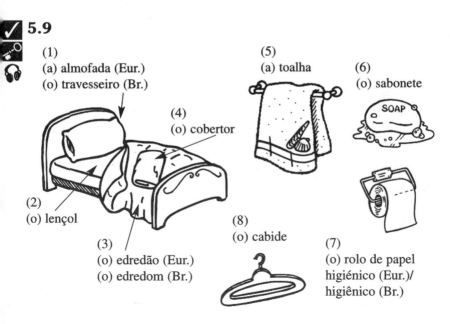

(1)
(a) almofada (Eur.)
(o) travesseiro (Br.)

(2)
(o) lençol

(3)
(o) edredão (Eur.)
(o) edredom (Br.)

(4)
(o) cobertor

(5)
(a) toalha

(6)
(o) sabonete

(7)
(o) rolo de papel higiénico (Eur.)/ higiênico (Br.)

(8)
(o) cabide

5.9.1   mais um / uma   *one more...*

Ask whether you can be brought one more of each item in the picture.

Examples:

> Por favor, pode me trazer mais uma almofada (Eur.)?
> Por favor, pode me trazer mais um travesseiro (Br.)?

Listen to the above examples on your cassette/CD. Then continue on your own.

5.9.2   mais dois / duas   *two more...*

Ask whether you can be brought two more of each.

5.9.3   Write a note to leave in your room asking for four extra hangers and two extra blankets. Start with **Por favor** and don't forget to finish with a thank you.

5.10

 (o) médico
doctor

 (o) dentista
dentist

 (o) enfermeiro
nurse

 (o) mecânico
mechanic

5.10.1   Há ... perto daqui?

Listen to your cassette/CD and (*a*) enter **Há** or **Não, não há** on the line above the following pictures, depending on whether there is, or not, one nearby; (*b*) then write down what you heard and say it aloud.

(i) _____   (ii) _____   (iii) _____   (iv) _____

5.10.2 Pode chamar um ... para mim?

Ask whether the following can be sent for, for you. Write down your questions and then read them aloud. The first one is on the cassette/CD.

(i)   (ii)   (iii)   (iv)

 5.11

You have tried to look up a word in the vocabulary at the end of the book, but it does not appear to be there. This may be because it is a verb, and, in order to find a verb in a dictionary, often you need to change it, from the form you have to its infinitive, e.g., from *is* to *(to) be*.

In the left-hand side column, there are a number of verb forms you have come across. Work out their respective infinitives and enter them in the right-hand side column. Remember that they will have to end in **-ar**, **-er** or **-ir**. Some irregular and other cases have been done for you.

WORD AS YOU HAVE SEEN IT	WORD AS A DICTIONARY ENTRY	
desculpe	(a)	
é, são	(b)	ser
está, estão, estou	(c)	estar
faça, faz	(d)	
fica, ficam, fico	(e)	
há	(f)	haver
parte	(g)	
pode	(h)	
queria	(i)	querer
tem, temos, tenho	(j)	ter

When you have completed this exercise, look up the obtained words (infinitives) in the Portuguese–English vocabulary at the end of the book.

5.12

This is the shopping
list (**a lista de compras**)
that you have written
and taken with you
to the local store.
Read it aloud.
Start with

Por favor, queria ...

> *pão x 3*
> *maçã 1 / 2 dúzia*
> *leite*
> *1 garrafa pequena*
> *água*
> *1 garrafa grande*

 5.13

 On the left are the courtesy words you have learned. On the right are their
respective replies.

Pode me fazer um favor?	Claro! Com certeza /Eur.) Pois não (Br.)	*Certainly*
Perdão Desculpe	Não tem importância Não faz mal (Eur.) Não foi nada (Br.)	*It's all right*
Com licença	Por favor Faz / faça favor (Eur.) Pois não (Br.)	*Please do*
Obrigado / obrigada Muito obrigado/a Agradecido / agradecida Muito agradecido/a	De nada Não tem de quê Eu é que agradeço	*Not at all* *It's I who must thank you*

5.13.1   Listen to the new words on your cassette/CD.

5.13.2 Practise saying aloud the different courtesy expressions and the appropriate response to each one.

5.14

Follow the clues and complete the courtesy crossword puzzle. Number 4 across and number 2 down have been done for you.

Palavras Cruzadas

Horizontais:
1 - Perdão
2 - Por favor
3 - Não tem importância
4 - Não tem de quê
5 - Obrigada
6 - De nada

Verticais:
1 - Muito obrigado
2 - Eu é que agradeço
3 - Muito obrigada
4 - Com licença

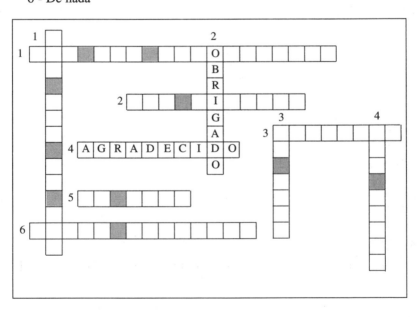

6 | VOCÊ ESTÁ DE FÉRIAS?

Are you on holiday?

In this unit you will learn how to:

- introduce a friend or relation
- say where you are from and talk about yourself
- find out about others

Na rua

Portuguese João is introduced to Brazilian Celso by a mutual friend, Tânia.

Tânia (*apresentando João a Celso*) Este é meu amigo João.
Celso (*apertando a mão*) Muito prazer.
João O prazer é todo meu.
Celso Você está de férias?
João Infelizmente não estou de férias, mas o trabalho também é bom.
Celso Está sozinho?
João Estou.
Celso Num hotel?
João Sim, num hotel.
Celso Então pode vir jantar em nossa casa, talvez amanhã.
João Muito obrigado.

apresentando *introducing*
(o) amigo *friend*
apertando a mão *shaking hands*
o prazer é todo meu *the pleasure is all mine*
você *you*
de férias *on holiday*
infelizmente *unfortunately*
(o) trabalho *work*

também *also, too*
sozinho *by oneself*
então *then*
vir jantar *come to dinner* (lit. *come to dine*)
em nossa casa *at home* (lit. *in our house*)
talvez *perhaps*
amanhã *tomorrow*

Num café

Two students who have joined the same course exchange information about themselves.

Lino   Desculpe, mas você … de onde é?

Rita   Eu sou de Lisboa. E você, de onde é?

Lino   Eu sou de São Paulo, mas moro no Rio de Janeiro há muito tempo. Você é de Lisboa, mas agora onde mora?

Rita   Moro aqui.

Lino   Com quem?

Rita   Com uma irmã.

Lino   Então você é solteira, não é?

Rita   Não sou casada, mas estou noiva. O nome dele é Luís.

de onde é? *where are (you) from?*	**com quem?** *with whom?*
eu sou de … *I am from …*	**(a) irmã** *sister*
há muito tempo *since long* (lit. *there is much time*)	**solteira, casada** *single, married*
moro, mora *(I) live, (you) live*	**não é?** *aren't you?* (lit. *isn't it?*)
agora *now*	**noiva** *engaged*
	dele (= **de** + **ele**) *his* (lit. *of him*)

Exercícios

6.1 Certo ou errado?

	C	E
1 João está de férias.	❏	❏
2 João está sozinho.	❏	❏
3 Rita não é de Lisboa.	❏	❏

6.2 Perguntas e respostas

1 Rita mora sozinha ou não mora sozinha?

  (a) Mora sozinha.   *(b)* Não mora sozinha.

2 Lino é de onde? E onde mora?

  (a) É do Rio de Janeiro mas mora em São Paulo.

  (b) É de São Paulo mas mora no Rio de Janeiro.

3 Rita é casada ou solteira?

  (a) É solteira.   *(b)* É casada.   *(c)* Está noiva.

🎧 Como se pronuncia

The letter sequence **qu** can be pronounced in more than one way. Practise after the voice on the cassette/CD.

> **qu** before **a** or **o** sounds like English *kw*: **qua**rto; **qua**tro; **qua**nto; **quo**ta (*quota, share*).

> **qu** before **e** or **i** sounds like *k*: **que**ria; **que**m; a**qui**; **qui**nze (*fifteen*) but, in some cases,

> **qu** before **e** or **i** sounds like *kw*, as in the word for *fifty*: cin**que**nta (Eur.) / cin**qüe**nta (Br.). Brazilians show the difference by changing the spelling to **ü**.

The end sound in el**e** /el**a**, *he/she*, influences the quality of the first sound. Follow the voice on the cassette/CD.

> **el**e (say *ey* in *they* but without the final glide)
> **el**a (say *e* in *tell*)

Similarly,

> d**el**e-d**el**a;
> **e**ste-**e**sta; **e**sse-**e**ssa (*that, that one*);
> aqu**el**e-aqu**el**a (also *that, that one*)

🔑 Expressões-chave

este – esse – aquele

In English, *this*, or *this one*, and *that*, or *that one*, establish a distinction between what or who is near you and what or who is away from you. Portuguese **este**, **esse** and **aquele** establish a further distinction as follows:

- **este** is near you or near you and the person/people you are talking to;
- **esse** is away from you but near the person/people you are talking to;
- **aquele** is away from both you and the person/people you are talking to.

esta, **essa** and **aquela** are the respective feminine forms.

Este é (o) Pedro, **esse** é (o) Paulo e **aquela** é (a) Maria.	*This is Peter, that is Paul and that one (over there) is Mary.*

(For **o/a** please refer to page 71.)

Muito prazer

When introducing someone, say **este é (o) meu amigo João / esposo** or **marido** (*husband*) / **pai** (*father*) or **esta é (a) minha amiga Joana / esposa** or **mulher** (*wife*) / **mãe** (*mother*). Brazilians will leave out **o/a**.

Muito prazer is the abridged version of **muito prazer em conhecê-lo** or **muito prazer em conhecê-la**, *delighted to meet you*, when you are talking, respectively, to a man or to a lady. Sometimes you may find that the abridged version is further reduced to **prazer**. This doesn't mean that you are not 'delighted' but is just a relaxed way of speaking. However, **muito prazer** or **igualmente** are the usual responses. If you wish to be very polite, then you can also say **o prazer é meu** or **o prazer é todo meu**, *the pleasure is (all) mine*.

Information about yourself

Both in a social situation and for official purposes, you may want to provide information about yourself. You may also wish to find out about other people. Below are some questions and answers that will help you.

Nome

Qual é o seu nome? (Eur.) / Qual é seu nome? (Br.)

has the following alternatives:

Como é o seu nome? (Eur.) / Como é seu nome? (Br.)
 (lit. *how is your name?*)
Como se chama você? (Eur.) / Como você se chama? (Br.)
 (lit. *how do you call yourself?*)

The word "você" is more likely to be used by a Brazilian speaker but omitted by a Portuguese speaker.

As for the reply:

O meu nome é... (Eur.) / Meu nome é... (Br.)

has the following alternative:

Chamo-me... (Eur.) / Me chamo... (Br.)   (lit. *I call myself*)

To reciprocate the question, instead of

E o seu?

on both sides of the Atlantic you can equally ask

E você, como se chama?   asking anyone
E o senhor, como se chama?   asking a man
E a senhora, como se chama?   asking a woman

The two last versions are more polite.

Local de nascimento, *Place of birth.*
Nacionalidade, *Nationality*

De onde é você? *or* De onde você é?

The word "você" is more likely to be used by a Brazilian speaker and
omitted by a Portuguese speaker.

Reply: Eu sou de Portugal.
       Eu sou do Rio, no Brasil.
       Eu sou da Inglaterra   *from England*
       Eu sou dos Estados Unidos   *from the United States*

Reciprocating:

E você, de onde é?
E o senhor / a senhora, de onde é?

Also: *Are you.....*
       Você é português? / Você é portuguesa? ... *Portuguese?*
       O senhor é brasileiro? / A senhora é brasileira? ... *Brazilian?*
       O senhor é inglês? / A senhora é inglesa? ... *English?*
       O senhor é americano? / A senhora é americana? ... *American?*

Reply: Sou sim.
       Não, não sou. Eu sou australiano / australiana.   *Australian*

Profissão, *Profession.* Ocupação, *Occupation*

Qual é a sua profissão?(Eur.) / Qual é sua profissão? (Br.)

Eu sou ...	*I am a ...*
estudante	*student*
professor / professora	*teacher*
engenheiro / engenheira	*engineer*
homem / mulher de negócios	*businessman/woman*
dona de casa	*housewife*
aposentado/aposentada	*retired* (from employment)
reformado/reformada (Eur.)	*retired*

Estado civil, *Marital status*

Você é solteiro?
A senhora é casada?
A senhora está noiva?
Eu sou viúvo / viúva   *a widower/ widow*
Eu sou divorciado / divorciada   *divorced*

Idade, *Age*

Quantos anos tem você? (Eur.) /
Quantos anos você tem? (Br.)   *How old are you?*
  (lit. *How many years have you got? i.e., have you completed?*)
Eu tenho vinte e cinco anos.   *I am twenty five years old.*
  (lit. *I have i.e., have completed twenty five years.*)

Filhos, *Children*

Você tem filhos?   *Have you got any children?*
Eu tenho dois filhos.   *I have two children.*
Eu tenho um filho e uma filha.   *a son and a daughter.*
Eu não tenho filhos.   *no children.*
Eu tenho um neto e uma neta.   *a grandson and*
            a granddaughter.

Endereço ou morada, *Address*

Onde mora você? *or* Onde você mora?
Onde mora a senhora? *or* Onde a senhora mora?
Eu moro no Brasil, no Rio.
Qual é o seu endereço? (Eur.) / Qual é seu endereço? (Br.)
Como é o seu endereço? (Eur.) / Como é o seu endereço? (Br.)
Qual é o número do seu telefone?(Eur.)
  / Qual é o número de seu telefone?(Br.)
  / Qual é (o) seu número de telefone?

Estada ou estadia, *Your visit*

Quanto tempo vai ficar?   *How long are you going to stay?*
Eu vou ficar um mês.   *I am going to stay for one month.*
Onde vai ficar?   *Where are you staying?*
Onde está?   *Where are you staying (now)?*
Com amigos.   *With friends.*

No Hotel Central.

Estou aqui de férias	... *on holiday*
em negócios (Eur.) /	
a negócios (Br.)	... *on business*

Como funciona

I, you, s/he...

With verbs, the subject pronoun (*I, you, s/he, etc.*) is optional. In fact it tends to be omitted where the verb ending itself shows whether it is *I, you*, etc.

☐ Moro em Lisboa.   *I live in Lisbon.*

However, use the pronoun with the verb where it could otherwise be ambiguous, or for emphasis.

Eu é que agradeço.   *It's I who must thank you.*

eu	I
você	*you* (both m. and f.)
o senhor / a senhora	*you* (m.) / *you* (f.) [POLITE]
tu	*you* (both m. and f.) [FOR CLOSE FRIENDS]
ele / ela	*he / she / it*
nós	*we*
vocês	*you* (both m. and f. plural)
os senhores / as senhoras	*you* (m. pl.) / *you* (f. pl.) [POLITE]
eles / elas	*they*

Note that 'os senhores' can be m. and f. together. See page 101.

Numbers 11 to 100

11	onze	21	vinte e um/uma
12	doze	22	vinte e dois/duas
13	treze	30	trinta
14	catorze	40	quarenta
15	quinze	50	cinquenta (Eur.) cinqüenta (Br.)
16	dezasseis (Eur.) dezesseis (Br.)	60	sessenta
17	dezassete (Eur.) dezessete (Br.)	70	setenta
18	dezoito	80	oitenta
19	dezanove (Eur.) dezenove (Br.)	90	noventa
20	vinte	100	cem

João *or* o João ?

The use of the definite article (**o/a**) with the name of a person is optional and is more widely heard on the eastern side of the Atlantic rather than in Brazil.

Este é o João   *or*   Este é João   *This is John.*

However, it is not used in a vocative, i. e., when calling someone.

João! *John!* (*come here*)

a civil servant and a vegetarian

Unlike English practice, the Portuguese indefinite article (**um/uma**) is not used before a noun denoting profession or occupation, affiliation, marital status or origin.

Sou funcionário público	*I am a civil servant*
vegetariano	*vegetarian*
católico	*catholic*

◢ Exercícios

6.3

Fill in the missing words in what Joana is saying to Paulo.

Paulo! Este é _____ , _____ Rosa e _____ Mariana.

Nuno   Joana   Paulo   Rosa   Mariana

6.4

José, Glória, Osvaldo and Amélia are explaining where they come from and talking about themselves.

6.4.1 Study the picture on the opposite page, listen to your cassette/CD and complete the table below writing in Portuguese the correct information about each individual. Number 1 has been done for you.

name	s/he comes from ...	age and occupation	married? children?
(i) José	*Faro, Algarve*	*22 anos, estudante*	*solteiro, não tem filhos*
(ii) Glória			
(iii) Osvaldo			
(iv) Amélia			

6.4.2 Listen again to what they say and transcribe their words. Then act out each one's role by reading aloud what you wrote.

6.5

Matthew has to provide some information about himself. Help him out and answer the following questions on his behalf.

   – Por favor, o senhor é americano?
   – (say *No, I am not, I am English*)
   – Como se chama e de onde é na Inglaterra?
   – (say *My name is Matthew Smith. I come from Manchester*)

– Quanto tempo vai ficar aqui e com quem?

– (say *I am on my own and I am going to stay for 8 days, on holiday*)

– Faça o favor de me mostrar um documento de identidade com o seu endereço de Manchester.

– (say *There you are* showing your driving licence)

José Fontes

Faro

ALGARVE

Natal

RIO GRANDE DO NORTE

Glória Fonseca

RIO GRANDE DO SUL

Porto Alegre

MADEIRA

Funchal

Osvaldo Medeiros

Amélia Sarmento

7 | QUANDO COMEÇA A EXCURSÃO?
When does the tour start?

In this unit you will learn how to:

- talk about time and the days of the week
- find out when a service is available
- identify a person you are going to meet for the first time

  ## Numa agência de viagens

Susana is in a travel agency enquiring about local tours.

Susana	Queria ver a lista das excursões nesta região.
Empregado	Algum local em particular?
Susana	Não, queria conhecer a região em geral.
Empregado	Então recomendo a excursão de dois dias. A próxima é na quarta-feira, partindo de manhã. Ficamos uma noite num hotel e regressamos quinta à tarde.
Susana	E a que horas começa a excursão na quarta-feira?
Empregado	Vamos partir às nove. A senhora quer fazer reserva? Hoje ainda tem lugar, mas amanhã talvez não.

ver *to see*	**ficamos** *(we) stay*
(a) excursão *excursion, tour*	**regressamos** *(we) return*
(a) região *region*	**(a) quinta(-feira)** *Thursday*
em particular *in particular*	**à tarde** *in the afternoon / evening*
em geral *in general*	**a que horas..?** *at what time...?*
recomendo *I would recommend*	**começa** *starts*
(lit. *(I) recommend*)	**às nove (horas)** *at nine (o'clock)*
(a) quarta-feira *Wednesday*	**a senhora quer...?** *do you want...?*
de manhã *in the morning*	**ainda tem lugar** *(you) still have a seat*

Falando com um amigo

Dulce is in charge of collecting David from the coach station and is trying to find out what he looks like.

Dulce   Pode me descrever a aparência física dele? Preciso saber como ele é.
Sílvio   Para quê?
Dulce   Ele vai chegar hoje à noite. Tenho que ir buscá-lo à estação.
Sílvio   A que estação?
Dulce   À rodoviária. Não sei como vou reconhecê-lo. Não sei se ele é gordo ou magro, alto ou baixo...
Sílvio   Oh! Não tem problema. Ele nem é gordo nem é magro, nem é alto nem é baixo.
Dulce   Mas que grande ajuda! Muito obrigada.

descrever *to describe*	**(a) rodoviária** *coach (station)*
aparência física *physical appearance*	**não sei como** *(I) don't know how*
preciso (de) saber *(I) need (to) know*	**reconhecê-lo** *to identify him*
como ele é *what he looks (lit. is) like*	**se** *whether, if*
ele vai chegar *he is going to arrive*	**gordo – magro** *fat – thin*
à noite *at night / in the evening*	**alto – baixo** *tall – short*
tenho que *(I) have got to*	**oh! não tem / há problema** *oh!*
ir, vou *to go, (I) go / am going*	*((you) have/there is) no problem*
buscá-lo *to fetch him*	**que grande ajuda!** *what a great help!*

Exercícios

7.1 Certo ou errado?

                                         C   E

1 Susana quer conhecer a região. ☐ ☐
2 Susana ainda tem lugar na excursão. ☐ ☐
3 David vai chegar amanhã à noite. ☐ ☐
4 Sílvio vai buscar David à estação rodoviária. ☐ ☐

7.2 Perguntas e respostas

1 Excursão para Susana: Quando é a partida? e o regresso?
   (a) A partida é quinta-feira de manhã e o regresso quinta-feira à noite.
   (b) A partida é quarta-feira de manhã e o regresso quinta-feira à tarde.
   (c) A partida é quarta-feira à tarde e o regresso quarta-feira à noite.

2 David: Qual é a aparência física dele?

    (a) Ele nem é gordo nem é magro mas é alto.

    (b) Ele nem é alto nem baixo mas é magro.

    (c) Ele não é alto mas não é baixo, não é gordo mas não é magro.

🎧 Como se pronuncia

Sounds spelt **s** or **z** can change depending on their position in the word and within the sentence. Practise the following after the speaker on the cassette/CD.

s- at the beginning of a word (like English *s* in *so*): **s**ol; **s**ou; **s**aber; **s**enhora.

-s- between vowels (like *z* in *zebra*): ca**s**a; bra**s**ileiro.

-s at the end of a word and often at the end of a syllable

    in Portugal (like *sh* in *push*): hora**s**; português, ficamo**s**; li**s**ta.

    in most of Brazil (like *s* in *so*): hora**s**; português, ficamo**s**; li**s**ta.

               but

    when the next word starts with a vowel, a fast speaker, on either side of the Atlantic, will change the final **-s** into a *z* for *zebra*:

         à**s** oito horas; vamo**s** amanhã à**s** oito horas.

    ➡   ➡   ➡

z sounds like *z* in *zebra* in general: **z**ero (*nought*)

-z at the end of a word or syllable sounds like *sh* in *push*: talve**z**; feli**z** (*happy*).

    but like *z* for *zebra* when the next word starts with a vowel:

         talve**z** amanhã; feli**z** ano.

    ➡   ➡

🔑 Expressões-chave

Days of the week

Que dia da semana é hoje?   *What day of the week is it today?*

É... *It is....*		**quarta-feira**	*Wednesday*
domingo	*Sunday*	**quinta-feira**	*Thursday*
segunda-feira	*Monday*	**sexta-feira**	*Friday*
terça-feira	*Tuesday*	**sábado**	*Saturday*

The days of the week may start with either lower case or capital letter. They are feminine except for the weekend days which are masculine; and so is (**o**) **feriado**, *public holiday*. In the compound word, **-feira** is often dropped and the first part is represented as **2ª**, **3ª**, **4ª**, **5ª** or **6ª**.

For something that happens regularly, you can say: **às segundas**, **aos fins de semana**, **todos os fins de semana**, and so on.

A excursão é **às quartas-feiras**. *The tour is on Wednesdays.*

Telling the time

For *What time is it?* say **Que horas são?** lit. *What hours are (they)?*

The answers:

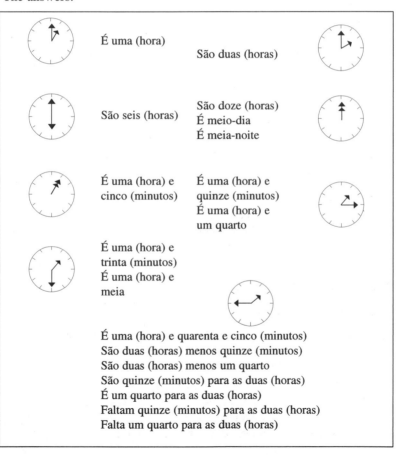

É uma (hora)

São duas (horas)

São seis (horas)

São doze (horas)
É meio-dia
É meia-noite

É uma (hora) e
cinco (minutos)

É uma (hora) e
quinze (minutos)
É uma (hora) e
um quarto

É uma (hora) e
trinta (minutos)
É uma (hora) e
meia

É uma (hora) e quarenta e cinco (minutos)
São duas (horas) menos quinze (minutos)
São duas (horas) menos um quarto
São quinze (minutos) para as duas (horas)
É um quarto para as duas (horas)
Faltam quinze (minutos) para as duas (horas)
Falta um quarto para as duas (horas)

For the hour, remember to use **é** for **meio-dia, meia-noite** and *one* (**é uma hora**) but **são** for the others (**são onze horas**). In the 24-hr clock reading, time past and time to the hour are expressed as hour + minutes or quarters (**são onze horas e trinta e cinco minutos**). In the more colloquial 12-hr reading, time past the hour finds expression in the same way (**são onze e vinte e cinco**). For time to the hour the **para** and the **menos** versions are both widely heard (**são vinte e cinco para a meia-noite** *or* **é meia-noite menos vinte e cinco**). Finally, *on the dot* has its Portuguese equivalent in **em ponto – É uma (hora) em ponto**.

Parts of the day

When using the 12-hr clock you can add **da manhã, da tarde** or **da noite** (**nove horas da noite** = *9 pm*). If you wish to refer to the different parts of the day with no mention of time, say:

de manhã	*in the morning*
à tarde or **de tarde**	*in the afternoon / early evening*
à noite	*in the late evening / at night*
A partida é na quarta-feira **de manhã**.	*The departure is on Wednesday a.m.*
De manhã como cereais com leite.	*In the morning I eat cereals with milk.*

De noite is better reserved for *at night* in the sense of *during the night*.

Está escuro **de noite**.   *It is dark at night.*

Hoje de manhã means *this morning*, **hoje de tarde** means *this afternoon* (or *early evening*) and **hoje à noite** means *tonight* (or *late evening*). However, **esta manhã, esta tarde** and **esta noite** are equally used.

For *see you tomorrow* say **até amanhã** (lit. *until tomorrow*) and for *see you tomorrow morning* **até amanhã de manhã**. For *see you on Monday* say **até segunda(-feira)** and so on.

Agências e estações

The word **agência** is used for a services office – **a agência de viagens**. **O turismo** and **o correio**, or **os correios**, are abridged versions of, respectively, **a agência de turismo** and **a agência dos correios**. Concerning the latter, **o posto dos correios** is also used.

A estação is used for both railway station and coach station. The full name for the former is **a estação rodoviária** and for the latter **a estação ferroviária** (Br.) or **a estação dos caminhos de ferro** (Eur.).

◻ Como funciona

Verbs: the three conjugations – present indicative

	I buy, etc.	*I sell, etc.*	*I leave, etc.*
S1 eu	compr**o**	vend**o**	part**o**
S2 você, o sr / a sra tu	compr**a** compr**as**	vend**e** vend**es**	part**e** part**es**
S3 ele / ela	compr**a**	vend**e**	part**e**
P1 nós	compr**amos**	vend**emos**	part**imos**
P2 vocês, os sres / as sras	compr**am**	vend**em**	part**em**
P3 eles / elas	compr**am**	vend**em**	part**em**

The three *S* (for singular) boxes are for just one person – *I, you (one)*, *he/she/it*. The three *P* boxes are for their respective plurals – *we, you (more than one), they*.

With exception of the **tu** endings (**-as, -es, -es**), *S2* and *S3* are the same (**-a, -e, -e**), and *P2* and *P3* are also the same (**-am, -em, -em**). They will be grouped together in the tables for verb tenses you will come across.

Use the present tense for:

- a description of something or someone
  A saída fic**a** em frente. *The exit is straight ahead.* (verb fic**ar**, with ending **-a** as for comprar *S3*)
- a description of a situation as it is now
  Mor**o** no Rio. *I live in Rio.* (mor**ar**)
- an habitual action or event
  Normalmente, as lojas abr**em** às 9h. *Usually, shops open at 9 am.* (abr**ir**)
- a constant fact
  Gost**o** de música. *I like music.* (gost**ar**)
- an accepted truth
  As pessoas que viv**em** num clima frio vest**em** roupa quente. *People who live in a cold climate wear warm clothes.* (viv**er**, vest**ir**)
- a factual statement about a future occurrence
  Part**imos** amanhã. *We are leaving tomorrow.* (part**ir**)
- something started sometime in the past and not yet completed
  Estud**o** português há um mês. *I have been studying Portuguese for one month.* (estud**ar**)

You

The tendency to omit the subject pronoun (*I, you s/he, etc.*), that you learned in Unit 6, is not affected much by the fact that the verb ending can be the same for *you* and *s/he* and for *you* (more than one) and *they*. The situational context is likely to make the meaning clear. If someone looks at you and asks **Fala português?**, it may be obvious that this means *Do you speak Portuguese?* not *Does s/he speak Portuguese?*

However, if you want to use a word for *you* which should you choose?

Você fala inglês? or **O senhor** fala inglês? or **Tu** falas inglês?

você

Use **você** in general and when talking to friends.

o senhor / a senhora

Use **o sr / a sra** with strangers you want to be particularly courteous to.

tu

Here we have to make a distinction. In Brazil **tu** is not widely used in this form but only in its oblique forms **te** and **ti**, e.g., **para ti**, *for you*. We shall come back to this in later units.

Other than in Brazil, **tu** is used by those who grow up together or who have become very close later in life. Native speakers use this form to address children, children use this form amongst themselves through their school days and beyond, in many families children use this form to address their parents, and most adults use it for someone they have become intimate with. Remember to use the different verb form! In Brazil these areas of meaning are covered by **você**.

Also please note the following:

- **vocês** is plural to both **você** and **tu**.

  Vocês falam português? *Do you* (more than one) *speak Portuguese?*

- **o senhor / a senhora** and **os senhores / as senhoras** are nouns used as pronouns for *you*.

  O senhor fala português? *Do you speak Portuguese?* (lit., *does the gentleman speak Portuguese?*)

- **vós** is an alternative to **vocês** and **os senhores / as senhoras**. It has not been mentioned before because it has become archaic in most of the Portuguese-speaking world. However, you can find its verb forms, in brackets, in the tables at the end of the book.

Ordinal numbers

1º/1ª	primeiro/a	20º/20ª	vigésimo/a
2º/2ª	segundo/a	30º/30ª	trigésimo/a
3º/3ª	terceiro/a	40º/40ª	quadragésimo/a
4º/4ª	quarto/a	50º/50ª	quinquagésimo/a (Eur.)
5º/5ª	quinto/a		qüinquagésimo/a (Br.)
6º/6ª	sexto/a	60º/60ª	sexagésimo/a
7º/7ª	sétimo/a	70º/70ª	septuagésimo/a (Eur.)
8º/8ª	oitavo/a		setuagésimo (Br.)
9º/9ª	nono/a	80º/80ª	octogésimo/a
10º/10ª	décimo/a	90º/90ª	nonagésimo/a
11º/11ª	décimo/a primeiro/a	100º/100ª	centésimo/a

as duas primeiras ruas à direita   *the first two roads on the right*
o vigésimo primeiro andar   *the twenty-first floor*

Note that the ordinals are used for the days of the week from Monday to Friday, but **terça** not **terceira** is used for Tuesday: **terça-feira**.

✓ Exercícios

7.3

Put the days of the week in the right order, starting with Sunday.

7.4

A que horas... ?	At what time...?
À uma hora.	At one o'clock.
Ao meio-dia.	At midday.
A um quarto para as cinco.	At a quarter to five.

7.4.1 Fill in with the correct from of the verb.

(i) Outside a shop with a FECHADO sign on the door
A que horas _____ esta loja? (verb abrir)

(ii) In a restaurant
A que horas _____ o restaurante? (fechar)

(iii) In a hotel
A que horas _____ o almoço? (começar)

(iv) At a coach station in Brazil
A que horas _____ o próximo ônibus (Br.) para o Rio? (partir)

(v) At a railway station in Brazil
A que horas _____ o próximo trem (Br.) de São Paulo? (chegar)

(vi) At a coach station in Portugal
A que horas _____ o próximo autocarro (Eur.) para Faro? (partir)

(vii) At a railway station in Portugal
A que horas _____ o próximo comboio (Eur.) de Coimbra? (chegar)

(viii) At a bus stop in Portugal
A que horas _____ o próximo autocarro (Eur.) para o centro? (passar)

7.4.2 Look at the times and answer the questions above, using the 12-hr clock. The first one has been done for you.

(i) Às nove da manhã.

| (i) 9h00 | (ii) 24h00 | (iii) 12h00 | (iv) 14h15 |
| (v) 22h30 | (vi) 13h00 | (vii) 10h20 | (viii) 15h45 |

7.5

Six people are describing their physical appearance.

7.5.1 Study the boxes below. They contain words you will hear in the descriptions of what people look like. Listen to your cassette/CD and tick each word as you hear it.

(o) cabelo *hair*	
louro *or* **loiro** *blond*	**liso** *straight*
castanho *brown*	**ondulado** *wavy*
ruivo *red*	**frisado** *or* **crespo** *curly*
preto *black*	**curto** *short*
grisalho *grey*	**comprido** *long*

(os) olhos *eyes*	
azuis *blue*	**castanhos** *brown*
verdes *green*	**pretos** *black*

(a) pele *skin*	
clara *light*	**morena** *dark*

7.5.2 Write down what the six people on the recording said about themselves.

7.5.3 Sérgio is describing Linda:

Ela tem
cabelo preto,
liso e comprido,
tem olhos pretos
e pele muito clara.

How would he describe the following people:

(i) Jane (*long, very straight, blond hair + blue eyes + light skin*)
(ii) Henry (*short, grey, wavy hair + black eyes + very dark skin*)
(iii) James (*very short, brown, curly hair + brown eyes + dark skin*)
(iv) Claire (*very long, red, wavy hair + green eyes + light skin*)

8 VOU ENCONTRAR-ME COM ELA AMANHÃ
I am going to meet her tomorrow

In this unit you will learn how to:

- say what you are going to do
- describe people's clothes as a form of identification
- describe the route to where you want to go

🎧 Falando com uma colega

Zaida is asking her colleague Abel about his reunion with an old friend.

Zaida Então quando vai chegar a sua amiga?
Abel Amanhã. Vou encontrar-me com ela ao meio-dia.
Zaida Oh! E onde vai ser o encontro?
Abel Na estação.
Zaida Muito bem! Ainda se lembra como ela é? Como vai reconhecê-la?
Abel Lembro. E tenho aqui a carta em que ela descreve como está agora e o que vai vestir para a viagem. (*lendo*) "Estou um pouco mais gorda e agora uso o cabelo comprido. Vou estar vestida de saia branca e casaco azul claro. Vai ser fácil reconhecer-me."

vou encontrar-me com *I am going to meet*	**vai vestir** *(she) is going to wear*
vai ser *is going to be*	**lendo** *reading*
muito bem! *well done!* (lit. *very well*)	**um pouco** *a little*
ainda se lembra...? *do/can (you) still remember...?*	**uso** *(I) wear*
	vou estar vestida de *(I) am going to be dressed in*
a carta *the letter*	**(a) saia branca** *white skirt*
em que *in which*	**(o) casaco azul claro** *light blue jacket*
descreve *describes*	

Na rua

Eduardo is looking for Hotel Baía and seeks help from a passer-by.

Eduardo Por favor, pode me dizer como se vai para o Hotel Baía?

Transeunte É um pouco longe. O senhor vira à esquerda ali naquela esquina, depois segue em frente e toma ... a quinta ou sexta rua à direita. É a Rua Augusta. O hotel fica à esquerda, no primeiro quarteirão, antes de um semáforo.

Eduardo Então, naquela esquina viro à esquerda, depois sigo em frente e tomo a Rua Augusta, que é a quinta ou sexta à direita. É isso?

Transeunte É isso mesmo.

---

como se vai...? *how does one get to...?*
ali *over there*
naquela (= em+aquela) *at that*
(a) esquina *corner*
o sr vira, segue, toma *you turn, go, take*

viro, sigo, tomo (*I*) *turn, go, take*
depois *next, afterwards*
(o) quarteirão *block*
antes de *before*
o) semáforo *traffic lights*
isso mesmo *that's it, exactly that*

Exercícios

8.1 Certo ou errado?

	C	E
1 A amiga da Zaida vai chegar amanhã.	❏	❏
2 Abel não vai poder reconhecer a sua amiga.	❏	❏
3 Eduardo pergunta como se vai para o Hotel Baía.	❏	❏

8.2 Perguntas e respostas

1 Como está a amiga que vai chegar amanhã?
 (a) Está um pouco mais gorda e com o cabelo comprido.
 (b) Está mais gorda e com o cabelo um pouco mais curto.

2 Como vai estar vestida a amiga do Abel?
 (a) De saia e casaco brancos.   *(b)* De saia e casaco azuis.
 (c) De saia branca e casaco azul claro.

3 Como se vai para o Hotel Baía?
   (a) Vira-se à esquerda naquela esquina, depois segue-se em frente e
   toma-se a quinta ou sexta rua à esquerda.
   (b) Naquela esquina vira-se à esquerda, depois segue-se em frente e
   toma-se a quinta ou sexta rua à direita.

🎧 Como se pronuncia

The spellings **gu** and **g** can alternate within the same verb. Practise after
the voice on the recording the different values of **g** and words with **gu**.

g   sounds like the first *g* in *garage* in general: che**g**ar; a**g**ora; **g**ordo
     but like the second *g* in *garage* before **e** or **i**: lon**ge**; **ge**ral; re**gi**ão.

gu sounds like *gw* in *arguing* – á**gu**a, **gu**arda-sol – except before **e** or **i**
     where it 'preserves' the first *g* sound in *garage*: se**gui**r (*to follow/
     go*). For example, in forms of the verb se**gu**ir, note that for **você** or
     ele you say se**gue** *but* for **eu** you say si**go**.

However, in some cases, the **u** is pronounced and Brazilians show the
difference by changing the spelling to **ü**: não a**gu**ento (Eur.) / não a**gü**ento
(Br.) (*I can't stand it*).

The different sounds represented by **x** have a lot to do with the different
origins the respective words have. Practise the following after the voice
on the recording.

x   sounds like *sh* in *show* at the beginning of a word and in some cases
     between vowels: **X**avier; **x**arope; **x**ícara (*cup*); pu**x**ar.

x   sounds like *s* in *so* between two vowels: pró**x**imo; má**x**imo (*maximum*);
     trou**x**e (*brought*).

x   sounds like *z* in *zebra* where **ex** comes before a vowel: e**x**ame (*exam*);
     e**x**emplo (*example*); e**x**austo (*exhausted*).

x   sounds like *ks* in *taxi* in some words: tá**x**i; fi**x**ar (*to fix, set*); se**x**o (*sex*).

x   before a consonant sounds like *sh* for *show* in Portugal but like *s* for *so*
     in most of Brazil: se**x**ta-feira (Eur.) / se**x**ta-feira (Br.).

Expressões-chave

Colours

Below you have the names for the colours. Some are different to what you have learned for physical appearance, e.g., **grisalho** for *grey* when applied to hair but not for *grey* in general. The word **castanho** in Brazil translates *brown* for hair and in Portugal for hair and in general.

branco/a	*white*
preto/a	*black*
vermelho/a – encarnado/a (Eur.)	*red*
amarelo/a	*yellow*
verde	*green*
azul	*blue*
cinzento/a (Eur.) **– cinza** (Br.)	*grey*
castanho/a (Eur.) **– marrom** (Br.)	*brown*
laranja	*orange*
cor-de-rosa	*pink*

To say that a colour is light or dark, add **claro** or **escuro: azul escuro**.

Colour names agree – **o**(**s**) or **a**(**s**) endings – with what they describe, but there is no m./f. change of ending in **verde** and **azul**. Also there is no change in expressions such as **cor-de-rosa**, (lit. *colour of the rose*). This is equally the case with **cor-de-laranja** (*colour of the orange*), or simply, **laranja**, and **cinza** (*ash*), despite the expression having been shortened.

Clothes

In general the same names are used on both sides of the Atlantic:

a saia; **a blusa**, *blouse*; **o vestido**, *dress*; **a camisa**, *shirt*; **a camiseta** or **a T-shirt**. There are, however, some distinctions to be made.

For anything that comes in pairs, for example shoes, the Portuguese will rather use the plural and the Brazilians the singular: **os sapatos** (Eur.) / **o sapato** (Br.). Similarly, for trousers, you may hear **as calças** (Eur.) or **a calça** (Br.). This also explains the following: **os jeans = as calças de ganga** (Eur.) but **o jeans = a calça de zuarte** (Br.). The change of gender (**a → o**) makes it clear you are not talking about Jean!

O casaco means basically *coat* or *jacket*, but the range of meaning covered is not quite the same in Portugal and in Brazil. If you are referring to the jacket in a suit, for a man or a lady, use **o casaco** in Portugal. In Brazil, it will be **o paletó** for a man and **a jaqueta** for a lady. For a casual jacket such as denim wear, you can say **o blusão** on both sides of the Atlantic.

For a man's suit, in Portugal say **o fato** (= **casaco** + **calças**) and in Brazil say **o terno** (= **paletó** + **calça**). For a lady's suit, you can simply say **saia e casaco** (Eur.) / **saia e jaqueta** (Br.). A tracksuit is **o fato de treino** (Eur.) / **o training** (Br.).

Como se vai para...?

In previous units you were given street directions as locations, with **fica/ ficam** or **é/são** – e.g., O hotel fica na segunda rua à esquerda – and you also learned how to ask to be shown on the map the place you want to go to – **faça o favor de me mostrar no mapa onde fica ...** – and the place where you are – **... onde estou**. Now you can also ask **como se vai para...?** or **por onde se vai para...?**

> **Por favor, como se vai para o Hotel Baía?** or
> **Por favor, por onde se vai para o Hotel Baía?**
> *Which way does one go to get to the Hotel Baía?*

For possible answers when the route is described to you, you will need the following verb forms:

vai *go*	**segue** *go, carry on*	**continua** *carry on*	**vira** *turn*	**toma** *take*
from **ir**	segu**ir**	continu**ar**	vir**ar**	tom**ar**

Landmarks are given depending on what stands out as a good reference point, e.g., **o semáforo** or **o sinal de trânsito** (*the traffic signal*). Also, geometric expressions for road layout are used, such as **paralela** (*parallel*), **perpendicular** (*at a right angle*), **transversal** (*cutting across*), e.g., **na segunda transversal**, *at the 2nd cutting across*.

Até

Até, meaning *as far as*, is another useful word when it comes to describing a route. (In Portugal **até a** is often preferred to just **até**.)

> A senhora segue em frente **até a**o segundo semáforo (Eur.)
> A senhora segue em frente **até** o segundo semáforo (Br.)
> *You carry on as far as the second set of traffic lights.*

Até is also used for time, with the meaning of *until, till.* It is so in expressions you have learned such as:

até amanhã; **até** segunda-feira; **até** a próxima.

In Portugal this last expression is often pronounced with an open sound, a bit like *a* for *arm* and spelt **à**, **até à** próxima (**à** = **a**, preposition + **a**, article).

Como funciona

Reflexive verbs

Sometimes the action of a verb is done to the subject of that verb. In Portuguese this is often shown with a reflexive construction, in other words, the subject and the object are the same. Below you have the present tense of the verb **lavar** (*to wash*) employed reflexively, i.e., *to wash oneself.*

eu	lavo-**me**
tu	lavas-**te**
você, o sr / a sra ele / ela	lava-**se**
nós	lavamo-**nos** (*)
vocês, os sres / as sras eles / elas	lavam-**se**

(*) Note the omission of **-s** at the end of **lavamos**.

Reflexive pronouns (**me, te, se** ...) are attached to the end of the verb by a hyphen or are placed before the verb and no hyphen is used.

Lava-**se** às sete horas. (*He*) *has a wash at 7 am.*
Ele **se** lava às sete horas. (Br.) *He has a wash at 7 am.*
    (In both cases, lit. *he washes himself at 7 am.*)

In Brazil there is a strong tendency to place the reflexive pronoun before the verb. In order to avoid starting a sentence with a reflexive pronoun, you can begin with e.g., **ele, nós**, etc.:

Ele se lava às sete horas. **Nós nos** lavamos às sete horas. (Br.)

Both in Brazil and elsewhere, the reflexive pronoun precedes the verb in the following cases:

(a) Negative sentence:
Não se lava às sete horas. *He doesn't have a wash at 7 am.*

(b) Question introduced by a question word or phrase:
Quando se lava? *When does he have a wash?*
A que horas se lava? *At what time does he have a wash?* but
Lava-se às sete horas? *Does he have a wash at 7 am?*

(c) Sentence introduced by a short adverb or an adverbial phrase:
Já se lavou. *He has already had a wash.*
Depois de se lavar. *After he has had a wash.*

(d) A subordinate clause introduced by a conjunction (e.g., *I think that...*) or a relative pronoun (e.g., *the person who...*):
Penso **que** se lava às sete horas. *I think that he has a wash at 7 am.*
Ele é a pessoa **que** se lava às sete horas. *He is the person who has a wash at 7 am.*

This still stands if a subject (**ele** or other) is being used:

Ele não se lava às sete horas.   Depois de **ele** se lavar.
Penso que **ele** se lava às sete horas.

Also note the following:

■ Portuguese employs the reflexive construction in a variety of cases where English finds a different kind of rendering:

To do with the 'self'

Como (você) **se** chama?	*How do you call yourself?* for *what is your name?*
Lavo-**me** e visto-**me** às sete.	*I have a wash and get dressed at 7 am.*
Ainda **se** lembra como ela é?	*Do you still remember what she looks like?*

You..., One...

Por onde **se** vai para o Hotel Baía?	*Which way does one go to get to Hotel Baía?*
Como **se** escreve esse endereço?	*How do you spell that address?*

Reciprocal action

A que horas nos encontramos amanhã?	*At what time are we meeting tomorrow?*

- In a question-answer situation, the reflexive can be dropped:
  – E ainda **se** lembra como ela é?
  – Lembro.

Verbs: the three conjugations – colloquial future

Future action or state is often expressed by using the present tense of the verb **ir**, *to go*, plus the infinitive of the verb you want to express –

Vamos part**ir** amanhã, *We are going to leave tomorrow*.

I am, etc. going to...   buy   sell   leave

		buy	sell	leave
eu	**vou**	compr**ar**	vend**er**	part**ir**
tu	**vais**			
você, o sr / a sra ele / ela	**vai**			
nós	**vamos**			
vocês, os sres / as sras eles / elas	**vão**			

(Note that verb **ir** is irregular)

In Unit 7 you learned that you could simply use the present tense for the future. How does this compare with the 'colloquial future'?

The former is a mere factual reference to an expected future action or event, the latter implies an element of determination or certainty.

Partimos amanhã.   *We are leaving tomorrow.*
  (That is what is likely to happen)

Vamos part**ir** amanhã.   *We are going to leave tomorrow.*
  (That is our intention)

Vou estar vestida de casaco azul.   *I am going to be dressed in a*
                                   blue jacket.
  (You can rely on it to identify me)

Note: the **vou** + infinitive sequence is not normally used with the verb **ir** itself. Therefore,

Vou para o Porto na 2ª-feira.   *I am going to Oporto on Monday.* or
                                  I am going to go to Oporto on Monday.

Tone of voice can be used to convey determination or certainty.

☑ Exercícios

8.3

Tricia would like to go to the swimming pool and has asked
Por onde se vai para a piscina?

8.3.1 Fill in the gaps in the route she has been told, choosing the words
you need from the list below.

toma – vira – segue
transversal – perpendicular

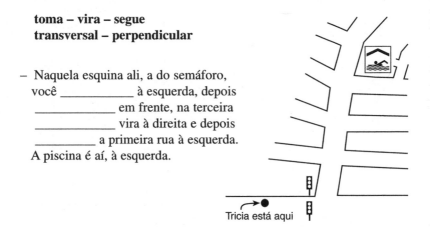

– Naquela esquina ali, a do semáforo,
  você _____ à esquerda, depois
  _____ em frente, na terceira
  _____ vira à direita e depois
  _____ a primeira rua à esquerda.
  A piscina é aí, à esquerda.

Tricia está aqui

8.3.2 What could you have said instead of **você...** to add a touch of
extra politeness?

🎧 8.4

Four people are talking about their clothes.

8.4.1 Listen to your cassette/CD and match up the pictures on page 93
with the description of what each individual is going to wear. Tick each
item as you hear it.

fato (Eur.) / terno (Br.)
[castanho (Eur.) / marrom (Br.) claro]

blusa [vermelho]

saia e casaco (Eur.) /
saia e jaqueta (Br.)
[cinzento (Eur.) / cinza (Br.)]

camiseta
[branco]

casaco
[laranja escuro]

calça(s)
[verde]

blusão [preto]

camisa
[amarelo]

calça(s) de ganga (Eur.) /
zuarte (Br.) [azul]

8.4.2 Listen to the recording again and write out a full description of what each person is going to wear.

8.4.3 How would they have said that, for travelling, this is the kind of clothes they usually wear. Number 1 is done for you:

Para viajar normalmente visto terno (ou um terno).

8.4.4 Out of the four individuals describing their clothes, which two come from Brazil?

8.4.5 You want to point out someone in a crowd. Complete the following sentences in Portuguese so as to explain who they are by reference to what they are wearing.

(i) É aquela senhora de _____(*pink blouse + green skirt*)_____

(ii) É aquele senhor de _____(*white shirt + brown trousers*)_____

8.5

The list of participants in a guided tour cannot be found and the guide is trying to sort out who is who. The questions, answers and statements below come from the group. Complete them, putting the jumbled-up words in the correct order.

1 O senhor, por favor, como __(chama / se)__ ?

2 Eu? __(Chamo / Valdemar Nascimento / me / -)__ .

3 Por favor! Esta é a pessoa que __(se / Mauro de Sá / chama)__ .

4 Aquele senhor? Eu penso que __(chama / Fernando Camargo / se / ele)__ .

5 Desculpe a pergunta, a senhora __(- / se / Flávia Couto / chama)__ ?

6 Não, __(Flávia Couto / . / me / Chamo / chamo / me / não / - / Rute Bento)__ .

9 | ONTEM FUI DE CARRO
Yesterday I went by car

In this unit you will learn how to:

- describe your daily routine or someone else's
- talk about the months, seasons and the weather
- talk about something you did or what happened in the past

Falando acerca do seu dia-a-dia

Alexandra is trying to find out about Reinaldo's daily routine.

Reinaldo	Levanto-me cedo, às sete e meia da manhã, e saio de casa às oito e meia. À noite volto para casa tarde, às nove, e deito-me pelas dez e meia.
Alexandra	E no fim de semana?
Reinaldo	Deito-me mais tarde.
Alexandra	Então levanta-se também mais tarde?
Reinaldo	Depende. Levanto-me mais tarde, quando faz mau tempo. Quando faz bom tempo, levanto-me às sete e meia como de costume mas para ir à praia. Gosto de chegar lá muito cedo.

---

levanto-me (*I*) *get up*
cedo – tarde *early – late*
saio de casa (*I*) *leave home*
volto para casa (*I*) *return home*
deito-me (*I*) *go to bed*
no fim de semana = aos fins de semana

mais tarde *later*
depende (*it*) *depends*
faz mau tempo *the weather is bad*
 (lit. (*it*) *makes bad weather*)
faz bom tempo *the weather is fine*
como de costume *as usual*
 (lit. *like of habit*)

Falando de como vai para o trabalho

 Nazaré is explaining to Marcos how she goes to work.

Marcos Onde é que você trabalha?
Nazaré Trabalho numa loja relativamente perto da minha casa.
Marcos E como vai para o trabalho?
Nazaré Normalmente vou a pé.
Marcos E quanto tempo leva?
Nazaré Levo meia hora. Mas às vezes, quando me levanto mais tarde ou faz mau tempo, vou de carro. Por exemplo ontem fui de carro. Levei mais ou menos dez minutos.

é que filler words, lit. (*it*) *is that*
trabalho (*I*) *work*
relativamente *relatively*
vou a pé (*I*) *walk*, (*I*) *go on foot*
quanto tempo leva? *how long does it take you?* (lit. *how much time (it) takes?*)

às vezes *sometimes* (lit. *at times*)
por exemplo *for instance*
ontem *yesterday*
fui de carro (*I*) *went by car*
levei *it took me* (lit. (*I*) *took/used up*)
mais ou menos dez minutos = uns dez minutos

✓ Exercícios

9.1 Certo ou errado?
                                                                    C   E
1 Reinaldo sai de casa às 8h30.   ❏   ❏
2 O Reinaldo volta para casa às 22h30.   ❏   ❏
3 Sabemos que a Nazaré gosta de ir à praia.   ❏   ❏

9.2 Perguntas e respostas
1 Reinaldo: Quando é que ele se levanta às 7h30?
   (*a*) De 2ª a 6ª feira.
   (*b*) Ao fim de semana quando faz bom tempo.
   (*c*) De 2ª a 6ª feira e nos fins de semana em que faz bom tempo.

2 Nazaré: Onde é que fica a loja em que ela trabalha?
   (*a*) A 15 minutos da casa dela, de carro.
   (*b*) A 30 minutos da casa dela, a pé.

3 Nazaré: Ontem como é que ela foi para o trabalho?

   (a) Foi a pé e levou uma meia hora.
   (b) Foi a pé e levou uma hora e meia.
   (c) Foi de carro e levou uns 10 minutos.

Como se pronuncia

You may wish to get your accent right for the side of the Atlantic where you are intending to speak the Portuguese you are learning.

In Units 7 and 8 you learned the *so*-versus-*push*-or-*show* sound differences. Now please also note that a large number of Brazilians pronounce the **t** and the **d**, particularly before spelling **e** or **i**, as, respectively, [tj] and [dj], a bit like the *ch* in *cheese* and the *j* in *jar*. The final **-e** then sounds like *i* in *cigarette*. Listen to the recording and practise the following examples which will be pronounced for you first by a Brazilian voice and then by a Portuguese voice:

   dia; tar**d**e; noi**t**e; universida**d**e (*university*); **t**ive (*I had*).

Expressões-chave

Months and dates

Que data é hoje?   *What is the date today?*

janeiro	January	**julho**	July
fevereiro	February	**agosto**	August
março	March	**setembro**	September
abril	April	**outubro**	October
maio	May	**novembro**	November
junho	June	**dezembro**	December

The names of the months may start with either lower case or capital letter. Unlike English, days of the month are expressed in cardinals except for **primeiro**, but not necessarily so in Portugal:

   no dia **um** de Novembro *or* no **primeiro** de Novembro
        (**um** - cardinal)   (**primeiro** - ordinal)

Also unlike English, years are not read in hundreds.

2999 = **dois mil, novecentos e noventa e nove,** *twenty nine ninety nine.*

Hoje é **cinco de Agosto.**	*Today it is the fifth of August.*
Pedro Álvares Cabral avistou o Brasil no dia **vinte e dois de abril de 1500.**	*Pedro Álvares Cabral sighted Brazil on the twenty second April 1500.*

Seasons

As quatro estações do ano (*the four seasons*)

(a) primavera	*spring*	**(o) outono**	*autumn*
(o) verão	*summer*	**(o) inverno**	*winter*

The names for the seasons may start with lower case or capital letter.

Em dezembro é **inverno** em Portugal mas **verão** na maior parte do Brasil.	*In December it is winter in Portugal but summer in most of Brazil.*

(Please remember that winter in the Northern hemisphere coincides with summer in the Southern hemisphere.)

Weather

Study the following ways of expressing the weather.

1. Está	nublado	*It is cloudy*
	quente	*hot*
	frio	*cold*
2. Faz	frio	*It is cold*
	calor	*hot*
	sol	*sunny*
	vento	*windy*
3. Há	nevoeiro	*It is foggy*
	neblina	*misty*
	geada	*There is ground frost*
	gelo	*ice (on the ground)*
4. Chove		*It rains*
Neva		*snows*

Some tips to help you describe the weather correctly:

1 Use **está** (verb **estar**) with an adjective (e.g., **quente**) or with a past participle (e.g., **nublado**).

2 Use **faz** (**fazer**) with a noun (e.g., **sol**). Note that **frio** can be both an adjective (**um dia frio** = *a cold day*) and a noun (**o frio** *the cold*). As a result it fits into both categories (1) and (2) above and can be used with both verb **estar** and verb **fazer**. By analogy, the verb **estar** is also used with **calor** (*heat*) as an alternative to **quente** (**está calor** = **está quente**).

3 Use preferably **há** (**haver**) with a noun for something that looks dense or static (e.g., **nevoeiro**, *fog*).

4 Use a verb expressing the weather condition - **chove** (**chover**), **neva** (**nevar**) – for forms of precipitation, i.e., rain, snow, etc., seen to be falling. However, frost or ice on the ground is better expressed with **haver** – **há geada / gelo**.

The notion of movement that may be behind the preference for a conjugated verb for rain, etc. can be extended to **vento**, *wind*, with the verb **ventar**, as is the case in Brazil (**está ventando**, *the wind is blowing*).

Children and adults

The English word *child* (and its plural *children*) finds a Portuguese translation in **criança/s**, in contrast with **adulto/s** (*adult/s*). The word **criança** is grammatically feminine even when applied to a male child; **adulto** is masculine even when applied to a female adult. There is also the word **menino/menina** which translates *litte boy/girl*. Note the different way a parent refers to his/her young children depending on whether s/he is talking about his/her family or buying tickets for them:

Tenho dois filhos, um menino de quatro anos e uma menina de dois anos.
but
Três, por favor, para um adulto e duas crianças.

Particularly the feminine **menina** can assume a courteous form of address.

O leite é para a menina. The milk is for the little girl (the young lady).

Also, **moço** (Br.) or **rapaz** can translate *young man, lad*.

Tenho dois filhos, dois rapazes. *I have two sons, two lads*.

The feminine of **rapaz, rapariga**, is better not used in Brazil, where it has acquired pejorative overtones. The safe alternative is **moça**.

⚙ Como funciona

Questions

You have come across two different types of question.

(a) Questions which are like a statement, with the same word-order. The only change is an inquisitive rising intonation.

Você está de férias. *You are on holiday.* (statement)
Você está de férias? *Are you on holiday?* (question)

(b) Questions which start with a question-word (**onde**, **quando**, **como**, **qual**, etc.), in which case the subject (e.g., *you*) may come before or after the verb.

Onde você trabalha?   *Where do you work?*
   subject(**você**)+verb(**trabalha**)
Onde trabalha você?   *Where do you work?*
   verb(**trabalha**)+subject(**você**)

Subject+verb is more widely heard on the American side of the Atlantic and verb+subject on the European side.

Please note that in both question type (a) and (b) the subject can also be omitted, as you learned in Unit 6, and therefore you are also likely to hear the following versions:

(a) Está de férias. (statement)   Está de férias? (question)
(b) Onde trabalha?   (question)

é que

These are merely filler words, meaning literally (*it*) *is* + *that*.

Eu **é que** agradeço. *It is I who must thank you.*

On both sides of the Atlantic, **é que** helps to fix the word-order in a subject+verb sequence. This means that with **é que** you will fit in with your question word-order wherever you speak Portuguese.

Onde é que você trabalha?

Note also that the subject can be omitted. **Onde é que** trabalha?

Gender

How to change masculine to feminine in nouns for people (or animals):

1 Words ending in **-o** (masc.) (but not **-ão**) substitute **-a** (fem.)
   amigo / amiga   *friend* (*male / female*)

2 Words ending in **-or** or **-ês** (masc.) add **a** (fem.)
  senhor / senhora   *gentleman / lady*
  inglês / inglesa (no accent ^ in the feminine) *English man/woman*

3 Words ending in **-eu** (masc.) in general substitute **-eia** (Eur.) / **-éia** (Br.) (fem.).
  europeu / europeia (Eur.), européia (Br.) *European*

4 Words ending in **-e** or **-a** do not change.
  estudante   *student* (*male / female*)   dentista   *dentist* (*male / female*)

5 A few words in **-ão** (masc.) drop the final **-o** (for the fem.).
  irmão / irmã   *brother / sister*

6 **ô** changes to **ó**.
  avô / avó   *grand father/mother*

7 A different word is used.
  pai / mãe   *father / mother*

Adjectives, past participles used as adjectives, and ordinals follow the above rules according to their particular endings.

  o sen**hor** in**glês** / **a** sen**hora** in**glesa**   *the English gentleman / lady*
  obriga**do** / obriga**da**   *thank you* (said by male / female)
  na pri**meira** rua   *in the first street*

Note the irregular formation of the following adjectives for *good* and *bad*.

  bom tempo (masc.) *good/fine weather*; **boa** tarde (fem.) *good afternoon*;
  mau tempo (masc.) *bad weather*; **boa** notícia (fem.) *good news*.

Plurals

A masculine plural noun may include both genders.

  os amigos   *male friends* but also *male + female friends*
  os pais   *fathers*, i.e., *male parents* but also *father + mother*
  os filhos   *male children* but also *male + female children*

Exception: os avós   *grandparents* (*male + female grandparents*)

Note that the word **parente** does not translate the English word *parent* but is the name for a 'related person'.

  Um tio é um parente.   *An uncle is a relation.*

A masculine plural adjective or past participle is required where nouns of both genders are to be covered.

  O fi**lho** e **a** fi**lha** casa**dos**.   *The married son and daughter.*

Verbs: the three conjugations – preterite indicative

	I bought *I have bought*	*I sold* *I have sold*	*I left* *I have left*
eu	compr**ei**	vend**i**	part**i**
tu	compr**aste**	vend**este**	part**iste**
você, o sr / a sra ele / ela	compr**ou**	vend**eu**	part**iu**
nós	compr**amos**	vend**emos**	part**imos**
vocês, os sres / as sras eles / elas	compr**aram**	vend**eram**	part**iram**

Use the preterite for:

■ an action/event (or a series of actions/events) which was completed at
  some definite time in the past

   Che**guei** ontem.   *I arrived yesterday.* (cheg**ar**)
   Ontem **fui** de carro.   *Yesterday I went by car.* (**ir**)

■ an action/event (or a series of actions/events) which has been
  completed at some indefinite time in the past, including recent past

   Che**guei** hoje.   *I have arrived today.* (cheg**ar**)
   Hoje sa**í** de casa cedo.   *Today I have left home early.* (sa**ir**)

(Check **ir** and **sair** in the section for special verbs at the end of the book)

✅ Exercícios

9.3

Complete the sentence below by putting the weather and season
pictures into words.

Onde eles moram...

 no , no

na   e   no

9.4

(a) terra	land, native country

On your cassette/CD you will find some people talking about what the months are like in their own and someone else's country.

9.4.1   From what they say, enter month(s) and weather in the grid below. The first one has been done for you.

no mês /
nos meses de...   normalmente...

(i)	Na minha terra	*maio*	*bom tempo*
(ii)	Na terra do meu marido		
(iii)	Na terra da minha esposa		
(iv)	Na terra dos meus avós		
(v)	Aquele rapaz é de uma terra onde		
(vi)	Estas crianças são de uma terra onde		

9.4.2   Listen again and make a written note of all they say.

9.4.3   Can you describe that summer holiday when the weather went terribly wrong? (Look up verbs **estar**, **fazer** and **haver** in the table of irregular verbs at the end of the book.)

> *The weather was bad. It was cold, it was windy, it rained, it was foggy and the sun didn't come out.*

9.5

In the pictures below you can see Tony's normal daily routine and how it changed yesterday.

Normalmente

7h00	8h00	20h30	23h00
levantar	sair de casa	voltar para casa	deitar

Ontem

8h00	9h00	22h00	24h00
levantar	sair de casa	voltar para casa	deitar

9.5.1   Help Tony explain his daily routine.
Start with **Normalmente eu...**

9.5.2   Now help him describe how things were different yesterday.
Start with **Ontem eu...**

9.5.3   How would his mother describe his daily routine?
Start with **Normalmente ele..**

9.5.4   How would she describe yesterday's changed routine?
Start with **Ontem ele...**

10 | LUGARES E PESSOAS
Places and people

In this revision unit there is more practice on how to:

- move around and meet people
- talk about times, dates and weather
- talk about the past and what is expected to happen in the future

10.1

You are intending to travel around the country and want to know which direction you have to take for the different places you would like to visit.

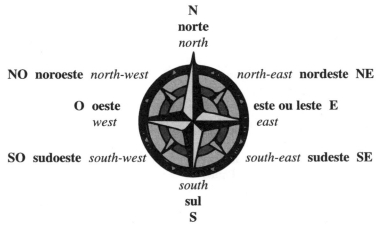

10.1.1 Study the above compass rose - **a rosa-dos-ventos** - and listen to your cassette/CD. Place a number, from 1 to 9, against each cardinal point as you hear it.

10.1.2 Check that you have understood everything the speakers on the recording have said. Write it down.

10.2

(os) graus centígrados	*degrees centigrade*

a temperatura está alta = está quente; a temperatura está baixa = está frio

10.2.1 Find a combination for the half-sentences below that will suit the weather forecast shown on the map of Portugal for the coming weekend.

No próximo fim de semana...

  (i) vai fazer sol
  (ii) vai fazer vento
  (iii) vai chover
  (iv) vai estar muito nublado
  (v) vão estar vinte e seis graus centígrados
  (vi) vão estar vinte e quatro graus centígrados

(*a*) no Porto
(*b*) em Lisboa
(*c*) nordeste-sudoeste
(*d*) a sul do Rio Tejo
(*e*) a norte do Rio Douro
(*f*) a norte do Rio Tejo

10.2.2 Re-write the forecast you have obtained above but as a report for last weekend. Start with:

No fim de semana passado...

10.2.3 Answer the following questions, giving full answers:

  (i) Fez mais calor no Porto ou em Lisboa?
  (ii) A temperatura esteve mais baixa em Lisboa ou no Porto?
  (iii) Fez bom tempo no norte ou no sul?
  (iv) Como é que esteve o tempo a norte do Rio Douro?
  (v) Fez vento de nordeste?
  (vi) Onde é que choveu?

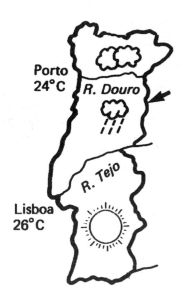

10.3

You may be travelling both in Portugal and Brazil.

10.3.1

(a) poltrona	*luxury seat*

Below is a ticket bought at a coach station in Brazil. Fill in the gaps in the dialogue between the lady traveller and the ticket clerk.

BILHETE PASSAGEM RODOVIÁRIO

SEGURO FACULTATIVO	LEI FEDERAL

DE	PARA	BILHETE Nº
MARINGÁ	CURITIBA	7500364

DATA EMBARQUE	HORÁRIO	POLTRONA
15 / 10	22:45	15

TIPO ÔNIBUS	PLATAFORMA	DATA EMISSÃO
EXECUTIVO	01	14/10

ônibus (Br.) = autocarro (Eur.)   plataforma (Br.) = cais (Eur.)

– Queria fazer uma reserva para Curitiba para amanhã à noite.
– À noite tem o Executivo.
– A que _____ parte?
– Às _____ e quarenta e cinco.
– Está bem. Queria "não fumante", somente ida.
– O ônibus é todo _____. É proibido _____.
– Certo.
– Aqui está a passagem da senhora. Poltrona _____ no Executivo das dez e _____ amanhã _____. O _____ sai da primeira plataforma.

10.3.2

(a) linha (Eur.) = (o) cais (Eur.) = (a) plataforma (Br.)

(o) lugar, lugar sentado	seat
junto à janela	by the window
(a) carruagem	train coach

Below is a ticket bought at a railway station in Portugal. Fill in the gaps in the dialogue between the lady traveller and the ticket clerk.

TIPO DE COMBOIO – IC

RESERVA   01.02   Nº 16 50050

BILHETE

1 LUGAR SENTADO   NÃO FUMADOR

COIMBRA - B → LISBOA - S.A.

PARTIDA   02.02   10:25   LINHA 2

CARR.   021   JANELA 22

---

comboio (Eur.) = trem (Br.)   fumador (Eur.) = fumante (Br.)

B – B station, as opposed to A station in the city centre, Coimbra.

S.A. – Santa Apolónia, northern line railway station in Lisbon.

  – Queria fazer uma reserva para Lisboa para amanhã de manhã.
  – De manhã tem o Intercidades.
  – _____ parte?
  – Às dez e _____.
  – Está bem.
  – "Fumador" ou _____?
  – "Não fumador", somente ida.
  – Quer lugar junto à janela?
  – _____, sim. Obrigada.
  – Aqui está o bilhete da senhora. Lugar _____ e dois na carruagem
     vinte e _____ do Intercidades das _____ e vinte e cinco amanhã
     _____. O _____ sai da linha número dois.

10.4

| Como é que se escreve? | How do you spell it? |
| A de África... | A for (lit. of) Africa... |

10.4.1 Practise saying the Portuguese names for the letters after the voice on the recording. You will hear the alphabet twice, in a Portuguese and in a Brazilian voice.

A, B, C, D, E, F, G, H, I, J, L, M, N, O, P, Q, R, S, T, U, V, X, Z

K, W, Y: These letters are found in some place names, words of foreign origin and international abbreviations.

10.4.2 Take Peter Ralph's place in the dialogue below and carry on, using the words in the box (these are words you already know).

– Como é que o senhor se chama?
– Peter Ralph.
– Peter... (*escrevendo*) E o outro nome, como é que se escreve?
– Escreve-se com R de rua...

praia	
	longe
homem	
	água

10.5

10.5.1 **Onde é que você mora?**

(i) Can you ask this question using **o senhor** for *you*?
(ii) Can you now ask the same question but using **tu** for *you*. Remember to change the verb endings too.

10.5.2 Look at the three road names and also at the three front door numbers.

Nº 21

Nº 95

Nº 42

a travessa = a rua pequena transversal

(i) Listen to the two people on the recording who are saying where they live and tick their road name and door number.

(ii) Play the role of the person who lives at the third address and say where you live.

 10.6

On your cassette/CD you will hear a lady talking to a taxi driver.

This is the piece of paper she is showing him.

> *Rua do Atlântico, nº 100*

10.6.1

(i) Listen to what she says and rearrange the words below so as to match her own words.

Pode / levar / para / me / ? / endereço / este

(ii) What did she ask?

(iii) Now, without showing the written note to the taxi driver,

(*a*) enquire whether he can take you to that address:

Pode...

(*b*) request to be taken to that address:

Faça o favor de...

 10.7

Three different people are looking for the public gardens Antero de Quental in the centre of Ponta Delgada in the Azores. They have asked:

Por onde se vai para o Jardim Antero de Quental?

10.7.1 Match the three sets of directions below with the three spots on the map where the question was asked - A, B, C.

(i) Esta rua é perpendicular à rua do jardim. Segue-se em frente até chegar lá.

(ii) Toma-se a primeira rua à direita, depois vira-se à esquerda e continua-se nessa rua. O jardim fica em frente.

(iii) Vai-se em frente. Na primeira transversal vira-se à esquerda. O jardim fica nessa rua, mas antes de chegar lá tem-se que passar duas ruas à direita.

10.7.2 These directions were given using **se** just like the question. What changes do you have to make to use **você** instead? Reword the three directions.

10.7.3 If you wish to be more courteous, what can you replace **você** with?

10.8

(os) calções de banho (Eur.)/ **a tanga** (Eur.) **(o) calção de banho** (Br.) / **a sunga** (Br.)	*male beachwear / bathing trunks*
(o) fato de banho (Eur.) / **(o) maiô** (Br.)	*bathing costume, bathing suit*
(o) biquíni	*bikini*

[cor-de-rosa]   [laranja]

10.8.1 Listen to the following mini-dialogues on your cassette/CD and write down the replies given to these questions.

(i) – Qual é a sua filha? (ii) – Qual é a sua irmã? (iii) – Qual é o seu pai?

10.8.2

em pé = de pé	*standing,* (lit. *on one's feet*)
deitado/a	*lying down* (lit. *laid*)
sentado/a	*sitting* (lit. *seated*)

Listen to the second set of mini-dialogues and write down the replies.

(i) – Qual é a sua neta? (ii) – Qual é a sua mãe? (iii) – Qual é o seu avô?

10.8.3 Following the above models, describe your:

 (i) female friend (*red bikini*; *very brown*; *standing*)
(ii) male friend (*green trunks*; *black hair*; *lying down*)

10.9

Sou de Maputo

← Maputo

Chamo-me Álvaro Maia. Sou de Maputo, em Moçambique. Tenho dezoito anos e sou estudante. Moro aqui na África do Sul há dois anos, com os meus pais, a minha irmã e o meu irmão. Os meus pais são portugueses e o negócio do meu pai tem uma agência grande no norte de Portugal. Vamos para lá no próximo ano e eu vou estudar na Universidade do Porto. Quero ser médico.

10.9.1   *What? Where? Where from? Where to? With whom? How long?*

Based on what Álvaro has said about himself and his family, what replies would he give to the following questions.

   (i)   Como é que você se chama?
  (ii)   De onde é que você é?
 (iii)   Quantos anos é que você tem?
 (iv)   Onde é que você mora?
  (v)   Há quanto tempo é que mora aqui?
 (vi)   Quando é que vai sair daqui?
(vii)   Com quem é que você mora?
(viii) Qual é que é a terra dos seus pais?
 (ix)   Para onde é que você vai no próximo ano?
  (x)   O que é que você quer ser profissionalmente?
 (xi)   Em que universidade é que você vai estudar?

10.9.2   **Você** *or* **tu**?

You are interviewing Álvaro for a school magazine in Portugal. Ask the same questions as above but with **tu** instead of **você**. Remember to change the verb endings accordingly.

The first question has been done for you: **Como é que tu te chamas?**

10.10

You may wish to send a Christmas card or express your good wishes verbally. Study the contents of the chart below and say the right words for each occasion after the speaker on the cassette/CD.

Natal *Christmas*	**Feliz Natal**
Ano Novo *New Year*	**Feliz Ano Novo / Próspero Ano Novo / Boas entradas**
Páscoa *Easter*	**Feliz Páscoa** *or* **Páscoa Feliz**
Aniversário *Birthday*	**Feliz aniversário / Parabéns**
Casamento *Wedding*	**Parabéns / Felicidades**
Aniversário de casamento *Wedding anniversary*	**Parabéns / Felicidades**
Nascimento *Newborn baby*	**Parabéns / Felicidades**
Falecimento *Bereavement*	**Sentidos pêsames**
Sucesso, êxito *Success, any happy event*	**Parabéns / Felicidades**

 ## 10.11

A birthday card for someone who is sixty years old reads:

Parabéns no seu sexagésimo aniversário. Muitas felicidades.

Re-write the birthday card for someone who is twenty-five years old.

10.12

Add your good wishes for the New Year to this Christmas card.

11 | SIGA EM FRENTE
Go straight on

In this unit you will learn how to:

- receive and give directions and instructions
- be specific about what you want in a shop
- talk about weights, measures and quantities

Na rua

Daniela stops two passers-by to ask the way to the local grocer's.

Daniela	Por favor, onde é a mercearia?
1° Transeunte	Não sei. Eu não sou daqui. Desculpe.
Daniela	Não tem importância. Obrigada.
	....
Daniela	Por favor, sabe me dizer onde é a mercearia?
2° Transeunte	Sei, sim. É perto. Siga em frente e no segundo semáforo vire à esquerda. A mercearia fica à direita.

> **a mercearia** *the grocer's shop* **siga** *go*
> **sabe me dizer...?** *can you tell me...?* **vire** *turn*
> (lit. *do you know to tell me...?*)

Na mercearia

The sales assistant at the grocer's serves Daniela and a second customer.

Daniela	Queria meio quilo de queijo.
Vendedor	Qual prefere?
Daniela	Prefiro esse à sua direita.

Vendedor Aqui tem o meio quilo de queijo. Mais alguma coisa?
Daniela   Não. Só isso. Quanto custa?

....

2ª Freguesa Queria meia dúzia de ovos, duzentos gramas daquele
queijo (*apontando*), uma garrafa de litro de água mineral e
salsicha em lata... uma daquelas latas na segunda prateleira
a contar de cima. E por favor dê-me um saco. (*pegando no
saco com as compras*) Obrigada. Quanto é tudo?

meio quilo de queijo 1/2 kilo of cheese	(a) **água mineral** mineral water
prefere (you) prefer	(a) **salsicha em lata** canned sausage
prefiro (I) prefer	**uma daquelas** (=de+aquelas) **latas** one out of those tins, cans
só = **somente**	(a) **prateleira** shelf
só isso that's all (lit. only that)	**a contar de cima** counting from the
quanto custa? = **quanto é?**	top (lit. at + to count + from)
duzentos gramas 200 grams	**dê-me um saco** give me a carrier bag
daquele (= de+aquele) **queijo** of (lit. from) that cheese	**pegando no saco** picking up the bag
apontando pointing	**as compras** the shopping
(a) **garrafa de litro** 1 litre bottle	**quanto é tudo?** how much does it come to? (lit. how much is (it) all?)

☑ Exercícios

11.1 Perguntas e respostas

1 Quem sabe onde é que a mercearia é?
(*a*) O primeiro transeunte.   (*b*) O segundo transeunte.

2 Por onde é que Daniela vai para a mercearia?
(*a*) Ela segue em frente e vira à esquerda no segundo semáforo.
(*b*) Ela segue em frente e vira à direita no segundo semáforo.

3 Qual é o queijo que a Daniela prefere?
(*a*) Ela prefere o queijo que está à direita dela.
(*b*) Ela prefere o queijo que está à direita do vendedor.

4 Quantas coisas é que a segunda freguesa quer comprar?
(*a*) Quatro: ovos, queijo, água e salsicha em lata.
(*b*) Cinco: ovos, queijo, água, salsichas e uma lata de outra coisa.

5 Onde é que está a lata que a segunda freguesa quer comprar?
    (a) Na quarta prateleira a contar de baixo.
    (b) Na segunda prateleira a contar da esquerda.
    (c) Na segunda prateleira a contar de cima

Expressões-chave

Being served

Someone entering a shop is normally received with expressions of welcome such as **faz favor** or **faça favor**, mainly in Portugal, and **pois não**, mainly in Brazil. These are polite phrases in an implicit invitation to the potential customer to express his/her request and are usually given a question-like intonation.

I would like...

As you have learned and practised in earlier Units, you can say the polite **queria...** , but you can equally say **quero....**, *I want...*

Also revise what you learned in Unit 4 about **tem...?** and **há...?** and on how to find out whether what you want is available.

Qual prefere?

Use **prefiro...** to express your preference, but if you don't mind one way or the other, say **Tanto faz**.

Prefiro esse à sua direita. *I prefer that one on your right.*

How much more?... or less?

Muito mais (*much more*), **muito menos** (*much less*), **um pouco mais** (*a little bit more*), **mais um/a** (*one more*).

Um pouco menos, por favor. *A little less, please.*

Enough and too much

Bastante (*enough*) is often used hyperbolically for *rather a lot.* **Muito** (*a lot*) is often used euphemistically for *too much.*

É bastante caro. *It is rather expensive.* É muito caro! *It is too expensive!*

But *enough* and *too much*, when controlling someone's actions, find a rendering in, respectively, **chega** and **é demais**.

| Chega. | *It's enough (stop there).* |
| É demais. | *It's too much (go back, take away a bit).* |

Is this all right? OK?

Está bem or **certo** will translate *all right* to express agreement.

Mais alguma coisa?

If you don't want anything else, you can say **não, só isso** or **não, é tudo**.

Something to carry your shopping in

For a *carrier bag* ask for **um saco** or in Brazil also **uma sacola**.

How much is it? and How much does it come to?

Just ask, respectively, **quanto é?** or **quanto custa?** and **quanto é / custa tudo?** or **quanto é / custa ao todo?**

Weights and quantities

The litre (**o litro**) is used for fluids and the kilogram (**o quilograma** or **o quilo**) for weights.

um litro de	*a litre of*
meio litro de	*half a litre of*
um quarto de litro de	*a quarter litre of*
um quilo (= quilograma) **de**	*a kilogram of*
meio quilo de	*half a kilogram of*

For smaller weights refer to grams (**os gramas**). Ham – **o fiambre** (Eur.) / **o presunto** (**cozido**) (Br.) – can also be bought by the slice – **a fatia**. Items such as eggs are usually bought by the dozen (**a dúzia**). For approximate weight or quantity use **mais ou menos** (*more or less*).

> Queria meio quilo de maçãs, mais ou menos 100 gramas de queijo, dez fatias de fiambre (Eur.) / presunto (Br.), uma dúzia e meia de ovos e uma garrafa de meio litro de água.

Bottles, cartons, jars, tins/cans, boxes and tubes

For beverages, **a garrafa** translates *bottle*; otherwise there is **o frasco** or **o vidro** (Br.). The word *jar* can be translated with **o boião** (Eur.) /

o **vidro** (Br.), but for a yoghurt ask for **um copo de iogurte** (Eur.) / **um pote de iogurte** (Br.). Other types of container and package include o **tubo**, *tube*, **a caixa**, *box*, e **o pacote**, *packet* or *paper carton*. Together with your tinned hot-dog sausages (salsicha em **lata**), you may also wish to buy some extras:

> Queria um pacote de manteiga (*butter*), um tubo de mostarda (*mustard*), um frasco de molho de tomate (*tomato ketchup*) e duas latas de cerveja (*beer*).

isto – isso – aquilo

Revise what you learned in Unit 6 about **este**, **esse**, **aquele** and their respective feminine forms. There is also a third set of forms: **isto** (*this thing here*); **isso** (*that thing there by you*); **aquilo** (*that thing over there away from both me and you*).

> Queria **isto**, **isso** e **aquilo**. *I would like this one, that one and that one over there.*

All these three sets of forms serve to point out something or someone. You will learn details of how they function later in this Unit.

⬛ Como funciona

Verbs: the three conjugations - imperative or command forms

buy!	*sell!*	*leave!*	
compr**a**	vend**e**	part**e**	one person (i)
compr**e**	vend**a**	part**a**	one person (ii)
compr**em**	vend**am**	part**am**	more than one person (iii)

When talking to:

(i) a person you would address with **tu**; (ii) a person you would address with **você** or **o sr / a sra**; (iii) more than one person in (i) or (ii).

> *Keep your voice down!* :
> **Fala** mais baixo! (i); **Fale** mais baixo! (ii); **Falem** mais baixo! (iii).

Handy Hints for the right 'command' endings

(i) tu: go back to the present tense (Unit 7) and take away the final -s:

compras→compra   vendes→vende   partes→parte

(ii) você or o sr / a sra: go back to the present and swap over the endings, i.e. -a to -e and -e to -a:

compra→compre   vende→venda   parte→parta

(iii) plural to (i) or (ii): just add -m to (ii):

compre→compre**m**   venda→vend**am**   parta→part**am**

(For other than regular verbs, always refer to the tables in the appendix)

Command forms and their alternatives

In Unit 2 you learned that public instructions are often given in the infinitive. You can use this - the infinitive - as the basis for different ways of telling someone verbally to do or not to do something.

For an instruction or invitation:

| EMPURRAR | on a door

You are standing by the door and are asked to push it open.

Faça o favor de **empurrar**   or
Queira **empurrar**

Similarly, when being offered a seat you may hear

Faça o favor de **sentar**-se   or
Queira **sentar**-se   and also
O sr / a sra quer **sentar**-se?   or
Você quer **sentar**-se?

The last two examples, though presented as a question in the present tense, are in fact an invitation. This format is used on both sides of the Atlantic, but the practice is further extended in Brazil where, depending on tone of voice, it can equally be used for a command – *Will you sit down?*

For a prohibition:

| NÃO FUMAR | on the wall

You haven't noticed the *No smoking* sign and have lit a cigarette. You may be told

   É favor não **fumar**   or
   Faça o favor de não **fumar**

You may also be reminded that this is a no smoking area by means of a statement in the present.

   Aqui não se fuma or Aqui não fuma (*here one doesn't / you don't smoke*) or, back to the infinitive you learned in Unit 2,

   Aqui é proibido **fumar**

In the examples above, if a direct command form had been used, this would have been, respectively,

   Empurre   Sente-se   Não fume

to which an expression such as **por favor** could be added for politeness.

   Empurre, **por favor**   Sente-se, **por favor**   **Por favor** não fume

The degree of politeness or assertiveness will vary with the tone of voice in which these words are said.

Both the infinitive and the command forms are used in public instructions, but the latter, being a more direct approach, tend to be given preference where the need is felt for a more forceful message, for example, where failing to observe the instruction may result in danger for yourself or others.

   Pare Olhe Escute *Stop Look Listen* (at a railway crossing)

Numbers 101 to 1,000

101	cento e um/uma	500	quinhentos/-as
102	cento e dois/duas	600	seiscentos/-as
121	cento e vinte e um	700	setecentos/-as
200	duzentos/-as	800	oitocentos/-as
300	trezentos/-as	900	novecentos/-as
400	quatrocentos/-as	1.000	mil

   cento e vinte e cinco gramas (o grama)
   cento e oitenta e duas pessoas
   duzentas pessoas
   mil pessoas

isto – este – esta

Despite its ending **-o**, **isto** is not masculine but neuter. It is for something (or someone) you have identified as being present but you don't know much about. Once you do, then it changes to **este** or **esta**, i.e., acquires a gender. The same happens with **isso-esse-essa** and **aquilo-aquele-aquela**.

– O que é **aquilo**?	*What is that* (neuter) *over there?*
– É uma lata de cerveja.	*It is a can of beer.*
– Ah! **aquela** lata de cerveja...	*Ah! that* (fem.) *can of beer over there...*

Also, **isto-isso-aquilo** is always singular, but the other forms can be plural, if you find out that there is more than one can of beer...

– Ah! **aquelas** latas de cerveja...	*Ah! those cans of beer over there...*

Finally, **isto-isso-aquilo** is always on its own, but the other forms can be on their own or accompany a noun

aquelas	(on its own)
aquelas latas	(with a noun)

  Exercícios

11.2

Ranging from a parking ticket to a cup of coffee, what you want may come out of a vending machine.

11.2.1 Study the information given on the coffee dispensing machine.

pressionar a tecla	*to press the key*
onde diz	*where it says*
retirar o troco	*to take out the change*

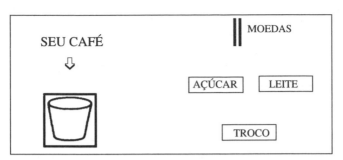

11.2.2 Mónica would like a cup of coffee with milk and no sugar. She is having trouble in operating the automatic dispenser and seeks help.

(i) Listen to the recording and read what she asks and what she is told. This is both on cassette/CD and transcribed below.

> – Desculpe, o que tenho que fazer para comprar café com leite e sem açúcar?
> – A senhora tem que introduzir as moedas, pressionar a tecla onde diz LEITE , esperar um pouco e depois retirar o troco e o café.

(ii) Give similar instructions but for a black coffee with sugar.
(Note that the instructions are given in the infinitive.)

11.2.3 Mónica tries but to no avail. She seeks help again, from someone else.

(i) Listen and read what she is told this time.
> – A senhora introduz as moedas, pressiona a tecla onde diz LEITE , espera um pouco e depois retira o troco e o café.

(ii) Explain how to operate the machine in a similar way but for a black coffee with sugar.
(Note that the different steps are described in the present.)

11.2.4 Still no good. Mónica seeks help for the third time.

(i) Listen and read how she is told to solve the problem.
> – Introduza as moedas, pressione a tecla onde diz LEITE , espere um pouco e depois retire o troco e o café.

(ii) Can you now give similar instructions but for a black coffee with sugar.
(Note that command forms are being used.)

11.2.5   Despite all the effort, the machine won't dispense any coffee.

Conclusion:

> A máquina está avariada.
> A máquina está com defeito (Br.) *or* a máquina está desarranjada (Br.).
> What does this mean?

11.3

Check that you remember how to say the following in Portuguese for when you are shopping for food over the counter:

1 I would like...
2 How much is it?
3 I would rather have...
4 A bit more / less, please.

5 It's all right.
6 Nothing else, thank you.
7 How much does it come to?
8 Can you give me a carrier bag?

11.4

You are in the grocer's shop. Some of the items you want are near you or near both you and the assistant (*location 1*); others are relatively distant from you but near the assistant (*loc. 2*); others are distinctively away from both you and the assistant (*loc. 3*).

Re-write the following sentences completing them with one of the three choices in brackets:

Queria...   *loc.*

(i)	_____ que está à sua frente. (isto / isso / aquilo)	*2*
(ii)	_____ lata de cerveja. (esta / essa / aquela)	*1*
(iii)	quatro fatias _____ fiambre(Eur.) / presunto(Br.) (deste / desse / daquele)	*3*
(iv)	mais ou menos meio quilo _____ maçãs. (destas / dessas / daquelas)	*1*
(v)	uma garrafa de vinho, uma _____ de litro. (destas / dessas / daquelas)	*2*
(vi)	250g _____ queijo, o terceiro a contar da esquerda. (deste / desses / daquele)	*3*

11.5

These are instructions on the escalator at an underground train station.

manter-se *to stand/stay still/keep*   **caminhar** *to walk, move forward*

MANTENHA-SE À DIREITA

CAMINHE PELA ESQUERDA

11.5.1 What does it say?

11.5.2 Advise a group who are with you. Start with: **Na escada rolante...** *On the escalator...* Complete the sentence by reading out the notice but remember to make the verb endings plural.

11.5.3 Give this set of instructions to someone you use **tu** with. It has been started for you: **Mantém-te ....**   Carry on.

12 QUANDO ESTARÁ PRONTO?
When will it be ready?

In this unit you will learn how to:

- deal with currency including large figures
- explain what you want as an alternative to self-service
- find different ways of expressing yourself about the future

 ## Numa agência dos correios

 Débora is with Alexandre at the post office and wants to buy some stamps.

Débora Não tenho trocado para a venda automática de selos. Você tem?

Alexandre Não, só tenho notas. A máquina não troca notas?

Débora Não, esta não. Apenas aceita moedas. Não faz mal. Posso comprar os selos no balcão.

....

Débora (*falando para o empregado do balcão*) Queria selos para enviar postais para o estrangeiro, por via aérea. São dois, um postal para a Europa e um para os Estados Unidos da América. Quanto é tudo?

(o) (dinheiro) trocado *small change*	**aceita** *accepts*
(a) venda automática *vending machine (lit. automatised sale)*	**não faz mal** *never mind (lit. (it) does not do harm)*
(o) selo *stamp*	**posso** *(I) can*
(a) nota *paper money, note*	**no/ao balcão** *at the counter*
trocar *to change*	**(o) postal** *postcard*
apenas = só, somente	**(o) estrangeiro** *abroad*
	por via aérea *by air mail*

Num posto de abastecimento

Carolina is at a filling station and wonders whether someone could check the tyre pressures for her.

Carolina Bom dia. É só auto-serviço ou pode verificar a pressão dos pneus?

Empregado Posso. Não há problema. A senhora pode deixar o carro que eu dou uma olhada nos pneus. Quer mais alguma coisa?

Carolina Não, muito obrigada, é tudo. Quando estará pronto?

Empregado Isso é rápido. Vai estar pronto daqui a dez minutos, mais ou menos. Enquanto espera, a senhora pode tomar um cafezinho. O bar é ali à esquerda.

(o) auto-serviço *self-service*	**pronto** *ready*
verificar *to check*	**rápido** *quick*
a pressão dos pneus *the tyre pressure*	**daqui (= de + aqui)** *from now*
deixar *to leave (something)*	**enquanto** *while*
dou *(I) give*	**tomar** *to have (drink)*
uma olhada/olhadela (Eur.) *a look*	**(o) cafezinho** *small black coffee*
	bar *bar*

Exercícios

12.1 Perguntas e respostas

1 Quem não tem dinheiro trocado para a venda automática de selos?
   (*a*) Débora.   (*b*) Alexandre.
   (*c*) Débora e Alexandre.

2 Para onde é que a Débora quer comprar selos?
   (*a*) Para a Europa.   (*b*) Para os Estados Unidos da América.
   (*c*) Para os EUA e a Europa.

3 O empregado pode verificar a pressão dos pneus?
   (*a*) Não, não pode. É só auto-serviço.
   (*b*) Pode e vai verificar a pressão dos pneus.

4 Quando é que o carro estará pronto?
   (*a*) Hoje.   (*b*) Hoje à noite.   (*c*) Amanhã de manhã.

5 A Carolina quer mais alguma coisa?
  (*a*) Não, não quer.
  (*b*) Quer, quer também gasolina.
  (c) Quer, quer tomar um cafezinho.

Expressões-chave

Self-service and automation

A vending machine can be simply referred to as **a venda automática de selos / bilhetes /** etc. and you don't normally say the whole name which is **a máquina de venda automática de...** You may need to get change (**trocar dinheiro**) for these and other coin-operated machines.

Onde posso trocar dinheiro para... *Where can I get change for...*
... a venda automática de selos? *... the stamps vending machine?*
... esta máquina? *... this machine?*

Also, you may prefer personal service where self-service is available. Start with **Pode...** or **Não se importa de...** , *if you don't mind...* (lit. *you don't mind...?*)

Pode... / Não se importa de ...
... verificar a pressão dos pneus? *... check the tyre pressure?*
... pôr gasolina no carro? *... put petrol in the car?*
... completar/encher? *... fill it up / top it up?*
  (the fuel tank)

here or there – now or then

isto	isso	aquilo	a
↓	↓	↓ — ↓	parallel
aqui = cá	**aí**	**ali lá**	concept
(here)	(there)	(there)	

There is no significant difference in meaning between **aqui** and **cá**; **ali** is nearer than **lá**; and **aí** is near the person/people you are talking to.

Also, **isso**, is what is near your interlocutor (**aí**) and/or in his/her thoughts or words:

É isso mesmo *It's exactly that* (i.e., *what you have said*)
Isso é rápido *That's a quick thing to do* (i.e., *what you have mentioned*)
Isso é boa ideia (Eur.) / idéia (Br.) *That is a good idea* (i.e., *your idea*)

Furthermore, **aqui**, **aí, ali** and **lá** can be applied to time.

Daqui (= de + aqui) a dez minutos   *In ten minutes from now*
Daqui (= de + aqui) a uma semana   *In a week's time*

Como funciona

Verbs: the three conjugations – future

I shall...	*buy*	*sell*	*leave*
eu	compr**arei**	vend**erei**	part**irei**
tu	compr**arás**	vend**erás**	part**irás**
você, o sr/a sra ele/ela	compr**ará**	vend**erá**	part**irá**
nós	compr**aremos**	vend**eremos**	part**iremos**
vocês, os sres/as sras eles/elas	compr**arão**	vend**erão**	part**irão**

The simple future is formed by attaching the endings **-ei**, **-ás**, **-á**, **-emos**, **-ão** to the infinitive of the verb. There are three exceptions – **dizer**, **fazer**, **trazer** – where the endings are added to shortened forms of the infinitive: **dir**ei etc., **far**ei etc., **trar**ei etc.

Handy Hints

Have you noticed that the endings for the simple future are basically the same as the present tense of the verb haver?

-ei	**-ás**	**-á**	**-emos**	**-ão**
hei	**hás**	**há**	**havemos**	**hão**

Verbs: the three conjugations – emphatic future

This is formed by the present tense of the verb **haver**, t*o exist / there to be*, plus **de** plus the infinitive of the verb you want to express.

I will/am etc. to...		*buy*	*sell*	*leave*
eu	**hei de**	compr**ar**	vend**er**	part**ir**
tu	**hás de**			
você, or sr/a sra ele/ela	**há de**			
nós	**havemos de**			
vocês, os sres/as sras eles/elas	**hão de**			

(Note that **haver** is an irregular verb.)

Comparing the 'futures'

Use the simple future

- in formal writing or speech as well as colloquially where futurity is the dominant notion:
  Part**iremos** amanhã. *We shall leave tomorrow.*
- to express uncertainty:
  Não sei se part**iremos amanhã**. *I don't know whether we shall leave tomorrow.*

Use the emphatic future

to express firm determination over a future action or firm conviction over a future event:

Havemos de part**ir** amanhã. *We will leave / are to leave tomorrow.*

Also revise what you learned in Unit 8 about the **colloquial future**.

Just imagine the following different outlooks on tomorrow's weather coming from three people who are planning to spend the day on the beach:

A – Não sei se **fará** sol amanhã. (simple future)
B – **Vai** faz**er** sol amanhã. (colloquial future)
C – **Há de** faz**er** sol amanhã. (emphatic future)

Speaker A is wondering whether the sun will come out; but speaker B knows that the weather forecast is for a sunny day; and speaker C trusts that the weather won't let them down.

Note:

The simple future can also be used as a courteous way of expressing someone's obligation.

O senhor dev**erá** reservar lugar. *You are advised to book a seat (you should really do it)*

The emphatic future can correspond to English *What shall I / we do?*

Que **havemos de** fazer? *What shall we do?*
Não sei o que **hei de** fazer. *I don't know what to do.*

Diminutives and Augmentatives

Diminutives and augmentatives are usually treated as single nouns and take plural ending **-s**.

(o) **cafezinho** (from **café**) *small coffee, for small cup of coffee*
um cafezinho – dois cafezinhos (**uma bica – duas bicas** (Eur.))

(a) **florzinha** (from **flor**) *little flower*
uma florzinha – duas florzinhas

(o) **casarão** (from **casa**) *big house*
um casarão – dois casarões *or* **um caseirão – dois caseirões**

Exception:

(o) **pãozinho** (from **pão**) *bread roll, i.e., small loaf*
um pãozinho – dois pãezinhos (from **pães**). See Plurals in Unit 4.

Numbers from 1,000 and Notes on numbers

1.001	mil e um/uma
1.022	mil e vinte e dois/duas
2.000	dois/duas mil
100.000	cem mil
1.000.000	um milhão
2.000.000	dois milhões
1.000.000.000	um bilhão/bilião (Eur.)
2.000.000.000	dois bilhões/biliões (Eur.)

Notes:

- **e** is used between digits in general, except after thousands when the hundreds plus either the tens or the units (or both) are greater than zero; and so on.

  vinte e um/uma (*21*); **mil e duzentos** (*1,200*); **mil, duzentos/-as e vinte** (*1,220*); **um milhão, duzentos/-as mil e sessenta e cinco** (*1,200,065*).

- **cem**, for 100, becomes **cento** when a number from 1 to 99 follows.

  cem pessoas (*100 people*); **cento e vinte pessoas** (*120 people*)

- where the number follows a noun, the masculine is used, as it agrees with the word (**o**) **número**, expressed or understood.

  (a) **porta número** vinte e **um** *door number 21*

  (a) **carruagem** vinte e **dois** *coach 22*

- the use of the comma – (**a**) **vírgula** – and dot is the reverse of English practice.

  1.001,5 – **mil e um vírgula cinco** (*1,001.5 – one thousand and one point 5*)

  For the thousands, etc. instead of using a dot you can leave a space.

  1 001,5 – **mil e um vírgula cinco** (*1,001.5 – one thousand and one point 5*)

 ## ✓ Exercícios

 ## 12.2

For centuries the word **escudo** was used in Portugal in connection with money and became the unit of currency, but **euro** (€) will be used in future.

o real (R\$)	*Brazilian currency*

12.2.1 Some digits are missing in the grid on page 133. Listen to your cassette/CD and fill in the gaps.

(i)						9	.	8	0	
(ii)					4		.	5		0
(iii)					7	0	.	1	2	
(iv)	1		.	6	3		.	7	1	
(v)		8	.		0	7	.		0	6
(vi)	9		.	3		0	.	8		

12.2.2 Listen to the recording again and write down what the speakers said.

12.2.3 Can you put into words the prices shown on these labels?

The first one has been done for you.

(i) Quarenta e dois reais e meio.

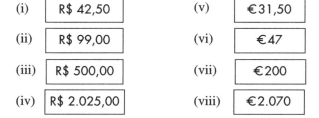

(i) R$ 42,50	(v) €31,50
(ii) R$ 99,00	(vi) €47
(iii) R$ 500,00	(vii) €200
(iv) R$ 2.025,00	(viii) €2.070

 12.3

Carlos has taken some friends to a café in Portugal. They are Portuguese Gabriela, Jorge and Judite and Brazilian Fábio and Eliana.

12.3.1   See below how Carlos went about finding out what each one wanted.

Carlos   Então o que é que vocês querem?

Eliana   Queria uma água mineral e um iogurte de banana.

Fábio   Por favor um café sem leite e com açúcar e um (Br.) sanduíche de presunto (Br.).

Jorge	Eu queria um café com leite e sem açúcar e uma sandes (Eur.) de fiambre (Eur.).
Gabriela	Queria uma cerveja e uma sandes (Eur.) de queijo.
Judite	Eu não quero nada, obrigada.

12.3.2 Take Carlos's place and make a list for the waiter (a Portuguese waiter), including a beer and a ham sandwich for yourself.

12.3.3 The group are invited to place their order.

Waiter	Façam favor?
You	*Read out your list.*

12.3.4 Put the following words in the right order so as to ask whether you will have to wait a long time:

Teremos / muito / ? / que / tempo / esperar

12.3.5 When the waiter comes with the order there is some confusion over who has ordered what. Explain that the mineral water and yoghurt are for the lady in the red T-shirt, and the white coffee and one of the ham sandwiches for the gentleman in the green shirt.

12.3.6 It is time to pay. Put the following words in the right order to ask for the bill (**a conta**):

A / por / . / favor / , / conta

12.3.7 Put the following words in the right order so as to tell the waiter he can keep the change (**o troco**):

Pode / o / ficar / . / troco / com

 # 12.4

incomodar	*to disturb, inconvenience*	**arrumar**	*to tidy up*

This is the card you found in your hotel room and you can hang on the door handle. On one side it has a 'do not disturb' message, on the other a message asking your chambermaid to tidy up your room.

É favor
não incomodar

É favor arrumar
o quarto

12.4.1   Someone has not noticed the sign hanging on your door and is making considerable noise in the corridor.

(i)   Use the words on the card so as to ask verbally not to be disturbed.

(ii)   Can you also ask not to be disturbed using the verb as a command instead? Add **por favor**.

12.4.2   You have turned over the card on your door handle and the other message is now showing. As you leave your room you meet the chambermaid in the corridor.

(i)   Starting with **Agora pode**... and using words from the card tell her that now the room is available to be done. Add **por favor**.

(ii)   Re-arrange these words to ask her when the room will be ready:
Quando / é / ? / quarto / pronto / o / que / estará

 # 12.5

This is the laundry form for nightwear and underwear that Craig and Barbara Howell had in their hotel room in Brazil.

LAVAGEM DE ROUPA – LAUNDRY SERVICE		
Quarto 405 Nome Howell Data 6 de fev.		
Quant. Qty	Roupa de noite e de baixo *Night and underwear*	Total (R$)
1	Pijama – *pyjamas*	
1	Camisola – *nightdress*	
2	Roupão – *dressing gown*	
	Camiseta interior – *vest*	
4	Cueca – *underpants*	
4	Calcinha – *panties*	
2	Sutiã – *bra*	
	Combinação – *slip*	
	Meia – *sock, stocking*	

Quant. = Quantidade
camisola (Br.) = camisa de noite (Eur.)
camiseta interior (Br.) = camisola interior (Eur.)

12.5.1 Read the form and see the items they have entered. The Howells haven't brought many clothes with them, and Barbara added a note asking whether all the washing could be done before Wednesday. Read her note.

> *Será possível ter tudo pronto antes de 4ª-feira? Obrigada*
> *B. Howell*

(i) If Barbara had wanted only the dressing gowns (**os roupões**), not everything, ready before Thursday, not Wednesday, what would she have written instead?

(ii) Write a similar note asking whether the pyjamas can be ready before Friday. Do not forget that unlike English **o pijama** is singular.

13 EU COSTUMAVA CALÇAR 43
I used to wear shoe size 43

In this unit you will learn how to:

- make comparisons and choices
- talk about what something is made of, design and pattern
- find different ways of expressing yourself about the past

Numa sapataria

Ricardo has entered a shoe shop and is interested in some footwear which is on display.

Ricardo	Queria um par destes sapatos e um destas sandálias, número 43.
Vendedor	O senhor quer sentar-se e esperar um momento?
	....
Vendedor	(*trazendo os dois pares*) Queira experimentar por favor.
Ricardo	(*experimentando um sapato e uma sandália*) Desculpe. Eu costumava calçar número 43, mas esta sandália está um pouco folgada e este sapato está muito apertado. Por favor traga-me outros iguais a estes mas a sandália no número abaixo e o sapato em dois números acima.

um par *a pair*	**iguais a estes** *like these*
(a) sandália *sandal*	**no número abaixo** *in the next*
experimentar *to try on*	*size down* (lit. *in one number*
eu costumava calçar *I used*	*below*)
to wear (footwear)	**em dois números acima** *in two*
um pouco folgada *a bit loose*	*sizes up* (lit. *in two numbers above*)
muito apertado *very tight*	

Numa loja de modas

Marlene is in a fashion shop looking for some clothes.

Marlene   Queria um conjunto de saia e blusa.
Vendedora   Temos vários. A senhora pode ver aqueles ali (*acompanhando a cliente*). O seu tamanho é 40 ou 42?
Marlene   42.
Vendedora   (*mostrando um conjunto*) Gosta deste?
Marlene   Gosto, mas preferia uma blusa com manga comprida e em roxo.
Vendedora   Em roxo não temos mas (*mostrando outro conjunto*) temos este aqui em rosa escuro e com manga comprida. Fica-lhe bem.
Marlene   Sim... talvez este. Posso provar?
Vendedora   Claro, as cabines de provas são ali à esquerda.
                ....
Marlene   (*voltando da cabine*) O conjunto assenta bem. Vou levá-lo.

---

um conjunto   *an outfit*
vários   *several*
acompanhando   *going with*
(o) tamanho   *size*
a cliente = a freguesa
gosta deste (= de+este)?   *do you like this one?*
(a) manga   *sleeve*

roxo   *purple*
fica-lhe bem   *it suits you*
provar = experimentar
(as) cabines de provas   *fitting rooms*
assenta / serve (Br.) **bem**   *is a good fit*
vou levá-lo   *I'll have it (lit. I am going to take it)*

✓ Exercícios

13.1 Perguntas e respostas

1 O que é que o Ricardo quer comprar?
   (*a*) Dois pares de sapatos.   (*b*) Dois pares de sandálias.
   (*c*) Um par de sandálias e um de sapatos.

2 Quais são os números que assentarão bem?
   (i) Sandália: (*a*) 44. (*b*) 45. (*c*) 42. (ii) Sapato: (*a*) 44. (*b*) 45. (*c*) 42.

3 Que tamanho é que Marlene veste?
   (*a*) 40. (*b*) 40 ou 42. (*c*) 42.

4 O que é que ela quer comprar?
   (*a*) Um conjunto com blusa de manga curta.
   (*b*) Um conjunto com blusa de manga comprida

5 De que cor é a blusa do conjunto que ela vai levar?
   (*a*) Roxa. (*b*) Rosa escuro. (*b*) Rosa claro.

Expressões-chave

Accessories

In addition to clothes you may also wish to buy some accessories such as:
a gravata, *tie*; **o lenço (de pescoço)**, *scarf* (square); **o cachecol**, *scarf*
(long); **o cinto**, *belt*; **o chapéu**, *hat*; **o boné**, *cap*; **a luva**, *glove*; **a bolsa /
a mala de mão** (Eur.), *handbag*. (Note that **mala** or **mala de viagem**
translates *suitcase*.)

um par de luvas *a pair of gloves;* **um chapéu de praia** *a beach hat*

What is it made of?

In order to ask this question, say **de que é feito**?

Isto aqui, de que é feito?	*This one here, what is this made of?*
De que são feitas aquelas	*What are those ties over there*
gravatas que estão ali?	*made of?*

The reply may come as: **de algodão**, *cotton*; **linho**, *linen*; **lã**, *wool*; **seda**,
silk; **couro / cabedal** (Eur.), *leather*; **pelica**, *kid*; **fibras sintéticas**, *man
made*.

Esta blusa é de seda	*This blouse is (made) of silk*
Aquelas blusas são feitas de	*Those blouses are made of cotton*
algodão	

Design and pattern

You may like something plain – **liso** – or not. Here are some alternatives
you can ask for: **listrado/a** or **com / às riscas** (Eur.), *striped*; **xadrez**,
checked; **estampado/a**, *with a printed pattern*.

uma camisa xadrez	*a checked shirt*
uma blusa em rosa, lisa	*a pink blouse, plain*
um vestido em tecido estampado	*a dress in a material with a*
	printed pattern

uma gravata listrada / às riscas *a striped tie in dark blue and white*
(Eur.) em azul escuro e branco

Como funciona

Comparatives

(i) mais
(ii) menos
(iii) tão

...

(do) que
como/quanto

(i) **mais ... do que**   *-er than, more ... than*

Peter é **mais** alto **do que** Mary.   *or*
Peter é **mais** alto **que** Mary.
Peter fala português **mais** fluentemente **(do) que** Mary.
Peter tem **mais** bagagem **(do) que** Mary.
Peter tem **mais** malas **(do) que** Mary.

(ii) **menos ... do que**   *less ... than, fewer ... than, no so ... as, not so much/many ... as*

Peter é **menos** alto **(do) que** Mary.
Peter fala português **menos** fluentemente **(do) que** Mary.
Peter tem **menos** bagagem **(do) que** Mary.
Peter tem **menos** malas **(do) que** Mary.

Note that in both (i) and (ii) above **do** in **do que** is often omitted.

(iii) **tão ... como ...   or tão ... quanto**   *... as ... as, so ... as*
There is a preference for the former on the European side of the Atlantic and for the latter in Brazil.

Peter é **tão** alto **quanto** Mary. = Peter é **tão** alto **como** Mary.
Peter não é **tão** alto **quanto** Mary. = Peter não é **tão** alto **como** Mary.
Peter fala português **tão** fluentemente **quanto** Mary.
= Peter fala português **tão** fluentemente **como** Mary.

Similarly,

tanto / tanta / tantos / tantas ... como   *or*
tanto / tanta / tantos / tantas ... quanto

as/so much and *as/so many ... as*

Peter tem **tanta** bagagem **quanto** Mary.
= Peter tem **tanta** bagagem **como** Mary.
Peter tem **tantas** malas **quanto** Mary.
= Peter tem **tantas** malas **como** Mary.

Verbs: the three conjugations – imperfect indicative

| *I was...* | *buying* | *selling* | *leaving* |
| *I used to...* | *buy* | *sell* | *leave* |

eu	compr**ava**	vend**ia**	part**ia**
tu	compr**avas**	vend**ias**	part**ias**
você, o sr/a sra ele/ela	compr**ava**	vend**ia**	part**ia**
nós	compr**ávamos**	vend**íamos**	part**íamos**
vocês, os sres/as sras eles/elas	compr**avam**	vend**iam**	part**iam**

The imperfect is formed with the above endings and is regular even for irregular verbs except in the case of **ser**, **ter**, **vir** and **pôr**, as well as their compounds e.g. con**ter** (*to contain*), su**por** (*to assume*).

Handy Hints

Note that there are only two sets of endings, one for verbs of the first conjugation (1st column, -ar verbs) and one for verbs of the second and third conjugations (2nd and 3rd columns, -er and -ir verbs). The latter is the same as the imperfect indicative of verb **ir**.

1st	**-ava**	**-avas**	**-ava**	**-ávamos**	**-avam**
2nd + 3rd	**-ia**	**-ias**	**-ia**	**-íamos**	**-iam**

Use for:

1 A continuous state or condition, action or event, in the past:

| Est**ava** / fa**zia** calor. | *It was hot.* |
| Eu **lia** o jornal. | *I was reading the newspaper.* |

2 An habitual action or event, in the past

Eu **lia** o jornal regularmente.	*I used to / would read the newspaper regularly.*
Eu tom**ava** chá todas as manhãs.	*I used to / would have tea every morning.*

or imperfect of **costumar** + infinitive:

Eu costum**ava** **ler** o jornal regularmente.	*I used to / would read the newspaper regularly.*

3 For politeness, often when asking for something:

Quer**ia** um pão.   *I wanted a loaf of bread.*
Meaning: *I would like a loaf of bread.*
Prefer**ia** uma blusa em roxo.   *I preferred a blouse in purple.*
Meaning: *I would like a blouse in purple.*

Comparing the 'pasts'

How does the imperfect compare with the preterite you learned in Unit 9?
In a nutshell, use the imperfect for a 'close-up' of something in the past
and the preterite for something finished with.

Imperfect
for something (state / condition / action / event) going on in the past:
Estava calor.   Eu lia o jornal.

Imperfect + imperfect
for something going on in the past at the same time as something else:

Eu lia o jornal enquanto ela estudava.
I was reading the newspaper while she was studying.

eu lia o jornal
|———————————————————————————|

ela estudava
|———————————————————————————|

Quando eu era criança, passava muito tempo na praia.
When I was a child, I used to spend a lot of time on the beach.

eu era criança
|———————————————————————————|

(eu) passava muito tempo na praia
|———————————————————————————|

Preterite + imperfect
for something that happened when something else was going on in the past:

Quando cheguei, estava calor. *When I arrived, it was hot.*

cheguei
↓
estava calor

|—————————————————————————————|

Preterite
for something that happened in the past when you look at it as a whole:

Cheguei na quarta-feira passada. *I arrived last Wednesday.*
Li o jornal esta manhã. *I read the newspaper this morning.*

Exercícios

13.2

Missanga is a young lady from Angola who spent some time in Portugal last year. She is talking about two T-shirts she bought from different places where she stayed for a while.

Algarve
no sul

Serra da Estrela
no centro leste

13.2.1   Listen to your cassette/CD and tick each T-shirt as you hear it being mentioned.

13.2.2   Listen again and write down all you hear.

13.2.3   In what two ways does Missanga talk about that time in the past? Why?

13.2.4 Missanga is now talking about her visit to Portugal globally rather than taking you through different stages in her stay. Listen to her next two sentences and rearrange the words below to match what she says.

Estive / ano / . / lá / passado / no
Fui / voltei /. / Março / Maio / em / em / dois / e / depois / , /meses

13.2.5 The two sentences above (in 13.2.4) are Missanga's reply to a question she has been asked.

(i) For the question, listen to the tape and unscramble the following words.
Quando / você / lá / é / esteve / que / ?

(ii) Can you reword this question for a friend who would address Missanga with **tu** instead of **você**?

13.3

Patrícia wants to buy a dress but cannot find one that will fit her.

13.3.1 This is what she says to the shop assistant:

Este vestido está muito comprido. Tem outro mais curto do que este?

Carry on on her behalf:
 (i) dress too short; a longer one (**curto**; **comprido**).
(ii) dress too tight; a wider one (**apertado**; **folgado**).

13.3.2 Now she says:
Este vestido está muito curto. Tem outro menos curto do que este?

Carry on:
(i) dress too long; not so long.   (ii) dress too wide; not so wide.

 ## 13.4

Jason is trying to buy a pair of boots – **a(s) bota(s)**– and tells the shop assistant his shoe size in his country.

13.4.1 Put the following sentences in the right sequence for his dialogue with the shop assistant.

(*a*) – Talvez o número acima, o 45.
(*b*) – No meu país calço n° 9 mas aqui não sei que número é.
(*c*) – Então quer experimentar o n° 44?
(*d*) – (*experimentando o n° 43*) Esta bota está muito apertada.
(*e*) – (*experimentando o n° 45*) Esta está bem, obrigado. Levo este par.

(*f*) – (*experimentando o nº 44*) Esta está menos apertada do que a 43, mas está um pouco apertada.

(*g*) – Nove... isso será número 43 ou 44. Eu trago três botas, uma em 43, uma em 44 e uma em 45.

13.4.2   Re-write the dialogue for Sarah. She wants training shoes – **o(s) ténis** (Eur.) / **o(s) tênis** (Br.). At home her size is 5 and the shop assistant suggests 37, 38 and 39 to choose from.

13.4.3   Later on Sarah tells a friend how she tried on different sizes until she found some trainers that fitted her. This is what she said. Fill in the gaps with the correct form of the verb estar.

O número 37 _____ muito apertado. O 38 _____ menos apertado que o 37, mas _____ um pouco apertado. Finalmente, o 39 _____ bem. Comprei o 39.

13.5

You are shopping for clothes, footwear and accessories and you are particular about material, pattern and colour.

13.5.1   What
                  you
               are buying

| uma camisa |
| uns sapatos |
| um vestido |
| uma gravata |
| uma saia |

Ask for:

(i) shirt; (ii) shoes; (iii) dress; (iv) tie; (v) skirt.
The first one has been done for you.

(i) Por favor, queria uma camisa.

13.5.2   Material

| algodão |
| pelica |
| linho |
| seda |
| fibra sintética |

Add the material you would like:

(i) cotton; (ii) kid; (iii) linen; (iv) silk; (v) man-made fibre.
(i) Por favor, queria uma camisa de algodão.

13.5.3   Pattern

> lisa
> lisos
> estampado
> listrada / às riscas (Eur.)
> xadrez

Add the pattern you would like:

(i) plain; (ii) plain; (iii) printed; (iv) striped; (v) checked.

(i) Por favor, queria uma camisa de algodão, lisa.

13.5.4   Colour

> em...
> branco
> azul escuro
> amarelo e verde
> preto e vermelho
> duas ou três cores diferentes

Add your choice of colour:

(i) white; (ii) dark blue; (iii) yellow and green; (iv) black and red; (v) two or three different colours.

(i) Por favor, queria uma camisa de algodão, lisa, em branco.

13.5.5   Your shopping has impressed your friends and they have some questions for you.

(i)   You are asked:
      Quando é que você comprou esses sapatos?
      Say:
      I bought these shoes last week.

(ii) You are asked:
      Quando é que você comprou essa camisa e essa gravata?
      Say:
      I bought this shirt last Monday and this tie last Wednesday.

(iii) Make the necessary alterations to change the questions in (i) and (ii) from **você** to **tu**.

14 | FAZENDO ISTO E AQUILO
Doing this and that

In this unit you will learn how to:

- meet someone socially
- fit in with local life and times
- talk about what is happening and express the idea of progression

Combinando um encontro

Marta and Tiago are arranging to go horse riding together.

Marta	Você ainda quer ir andar a cavalo esta semana?
Tiago	Quero. Quando e onde é que nós nos encontramos?
Marta	Quando, talvez 6ª.-feira.
Tiago	Ou sábado de manhã?
Marta	Pode ser sábado de manhã. Eu não me importo.
Tiago	E onde? Eu escolhi o dia, você escolha o lugar e a hora.
Marta	No correio, às 9 e meia.
Tiago	Dentro ou fora?
Marta	Dentro, junto das máquinas de venda automática.
Tiago	Sábado, às 9 e 30, junto das máquinas dentro do correio.
Marta	Combinado. Até sábado.

andar a cavalo	*to ride a horse*	**você escolha**	*you choose*
eu não me importo	*I don't mind*	**dentro ou fora**	*inside or outside*
(conceding)		**junto de = junto a**	*by, close to*
eu escolhi	*I have chosen*	**combinado**	*agreed*

Tomando alguma coisa

 Artur and Lúcia have arranged to meet at the café for a snack and a chat.

Lúcia   (*chegando*) Como vai?
Artur   (*sentado a uma mesa*) Bem, obrigado, e você?
Lúcia   Tudo bem. Desculpe se estou um pouco atrasada. Tive que fazer umas compras antes de vir.
Artur   Não, não está. Eu é que cheguei muito cedo. Enquanto estava sozinho, pensei em perguntar se você queria ir ao cinema.
Lúcia   Quero, sim. Ainda temos bastante tempo antes da segunda matiné.
Artur   Temos. E agora, o que é que havemos de pedir?
Lúcia   Para mim, um sorvete misto e depois um chá. E para você?
Artur   Uma água mineral com gás e uma porção de batatas fritas.

como vai? = como está? *how are you? how are you keeping?*	**pedir** *to ask for, order*
atrasada *late*	**para mim** *for me*
fazer umas compras *to do some shopping*	**um sorvete misto** *an ice cream in assorted flavours*
pensei em *I thought about*	**com gás** *fizzy*
(o) cinema *cinema*	**uma porção** *a portion*
matiné *afternoon session*	**(as) batatas fritas** *chips*

✓ Exercícios

14.1 Perguntas e respostas

1 Em que dia é que Marta e Tiago se vão encontrar?
   (*a*) Na sexta-feira.   (*b*) No sábado.   (*c*) No domingo.

2 A que horas?
   (*a*) Às oito e meia.   (*b*) Às nove.   (*c*) Às nove e meia.

3 Onde?
   (*a*) Fora do correio.   (*b*) Dentro do correio.

4 Quem está atrasado?
   (*a*) Artur.   (*b*) Lúcia.   (*c*) Ninguém.

5 O que é que Artur e Lúcia vão pedir?
   (*a*) Uma água mineral sem gás, meia porção de batatas fritas, um sorvete de chocolate e um chá.
   (*b*) Uma água mineral com gás, uma porção de batatas fritas, um sorvete misto e um chá.
6 O que é que eles vão fazer depois?
   (*a*) Vão para a praia.   (*b*) Vão para o cinema.   (*c*) Vão fazer compras.

Expressões-chave

de carro *but* a cavalo

For travelling we have been using the phrase **de** + means of transport: **de** carro; **de** táxi; **de** autocarro (Eur.) / ônibus (Br.); **de** comboio (Eur.) / trem (Br.).

Similarly,

de metro (Eur.) / metrô (Br.) (*by underground train*); **de** eléctrico (Eur.) / bonde (Br.) (*by tram*); **de** barco (by boat); **de** navio (by ship); **de** avião (*by aeroplane*); **de** moto, i.e., motocicleta (*on a motorbike*); **de** bicicleta (*on a bicycle*); **de** boleia (Eur.) / carona (Br.) (*hitchhiking, getting a lift*).

In Portugal:	*In Brazil:*
– Onde é que você foi ontem?	– Onde é que você foi ontem?
– A Braga.	– A Brasília.
– E como é que você foi?	– E como é que você foi?
– De carro.	– De avião.

You have also been using the phrase **a pé** (*on foot*) for when you are walking rather that using a means of transport – **andar a pé** meaning lit. *to go / move along on foot*. Similarly, **andar a cavalo** or **ir a cavalo** is used for *to ride a horse*, where **a cavalo** corresponds to *on horseback*.

Late, early, slow and fast

For late, use **atrasado/a** for a person and **tarde** for an action or event. For early, use **adiantado/adiantada** for a person and **cedo** for an action or event.

Desculpe se estou um pouco atrasada.	*Sorry if I am a little late.*
Eu é que cheguei muito cedo.	*It's I who arrived too early.*

You may also hear **atrasado** or **adiantado** in connection with an action, in which case what is being described is the person involved, not the action.

Eu é que cheguei muito adiantado.   *It's I who arrived too early.*

For clock reading, use **adiantado** for *fast* and **atrasado** for *slow*.

– **Que horas são no seu relógio?**   *What is the time by (lit. on) your watch?*
– **Uma e dez.**   *Ten past one.*
– **Está adiantado. É uma em ponto.**   *It is running fast. It is one on the dot.*

What about having the right time and arriving on time?

For clock reading, use **certo**, and for an action or event, use **na hora** or **a tempo** or **a horas**.

Este relógio está certo.   *This watch/clock is right,* i.e., *telling the right time.*

Cheguei na hora. *or* **Cheguei a tempo.** *I have arrived on time.*

Como vai?

When you greet someone you already know, you may wish to make some additions to what you learned in the introductory Unit at the beginning of this course.

For *How are you?* or *How are you keeping?* use **Como está?** and **Como vai?**. The latter is the general practice in Brazil but can also be used anywhere else. Another alternative is **Como passa?**

Although the expected reply may be *Well, thank you*, you may hear *Awful* instead. Usually they don't mean it!

Possible replies, in decreasing order of well-being, will be: **Óptimo** (Eur.) / **Ótimo** (*spendid*); **Muito bem** (*very well*); **Tudo bem** (*everything fine*); **Bem** (*well*); **Mais ou menos** (*so so*); **Não muito bem** (*not too well*); **Mal** / **Ruim** (Br.) / **Muito mal** (*not well / rather unwell*); **Terrível** (*awful*).

To enquire about a third person, say: **Como está / vai / vai passando** + the person's name. To send regards to someone, you can say **Dê** or **Faça o favor de dar cumprimentos meus a** + the person's name. For children, say **Beijos para as / nas** (Br.) **crianças**.

When parting, you can add to what you already know **Passe bem** (*keep well*) and **Adeus** (*goodbye*). The latter tends to suggest a longer separation in Brazil where **Tchau** is the most popular for just a brief *bye!*

– Como vai?
– Eu vou bem. E você, tudo bem?

– Olá! bom dia. Como está e como vai a sua mãe?
– Vamos bem, obrigada.

– Adeus. Dê cumprimentos meus a/à (Eur.) sua esposa. E beijos para as crianças.

Como funciona

Verbs: the three conjugations – continuous present and past

I am, etc. ...		*buying*	*selling*	*leaving*
eu etc.	**estou** etc.	**a** compr**ar** (Eur.) compr**ando** (Br.)	**a** vend**er** (Eur.) vend**endo** (Br.)	**a** part**ir** (Eur.) part**indo** (Br.)

I was, etc. ...		*buying*	*selling*	*leaving*
eu etc.	**estava** etc.	**a** compr**ar** (Eur.) compr**ando** (Br.)	**a** vend**er** (Eur.) vend**endo** (Br.)	**a** part**ir** (Eur.) part**indo** (Br.)

These are colloquial alternatives to the present indicative (Unit 7) and the imperfect indicative (Unit 13) in some cases.

The **continuous present** is formed with the present indicative of **estar** followed by (i) **a** + infinitive of the verb you wish to express (Eur.); (ii) the gerund (-ing form) of the verb you want to express (Br.).

The **continuous past** is formed with the imperfect indicative of **estar** followed by (i) **a** + infinitive of the verb you wish to express (Eur.); (ii) the gerund (-ing form) of the verb you want to express (Br.).

The continuous forms are more exact for the unfolding of an action or event which is happening now or was happening some time ago.

Eu est**ou a** l**er** a lição 14 neste momento (Eur.).
/ Eu estou l**endo** a lição 14 neste momento (Br.).
I am reading lesson 14 *at this moment.*
Eu est**ava a** l**er** o jornal quando ele chegou (Eur.)
/ Eu est**ava** l**endo** o jornal quando ele chegou (Br.)
I was reading the newspaper when he arrived.

Instead of the verb **estar** (**eu estou**, etc. *and* **eu estava**, etc.) you are likely to also hear the verb **andar** (**eu ando**, etc. and **eu andava**, etc.). Preference is given to the latter where the notion of 'lately' is involved.

Eu ando **a** estud**ar** muito (Eur.). / Eu and**o** estud**ando** muito (Br.).
I have been studying hard lately.

Ir is another verb you are likely to hear as an auxiliary for the continuous present and the continuous past (**eu vou**, etc. and **eu ia**, etc.). In this case there is no difference between European and Brazilian Portuguese.

I am / was, etc. ...		*buying*	*selling*	*leaving*
eu, etc.	**vou / ia,** etc.	compr**ando**	vend**endo**	part**indo**

– Como **vai**?   *How are you keeping?*
– Eu **vou indo** bem. E você?   *I am keeping well. And you?*

The verb **ir** option can emphasize progression.

Vou indo um pouco melhor.   *I am getting a little better* (after an illness).

Vou faz**endo** progressos.   *I am making progress* (in my studies).

Passive voice

The Portuguese passive voice is formed as follows:

verb **ser** + past participle of the verb you want to use
  ↓   ↓

Cadeiras de rodas são transportadas gratuitamente
Wheelchairs are carried free of charge

The past participle (**transportadas**) agrees in gender (feminine or masculine) and number (singular or plural) with the subject of the sentence (**cadeiras de rodas**).

As in English, the agent – who does the action – may or may not be expressed. When expressed, it is introduced by preposition **por**:

> **Cadeiras de rodas são transportadas gratuitamente pelo pessoal da Companhia** (por+ o)
> *Wheelchairs are carried free of charge **by** the Airline's staff*

However, in some cases the English passive voice finds a Portuguese translation in the reflexive construction you learned in Unit 8.

Como se escreve isto?	*How is this spelled?*
Fala-se inglês.	*English (is) spoken.*
Vendem-se selos postais aqui.	*Postage stamps are sold here.*
Aceitam-se cheques.	*Cheques are accepted.*
Aceitam-se cartões de crédito.	*Credit cards are accepted.*

half a...

Have you noticed that English *a* is left out in the translation of *half a...*: **meia hora**; **meia dúzia**; **meio quilo**; **meia porção**.

Temos que esperar meia hora.	*We have to wait half an hour*
Queria meia dúzia de pãezinhos.	*I would like half a dozen of bread rolls.*
Queria meio quilo de laranjas.	*I would like half a kilo of oranges.*
Traga-me meia garrafa de vinho.	*Bring me half a bottle of wine.*
Traga-me meia porção de batatas fritas.	*Bring me half a portion of chips.*

Exercícios

14.2

14.2.1 Look at the picture and answer the following questions about Sally:

(i) Ela vai de carro?
(ii) Como é que ela vai?

14.2.2 Use the words in brackets to say the following in Portuguese, on Sally's behalf:

(i) *I like horse riding.*
(Gosto / a / andar / cavalo / . / de)

(ii) *I go horse riding every Saturday.*
(Ando / sábados / todos / cavalo / a / os / .)

(iii) *I went horse riding last Saturday.*
(Andei / cavalo / sábado /. / a / no / passado)

14.2.3 Fill in the gaps in what Sally says next in Portuguese.

Eu encontrei o Raul quando _____ *(I was horse riding)* _____
_____ no sábado passado. Ele também ___ *(was riding a horse)* _____ .

14.2.4 What did she say? What happened when?

 14.3

Você fala português muito bem – *Your Portuguese is very good*

amável	*kind*	**aprender**	*to learn*
fazer erros	*to make mistakes*	**conseguir**	*to manage*
corrigir	*to correct*		

14.3.1 Put the following sentences in a different order so as to make a dialogue.

(*a*) – Você fala português muito bem.

(*b*) – Há dois meses.

(*c*) – Está. Há quanto tempo aprende português?

(*d*) – Estudando um pouco todos os dias.

(*e*) – Há só dois meses!? Como consegue aprender tão rapidamente?

(*f*) – Obrigado. Você é muito amável. Eu ainda faço muitos erros. Corrija-me, está bem?

14.3.2 Rewrite the dialogue for two people who address each other with **tu**.

14.4

14.4.1 Read the following question and reply which took place
at a shop with this notice in the window:

– Aceitam este cartão de crédito?
– Aceitamos.

> Aceitam-se cheques
> e cartões de crédito

What did these two people say?

14.4.2

a dinheiro	*cash*

In the same shop, other people are trying to find out how they can pay for
their shopping. Write down the reply that is likely to be given to each
question.

(i)   – Aceitam este cheque? (acei**tar**)
(ii)   – Posso pagar com este cheque? (pod**er**)
(iii) – Tenho que pagar a dinheiro? (**ter** que)

14.5

14.5.1 Study the notices on the page 156.

14.5.2 Answer the following questions, in Portuguese. Give full answers.

(i)   – A que horas é que o clube abre?
(ii)   – A que horas é que o jantar começa?
(iii)   – Até que horas é que o museu está aberto?
(iv)   – Quando é que a primeira matiné começa?
(v)   – Em que dia da semana há futebol?
(vi)   – A piscina está aberta à noite?
(vii)   – A partir de que horas é que a piscina está aberta?
(viii)   – A que horas é que a biblioteca fecha?
(ix)   – Posso estudar na biblioteca de manhã?
(x)   – A farmácia está fechada às dez horas da noite?
(xi)   – Qual é o horário de atendimento do médico de clínica geral?
(xii)   – Vou pôr uns postais no correio antes das vinte horas. Ainda vou
         a tempo para a terceira tiragem (Eur.) / coleta (Br.)?

14.5.3 Listen to your cassette/CD. You will hear four people, each one
asking a question about local facilities. Find the answers on the notices on
page 156. Give informative but brief answers.

14.5.4 Listen again to the four people on the recording and write down what they said.

14.5.5 Can you say the following in Portuguese:

(i) *At what time does the restaurant open?*
(ii) *At what time does the evening performance start?*
(iii) *Up to what time is the chemist's open tonight?*
(iv) *At what time does the museum close?*

CLUBE – RESTAURANTE
Club – Restaurant
ABRE ÀS 8 H DA NOITE
SERVE-SE JANTAR
A PARTIR DAS 8:30 H

CINEMA
1ª matiné   15h00
2ª matiné   18h00
soiré   21h30

ESTÁDIO
Stadium
FUTEBOL DOMINGO
À TARDE

MUSEU – GALERIA DE ARTE
Museum – Art Gallery
HORAS DE ABERTURA
Opening hours
DAS 11H00   ÀS 16H00

BIBLIOTECA
Library
DAS 9 HORAS DA MANHÃ
ÀS 9 HORAS DA NOITE

PISCINA
Swimming Pool
ABERTA
DAS 8 H DA MANHÃ
ÀS 6 H DA TARDE

Farmácia de Serviço
Duty Chemist
Aberta toda a noite

MÉDICO–CLÍNICA GERAL
Doctor – General Practice
HORÁRIO DE ATENDIMENTO
17:00H – 20:00H

CAIXA DE CORREIO
Tiragens (Eur.) / Coletas (Br.)
Collection Times
7h00   12h00   21h00

15 | ONTEM, HOJE E AMANHÃ
Yesterday, today and tomorrow

This is a main revision unit that will take you across the different topic areas you have been studying. You will be given extra practice on what you have learned about expressing yourself in the present, past and future and you will be using the language structures you already know in a variety of new ways.

 15.1

The words on the right mean the opposite of the words on the left, but they are in a different order. Can you pair up each word on the left with its opposite on the right? One has been done for you.

1 antes	(*a*) tarde
2 cedo	(*b*) depois
3 adiantado	(*c*) amanhã
4 ontem	(*d*) atrasado
5 na 2ª.-feira passada	(*e*) no próximo ano *or* no ano que vem
6 no ano passado	(*f*) no próximo mês *or* no mês que vem
7 no mês passado	(*g*) na próxima 2ª.-feira *or* na 2ª.-feira que vem

15.2

> **SÁBADO**
> *trabalhar*

This diary note is our starting point. But will working on Saturdays mean the same for everyone?

Aline, Guilherme, Ester and Rafael work in the same shop. Rearrange the words in brackets and find out how they view their Saturday work.

1 *Sexta-feira*. Aline always goes in Saturdays and she is referring to tomorrow's work factually, just as what is expected to happen.
(Amanhã / , / , / sábado /. / trabalho)

2 *Sexta-feira*. Guilherme doesn't always work on a Saturday. But he has committed himself to doing so tomorrow.
(Amanhã / . / trabalhar / vou)

3 *Sexta-feira*. Ester does not know yet for certain whether she will be working tomorrow, but she is likely to.
(Provavelmente / . / amanhã / trabalharei)

4 *Sexta-feira*. Rafael has always been reluctant about working on a Saturday, but he has made a new resolution and is determined to put it to practice tomorrow.
(Amanhã / . / de / trabalhar / hei)

5 *Sábado*. Aline is working when Hugo phones inviting her to take a break. Aline feels she can't now.
(Agora / . / não / posso / Estou / . / trabalhar / a) (Eur.)
(Agora / . / não / posso / Estou / . / trabalhando) (Br.)

6 *Domingo*. Aline is explaining to a friend that she worked yesterday, Saturday.
(Trabalhei / , / ontem / . / sábado)

7 *Domingo*. Aline is telling her friend about Hugo's phone call yesterday when she was working.
(Hugo / telefonou / eu / a / . / quando / trabalhar / ontem / estava) (Eur.)
(Hugo / telefonou / eu / . / quando / trabalhando / ontem / estava) (Br.)

8 *Umas semanas depois*. Aline is now going out with Hugo. She has given up working on Saturdays.
(Eu / aos / , / agora / não / trabalhava / sábados / mas / . / trabalho)
                                        or
(Eu / aos / , / costumava / agora / não / trabalhar / sábados / . / mas / trabalho)

15.3

Your watch may be right or not, you may be on time... or not.

Gonçalo's watch and Bernardo's are not showing the same time.

o relógio do Gonçalo   o relógio do Bernardo

The 'speaking clock' – **a informação horária** – tells us that the following is the right time:

> vinte horas e quarenta e cinco minutos

15.3.1   Give brief answers in Portuguese to the following questions:

(i) O relógio do Gonçalo está certo, atrasado ou adiantado?
(ii) O relógio do Bernardo está certo, atrasado ou adiantado?

15.3.2   Gonçalo and Bernardo had arranged to meet at a café halfway between where each one lives. Leaving home at the same time should result in arriving at the same time. They both set off at 8.30 pm by their respective watches. Who is likely to have thought the following on arrival:

(i)   (ii)

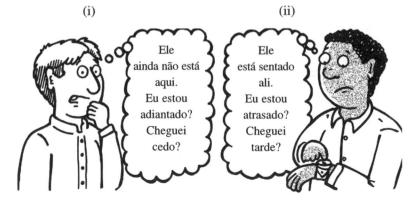

15.4

You don't want wrong figures in your bill, particularly if it adds up to more than expected.

You are paying for cakes (**bolos**), drinks (**bebidas**) and your bill includes 10% service (**dez por cento de serviço**), but there is a problem, the bill is wrong (**errada**).

uma conta errada   **uma conta certa**

Bolos	*1 600*
Bebidas	*1 760*
	3 360
Serviço 10%	*335*
Total	*3 795*

Bolos	*1 600*
Bebidas	*1 760*
	3 360
Serviço 10%	*335*
Total	*3 695*

15.4.1 To argue your point over the wrong bill enter the missing words in the gaps below.

Esta conta está errada. Três mil, _____ e sessenta de bolos e bebidas mais _____ e cinco de serviço não são _____e cinco. São _____e cinco.

15.4.2

> $2 + 3 = 5$
> dois mais três igual a cinco
> *or*
> dois mais três são cinco

Still about the mistake on the bill, say this in Portuguese:

$$3 + 3 = 6, \text{ not} = 7$$

15.5

Júlio is trying to concentrate and get on with his work but his colleagues are being somewhat noisy. Rearrange the words in brackets and find out how he starts by being very polite and ends up turning a bit dictatorial.

1 In a very polite tone, Júlio asks his colleagues to keep their voice down.
(Façam / baixo / mais / . / o / favor / de / falar)

2 They do but soon appear to forget and the noise comes back. Júlio asks again, still very politely.
(Por / , / falar / baixo / favor / . / queiram / mais)

3 They oblige, but it's not long before they forget once more. Júlio places his request a third time.
(Querem / mais / , / por / falar / baixo/ ? / favor)

4 There is silence for a few moments but peace and quite does not last long. Júlio is beginning to lose his patience and politeness is no longer a priority. He shouts:
(Falem / ! / baixo / mais)

15.6

carregue (Eur.) = aperte (Br.) = pressione

15.6.1 Look at the photographs on page 162. They were taken in Portugal. Photo (A) shows an instruction notice on a train, by the door, photo (B) shows an instruction notice by a pedestrian crossing.

(i) What 'command' word is shared by both instructions?
(ii) What does the writing in (A) say?
(iii) What does the writing in (B) say?
(iv) Rewrite the two instructions – (A) and (B) – using the infinitive you first learned in Unit 2.

(A)   (B)

15.6.2 Listen to your cassette/CD. You will hear people trying to help someone who does not appear to have noticed the instructions for the train door. Advice comes in five different ways. Write them down.

15.6.3 Continue listening. You will hear five different pieces of advice on the pedestrian crossing. Write them down.

15.6.4 Refer to the photos again.

(*a*) Rewrite notice (A) for Brazil, using the 'command' form.
(*b*) Rewrite notice (B) for Brazil, using the 'command' form.

15.6.5 Rewrite the two instructions – (A) and (B) – for Brazil, using the infinitive.

15.6.6 Listen to what comes next on your recording. Write down the new five pieces of advice on the train door.

15.6.7 Listen further. Write down the new five pieces of advice on the pedestrian crossing.

15.7

Joyce is explaining how she always (**sempre**) goes to the language school (**colégio**).

15.7.1 Look at the picture of Joyce going to school and fill in her missing words in the dialogue.

– Como é que você vai para as aulas de português?
– Vou _____.
– Normalmente ou sempre?
– Sempre. O colégio fica muito perto de minha casa.

15.7.2 Talking about the previous day, how would she describe how she went to school. Start with **Ontem**...

15.7.3 And what would she say about tomorrow: **Amanhã**...

15.7.4 How would you have asked the first question above if you were addressing her as **tu** instead of **você**?

15.8

> **(o) horário *or* (a) tabela de horário** (Br.)   *timetable*

a camioneta (para passageiros) (Eur.) = o autocarro (interurbano) (Eur.) = o ônibus (interurbano) (Br.)

Pode me dar o horário dos autocarros? (Eur.)
Pode me dar o horário das camionetas? (Eur.)
Pode me dar a tabela de horário dos ônibus? (Br.)

Following the above models, ask for the timetable for the trains:

(*a*) in Portugal   (*b*) in Brazil

15.9

> **(o) voo** (Eur.) **/ vôo** (Br.)   *flight*   **fazer escala em**   *to call at*
> **sem escala**   *non-stop*

15.9.1 Brazilian Antônio is in Lisboa enquiring about his flight back home to Brasília. Listen to your cassette/CD and write down both what he asks and the information he is given.

15.9.2 Portuguese António is in Brasília enquiring about his flight back home to Lisboa. Listen to your cassette/CD and write both question and answer.

 15.10

directo (Eur.) **/ direto** (Br.)   *direct*   **(o) transbordo**   *passenger transfer*

DIR = directo (Eur.) / direto (Br.)

In Portugal

– O comboio das 15.25
  para o Porto é directo
  ou tem transbordo?
– É directo.

> **PARTIDA**
>
> **PORTO (CAMPANHÃ)**
> **GUARDA – TOMAR**
> **DIR 15h25**

Campanhã – railway station in Porto

1 Taking the above mini-dialogue as a model and referring to the picture, say question and answer for:

(i) Tomar.
(ii) Guarda.

2 What word would you have said in Brazil instead of **comboio** ?

 15.11

When talking about coach and train stations, some people prefer using colloquial alternatives to **a estação rodoviária** and **a estação dos caminhos de ferro** (Eur.) / **ferroviária** (Br.). These alternatives are in the column on the right. Can you match the words on the left with their synonyms on the right?

1 estação rodoviária   (*a*) estação dos comboios (Eur.)
                                         (*b*) estação dos autocarros (Eur.)

2 estação dos caminhos de ferro (Eur.)   (*c*) estação dos trens (Br.)

(*d*) estação das camionetas (Eur.)

3 estação ferroviária (Br.)   (*e*) estação dos ônibus (Br.)

15.12

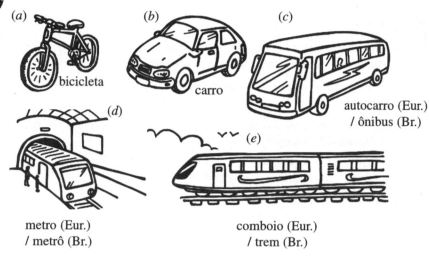

(*a*) bicicleta

(*b*) carro

(*c*) autocarro (Eur.) / ônibus (Br.)

(*d*) metro (Eur.) / metrô (Br.)

(*e*) comboio (Eur.) / trem (Br.)

15.12.1   On your cassette/CD you will hear six people talking about how they travel, where they travel to and how long it takes them.

15.12.2

(*a*) Listen to what they say and enter the information they give in the grid below. One has been done for you.

	where to?	how?	how long?
1			
2			
3			
4			
5			
6	*praia*	*bicicleta*	*+/–5 minutos*

(*b*) Listen again to what they said and write down all you hear.

15.12.3   Refer to the pictures and use the combinations below so as to compare how you usually go to work now and how you used to go to work over a period of time in the past. The first one has been done for you.

(i) (*b*) mas (*a*). (ii) (*c*) mas (*d*). (iii) (*e*) mas (*b*). (iv) (*c*) mas (*a*).

(i) Agora normalmente vou de carro mas costumava ir de bicicleta.

✓ 15.13

Point out the following people in a crowd by describing their physical appearance / clothes / where they are / what they are doing:

1 Four-year old Mariazinha **Aquela menina ....**
   (*long, blond hair + red and white dress*)

2 Teenage Bruno **Aquele rapaz ...**
   (*standing by the coffee vending machine*)

3 Adult Cecília **Aquela ...**
   (*black bikini + talking + by the yellow car*)

4 Adult Rúben **Aquele ...**
   (*short black hair + striped shirt + sitting down + reading the paper*)

✓ 15.14

 You are in Portugal booking in at a hotel for a group.

15.14.1   Try this for a tongue twister:

Quero quatro quartos no quarto andar para quatro noites.

15.14.2

o rés-do-chão (Eur.) **/ o andar térreo** (Br.)	*ground floor*
a cave (Eur.) **/ o subsolo** (Br.), **o porão** (Br.)	*basement*

You are inside the hotel lift going down. You are standing by the operating buttons and ask the other three guests joining you **Para que andar?** Listen to your cassette/CD and make a note of the floor where each one wants to get out.

4	❏
3	❏
2	❏
1	❏
r/c	❏
c/v	❏

15.14.3   When you come back to the hotel you want to ask for your room key you had handed in: **Por favor, pode me dar ...** Complete the sentence and say your room number:

   (i) the easy way *(4-3-9)*.   (ii) the not-so-easy way *(four hundred ...)*.

15.15

Below is your hotel breakfast order form, in Portugal.

15.15.1   You would like breakfast in bed between 8 and 8.30 am and you have decided on toast, jam, butter, orange juice, coffee, milk, boiled egg and bacon. Complete the form accordingly. Also, use the space provided and enter your three special requirements: hard-boiled egg (**ovo bem cozido**), skimmed milk (**leite magro** (Eur.) / **leite desnatado** (Br.)) and wholemeal bread (**pão integral**).

É favor servir entre as   *Please serve between the following times*
   07.00-07.30 ❏   08.00-08.30 ❏   09.00-09.30 ❏

pãezinhos quentes *hot bread rolls* .... ❏   mel *honey*.................... ❏
torradas *toasted bread slices* .... ❏   geleia *jelly/jam* ....❏
manteiga *butter* .... ❏   margarina *margarine* .. ❏

sumo de fruta *fruit juice*: laranja ❏ outro: indicar *specify* _____
              café ❏   chá ❏   leite ❏   chocolate ❏
              cereais *breakfast cereal* ❏   iogurte ❏
        ovos: cozidos *boiled* ❏   mexidos *scrambled* ❏
              estrelados *fried* ❏   omelete *omelette* ❏
                    presunto *bacon* ❏

Dieta ou outros requisitos *Diet or other requirements*:_____
_____

> geleia (Eur.) = geléia (Br.)   ovo estrelado (Eur.) = ovo frito (Br.)
> sumo (Eur.) = suco (Br.)   presunto (Eur.) = bacon (Br.)

15.15.2 The breakfast order form is on a long rectangular card with a large circular perforation at the top and says: **Antes de se deitar, queira pendurar na maçaneta exterior da porta**. Can you work out what this message means?

15.15.3 When you wake up at 8 o'clock the following morning you realise that the form is still lying on your bedside table. You phone reception to explain what happened and place the order verbally.

   esquecer-se (de) is the opposite of **lembrar-se (de)**

Fill in the gaps in your dialogue with the receptionist.

– Bom dia. Esqueci-me de pendurar na maçaneta da porta o cartão para pedir o _____*(breakfast)*_____. Ainda posso pedir?
– Pode, sim. O que deseja?
– Queria _*(boiled egg, toast, bacon, butter, jam, orange juice, coffee and milk)*_ .
– Prefere o ovo bem ou mal cozido?
– _*(well done)*_ . E só mais duas coisas, desculpe. Prefiro _*(skimmed milk, wholemeal bread)*_. Terei que _____ muito tempo?
– Não, meia hora mais ou menos.

✓ 15.16

Using words to locate what you want...

Can you pair up the positional words on the left with their opposites on the right?

1 à direita	(a)	atrás de
2 em frente de	(b)	dentro de
3 acima de	(c)	à esquerda
4 em cima de	(d)	abaixo de
5 do lado de cá	(e)	no fundo
6 fora de	(f)	ao fundo
7 do lado de fora	(g)	do lado de lá
8 em volta de	(h)	no lado interior de

9	à superfície	(*i*)	a contar de baixo
10	em primeiro plano	(*j*)	do lado de dentro
11	no lado exterior de	(*k*)	de baixo para cima
12	de cima para baixo	(*l*)	o último a contar de cima
13	a contar de cima	(*m*)	no meio de *or* no centro de
14	o primeiro a contar de cima	(*n*)	em baixo de (Eur.) / embaixo de (Br.)

15.17

no canto *in the corner*	**nas traseiras (Eur.) / nos fundos**
na parede *on the wall*	**(Br.)** *in the back (of house)*
no chão *on the floor*	**no balcão** *on the counter*
no tecto (Eur.) / no teto (Br.)	**na montra (Eur.) / na virtrine**
on the ceiling	**(Br.)** *in the shop window*

no lado exterior = no lado de fora
ao lado de = junto de/a
de um e do outro lado de = em ambos os lados de

15.17.1   Read the following description of a shop. Then check your comprehension of the text by answering the questions in English.

No lado exterior da loja vê-se a palavra ALIMENTAÇÃO na parede, acima da porta, que fica ao lado da montra (Eur.) / vitrine (Br.). Dentro da loja, há, no centro, um balcão. Na parede atrás do balcão há três prateleiras. Nas paredes de um e do outro lado do balcão há prateleiras, do chão até ao tecto (Eur.) / o teto (Br.). Abaixo da montra há uma prateleira. No canto direito ao fundo há uma porta para as traseiras (Eur.) / os fundos (Br.) da loja.

(i)   What can you read above the front door as you approach the shop?
(ii)   As you approach the shop, what can you see next to the door?
(iii) Where exactly inside the shop is the counter?
(iv)   What can you see on the wall behind the counter and the walls either side of it?
(v)   What is there in the right corner, at the far end of the shop?

15.17.2   Four different customers (*A*, *B*, *C* and *D*) enter the shop. They all want boxes of chocolates.

(i)   Read their words to find out who wants which box.

A: Queria a caixa grande que está em cima do balcão.

B: Quero a segunda caixa a contar da esquerda na prateleira abaixo da montra (Eur.) / vitrine (Br.)

C: Queria a caixa grande que está entre as duas caixas pequenas na prateleira do meio atrás do balcão.

D: Prefiro uma das caixas pequenas que estão em volta da caixa grande, na prateleira dentro do balcão.

(ii)   Answer the following questions, using full sentences in Portuguese:

(*a*)   Onde é que está a caixa que *A* quer?

(*b*)   A caixa que *B* quer está perto ou longe da montra (Eur.) / vitrine (Br.)?

(*c*)   A caixa que *D* quer está fora ou dentro do balcão?

(*d*)   Qual é a pessoa que prefere uma das caixas pequenas em volta da caixa grande?

(*e*)   Quem quer uma caixa que está na segunda prateleira a contar de baixo, atrás do balcão?

 15.18

Browsing and buying

15.18.1   In a shop, you want to explain that you are just looking. Do so by using the verbs in brackets and filling the gaps with the correct words.

   Estou só _____ (**ver**) (Eur.) / Estou só _____ (**olhar**) (Br.)

15.18.2   You are having difficulty in finding the right shop. Fill the gaps in the following sentence with the correct form of the words in brackets, so as to ask where you can find a shop that sells parasols.

   Onde _____ (**poder, encontrar**) uma loja que (**vender, guarda-sol**) _____ .

15.18.3   You are about to complete a purchase but you are asked to produce a voucher (**o talão**) as proof of payment before your shopping can be handed over to you. This is what the shop assistant says:

   Por favor, quer pagar ali na caixa? Depois traga-me o talão.

   What must you do?

15.19

(a) maré *tide* **(a) maré alta** *or* **preia-mar** *high tide*	**(a) maré baixa** *or* **baixa-mar** *low tide*

marés

preia-mar   02.50 e 15.15
baixa-mar   08.43 e 20.55

terminar means the opposite of **começar**

15.19.1   Answer the following questions, using the 24-hr clock reading.

(i)   A que horas começa a maré baixa?
(ii) A que horas termina a maré baixa?
(iii) A que horas começa a maré alta?
(iv) A que horas termina a maré alta?

15.19.2   What is the answer to the following questions:

(i)   Ao meio-dia a maré estará mais alta do que está agora ?

(agora são 10 horas da manhã)

(ii) Às seis horas da tarde a maré estará mais baixa do que está agora?

(agora são 4 horas da tarde)

15.20

o toldo de praia   **a barraca de praia**
beach awning, shade   *canvas beach hut*

15.20.1 Can you ask for the shade and beach hut hire? Start with

Pode me dizer onde ...

15.20.2 Unscramble the following sentences to say that you would like to hire:

(i) beach hut for one day.
   (Queria / alugar / barraca / . / dia / por / uma / um)

(ii) a shade for half a day.
   (Queria / dia / meio / um / alugar / . / toldo / por)

15.20.3 Ask how much it is:

(i) for the beach hut for one day;   (ii) for the shade for half a day.

16 ESPERO QUE A CONSULTA SEJA HOJE
I hope you can book me in for today

In this unit you will learn how to:

- cope in the case of illness or injury
- distinguish between a wish, an invitation, a suggestion and an order
- use a new way of expressing yourself about something in the future

Marcando consulta pelo telefone

Leonor is phoning for an urgent medical appointment.

Leonor	Eu queria marcar consulta para hoje.
Recepcionista	Por quê hoje?
Leonor	Porque não me sinto nada bem. É urgente. Agradeço que a consulta seja hoje, mesmo que seja tarde.
Recepcionista	Então... às 20 horas e 30.

---

por quê? / porquê (Eur.) *why?*
porque *because*
não me sinto nada bem *I don't feel at all well*
seja *may be, could be*

agradeço que a consulta seja hoje *I'd appreciate it if the appointment could be today* (lit. *I thank that...*)
mesmo que *even if*

No consultório do médico e depois na farmácia

Leonor is now at the doctor's surgery explaining her problem.

Leonor	Tenho uma dor forte no estômago.
Médico	É a primeira vez que tem essa dor?
Leonor	Não, a primeira vez foi há um ano. Estive no hospital.
Médico	Foi operada?

Leonor	Não, não fui.
Médico	Por favor, dispa-se e deite-se para ser examinada.
	(*examinando Leonor*) Dói aqui?
Leonor	Ai! Dói, sim.
Médico	(*escrevendo a receita*) Deve tomar este medicamento de 4 em 4 horas. Se não se sentir melhor dentro de dois dias, marque consulta novamente. (*despedindo-se*) Estimo as suas melhoras.
	....
Leonor	Para quando é que pode aviar esta receita?
Farmacêutico	Isso é rápido. O medicamento vai estar pronto daqui a um quarto de hora o mais tardar.

uma dor forte no estômago *a sharp /strong pain in my stomach*	**deve tomar** *you must take*
(a) vez *time, occasion*	**de 4 em 4 horas** *every 4 hours*
há um ano *one year ago*	**se não se sentir melhor** *if you don't feel better*
foi operada? *were you operated on?*	**marque** *book*
dispa-se *get undressed*	**despedindo-se** *saying good-bye / parting words*
deite-se *lie down*	**aviar esta receita** *to make up this prescription*
dói aqui? *does it hurt here?*	**o mais tardar** *at the latest*
ai! *(exclamation of pain)*	
(a) receita *prescription*	

✓ Exercícios

16.1 Perguntas e respostas

1 Leonor quer falar com o médico. Por quê? / Porquê? (Eur.)
   (*a*) Porque não foi operada.   (*b*) Porque toma um medicamento.
   (*c*) Porque tem uma dor no estômago.

2 Quando é que a Leonor esteve no hospital?
   (*a*) Há seis meses.   (*b*) Há um ano.   (*c*) Há um mês.

3 Quantas vezes por dia é que a Leonor deve tomar o medicamento?
   (*a*) Duas vezes.   (*b*) Seis vezes.   (*c*) Quatro vezes.

4 Que mais é que a Leonor deve fazer?
   (*a*) Marcar consulta o mais tardar daqui a dois dias.
   (*b*) Marcar consulta se não se sentir melhor dentro de dois dias.

5 Quando é que o medicamento estará pronto?
(*a*) Dentro de 10 minutos.   (*b*) Daqui a 15 minutos ou menos.

🔑 Expressões-chave

A telephone call

Ways of answering the telephone

You may hear:

(*a*) the number, e.g., 104 99 23 56
um zero quatro, nove nove, dois três, cinco seis(Eur.) / meia(Br.)
In Brazil there is the general practice of saying **meia** (from **meia dúzia**) instead of **seis** when you give a number digit by digit.

(*b*) the name of the subscriber
Consultório do doutor Armando Gonçalves.

(*c*) hello!
(i) Está? (Eur.) or Está lá? (Eur.) (lit. *are you / is anyone there?*)
(ii) Alô? (Br.)

How to announce yourself

Say **Fala...** You can also say **Daqui fala...** (Eur.) / **Aqui fala...** (Br.)
Fala Henrique Bernardes

The intention of your call

You can start with **Queria...** (*I would like...*) or **Posso...** (*May I...*)

Queria marcar uma consulta	*I would like to book an appointment* (e.g. for a medical appointment)
Queria marcar hora para....	*I would like to book an appointment for...* (e.g. with the hairdresser)

vez

You will come across the word **vez** and its plural **vezes** meaning *time(s)*, *occasion(s)*, *turn(s)*, depending on the context.

		alternatives
quantas **vezes**?	*how many times? how often?*	
duas **vezes**	*twice, two times*	
às **vezes**	*sometimes*	**ocasionalmente**
muitas **vezes**	*often*	**frequentemente/**
		freqüentemente (Br.)
poucas **vezes**	*seldom*	**raramente**
outra **vez**	*again*	**novamente**

Also, you wait your turn (**a sua vez**) in the doctor's or the dentist's waiting room. In the supermarket, you help yourself to a 'your turn' ticket instead of queuing up for the delicatessen counter; your ticket shows the words **sua vez** and a number.

Economising on words

Small words such as the articles – **o** (*the*), **um** (*a/an*) – and others are sometimes dispensed with in everyday speech and writing, particularly in brief messages.

> **Faça** ☐ **favor de...** *for* Faça o favor de... *please...*
> **Queria fazer** ☐ **reserva.** for Queria fazer uma reserva. ...*a reservation.*
> **Queria marcar** ☐ **consulta.** for Queria marcar uma consulta.
> ...*a medical appointment.*
> **Apertar** ☐ **cintos**, the lit up *Fasten your belt* sign facing your plane seat.

Clothes, shoes, hats on and off

Study the following Portuguese renderings:

vestir-se despir-se	vestir despir	o casaco, etc.	*it will cover your body*
calçar-se descalçar-se	calçar descalçar	o sapato, etc. a luva	*you slip it on your feet or hands*
	pôr tirar	o chapéu, etc.	*you put it on your head, etc.*

Note that **pôr / tirar** can be used as an alterantive to **vestir / despir** and **calçar / descalçar**, but the reverse does not apply.

> Quer tirar (=despir) o seu casaco? *Do you want to take your coat off?*

Emergency treatment and 'emergency' words

The following are usual ways of signposting a hospital accident department and a first-aid post.

EMERGÊNCIA	PRONTO-SOCORRO

Also note the following 'emergency' words: **Cuidado!** (*Watch out!*); **É perigoso!** (*It's dangerous!*); **Há /Tem perigo** (*There is danger!*); **Fogo!** (*Fire!*); **Depressa!** (*Hurry!*); **Socorro!** (*Help!*).

Como funciona

Verbs: the three conjugations – present subjunctive

I may...	*buy*	*sell*	*leave*
eu	compr**e**	vend**a**	part**a**
tu	compr**es**	vend**as**	part**as**
você, o sr/a sra ele/ela	compr**e**	vend**a**	part**a**
nós	compr**emos**	vend**amos**	part**amos**
vocês, os sres/as sras eles/elas	compr**em**	vend**am**	part**am**

The present subjunctive of regular verbs and the majority of irregular verbs is formed by dropping the final **-o** of the first person singular (the verb form for **eu**, *I*) of the present indicative (see Unit 7) and adding the endings highlighted in the above box.

Handy Hints

Have you noticed how close the present subjunctive is to the command forms, except for the **tu** form? (see Unit 11). In fact, it is the other way round. The command forms have been 'borrowed' from this tense.

Today's **tu** command form is the only remainder of the original command, or imperative, forms of the verb. Its plural counterpart, for **vós** (see Unit 7), is normally no longer used.

Use for:

1 The expression of a wish or hope.
   Espero que a consulta s**eja** hoje. *I hope that the appointment be toda*y.

2 The expression of sorrow or sympathy.
   Sinto muito que ela est**eja** doente. *I am very sorry that she is ill.*

3 An action or event regarded as a possibility.
   Ela talvez tome uma bebida quente. *She may perhaps have a hot drink.*

4 After a statement that implies influence upon other people or things.
   A hospedeira (Eur.) / aeromoça (Br.) pede ao passageiro que aperte o
   cinto de segurança. *The stewardess asks the passenger to fasten his
   safety belt.*

   Peço a/à (Eur.) Maria que compre o jornal. *I ask Mary to buy the paper.*

   Peço a/à (Eur.) Maria que faça o favor de comprar o jornal. *I ask Mary
   to be so kind as to buy the paper.*

(Note the different sentence construction in English – *to buy* / *to b*e)

A wish, a hope... and a 'polite imperative'

wish → hope → expectation

The command forms borrowed from the present subjunctive are a wish
made expectation. They are often referred to as the 'polite' command, or
imperative, forms.

   Compr**e** o jornal.   *Buy the paper.*

Unless tone of voice indicates otherwise, this does not bear the harshness
of tone the English translation may suggest, bearing in mind the inbuilt
uncertainty of the subjunctive forms.

Command form let's go!

The verb endings for **nós** (*we*) – **-emos, -amos** – render English *let's*.

   compr**emos** / vend**amos** / part**amos**   *let's buy / sell / leave*

These days this format is used mainly for verb **ir**.

   Vamos! *Let's go!*

Don't

For a command in the negative – *don't...* – just use **não** before the verb (see Unit 11).

Não compre isso. *Don't buy that.*   Não fume. *Don't smoke.*

In this case, the command for the **tu** approach borrows from the present subjunctive just like the others.

Não compres isso. *Don't buy that.*   Não fumes. *Don't smoke.*

Verbs: the three conjugations – future subjunctive

	if / when	*I buy*	*I sell*	*I leave*
eu		compr**ar**	vend**er**	part**ir**
tu		compr**ares**	vend**eres**	part**ires**
você, o sr/a sra ele/ela		compr**ar**	vend**er**	part**ir**
nós		compr**armos**	vend**ermos**	part**irmos**
vocês, os sres/as sras eles/elas		compr**arem**	vend**erem**	part**irem**

The future subjunctive is formed by dropping the final **-ram** of the third person plural (for **eles/elas**, *they*) of the preterite (see Unit 9) and by adding **-r, -res, -r, -rmos, -rem**.

Handy Hints

Does what you want to say start with *when* (**quando**) or *if* (**se**) and hasn't happened yet? Then use the future subjunctive.

Use for:

An action or event the realisation of which will determine the viability or purposefulness of another action or event.

Quando cheg**arem** lá, atravessem. *When you get there, cross over.*(they must get 'there', before crossing)

Pode me dizer por favor quando cheg**armos** lá. *Can you please tell me when we get there?* (the bus-top where you want to get off)

Se qu**iser**, podemos/poderemos ir ao cinema amanhã. *If you wish, we can/shall be able to go to the cinema tomorrow.*

The future subjunctive can be used for a very elegant way of saying *please*: **se fizer favor**. This expression is sometimes simplified to **se faz favor** which you learnt on page 16.

Note the use of, respectively, the present and the future subjunctive with the meaning of *God bless!*

■ As a warm wish for someone's well-being or as a warm expression of gratitude, *God bless!* finds a translation in **Bem haja!** (addressing one person) and **Bem hajam!** (addressing more than one) – verb **haver**.

■ *Good night, God bless!* Calling upon divine protection in the hours of darkness finds a different rendering, i.e., **Boa noite! Até amanhã, se Deus quiser**. Literally **se Deus quiser** means *if God so wishes* – verb **querer** – and corresponds to English *God willing*.

Irregular comparatives

Some adjectives and adverbs have irregular comparatives.

bom (*good*), **bem** (*well*)	**melhor** (*better*)
mau, ruim (*bad*), **mal** (*badly, poorly*)	**pior** (*worse*)
grande (*big, large*)	**maior** (*bigger*)
pequeno (*small*)	**menor** (*smaller*)
muito (*much*)	**mais** (*more*)
pouco (*little*)	**menos** (*less*)

However, sometimes both regular and irregular forms coexist. It is so with **mais pequeno** which is often preferred to **menor** in Portugal.

✓ Exercícios

16.2

A	B	C	D

The person in (A) is being invited to sit down – **Quer sentar-se?** – , the person in (B) to lie down – **Quer deitar-se?** –, and the person in (C) to stand up – **Quer levantar-se?**

16.2.1   Ask the following:

(i)   the person in (D) to lie down;
(ii)   the person in (C) to get up and sit down;
(iii)   the person in (B) to stand up.

16.2.2   Starting with **Faça favor de...** ask the following:

(i)   the person in (A) to take position (B);
(ii)   the person in (B) to take position (C);
(iii)   the person in (C) to take position (D).

16.2.3   Ask the same as in 16.2.2 above but starting with **Queira... .**

16.2.4   Ask the same as in 16.2.2 above but using the command form.

16.2.5   Ask the same again in the command form but talking to more than one person. (i) **Sentem-se**. Carry on.

16.2.6   Ask the same again in the command form but talking to a person you would use **tu** with. (i) **Senta-te**. Carry on.

16.2.7   Ask the same yet again in the command form but talking to more than one person you would individually use **tu** with.

16.3

Starting with **Queira...** ask someone to take off his/her:

(i) coat   (ii) boots   (iii) hat

16.4   Dores – *Aches and pains*

16.4.1   Put together the broken-up sentences in the box below so as to complain of the following:

(i)   a very bad sore throat since last Sunday.
(ii)   an aching tooth for the past two days.
(iii)   a severe ear-ache in your right ear since last night.
(iv)   a slight pain 'here' since last Wednesday.

Dói-me	muito um pouco	a garganta um dente o ouvido direito aqui	há dois dias desde ontem à noite domingo passado 4ª.-feira passada

16.4.2 The doctor is waiting for you to remove your clothes so you can be examined. To say you have done so insert the correct form of the verb:

Já me _____ . (**despir**)

16.4.3 Can you tell how often the following medicines must be taken?

(i) de 6 em 6 horas   (ii) 2 vezes por dia   (iii) dia sim dia não

16.5

Read the health information card completed by Kelly, who has a heart complaint and is allergic to penicillin. She has also entered her GP's name and phone number and that of her next of kin to be contacted in case of accident.

On Kelly's behalf, write the answers to the following questions.

1 É doente?
2 De que sofre?
3 É alérgica a algum medicamento?
4 Tomou alguma vacina recentemente?
5 Em caso de acidente, quem devo informar? Qual é o número do telefone?

MÉDICO ASSISTENTE *dr. Rui Vasco*

TEL.: *4571096*

VACINA _____ EM __ / __ / __

VACINA _____ EM __ / __ / __

EM CASO DE ACIDENTE, POR FAVOR INFORMAR
meu marido, Óscar Campos TEL.: *4381022*

OUTRA INFORMAÇÃO *sofro do coração;*
sou alérgica a penicilina.

 16.6

Listen to your cassette/CD and you will hear seven people saying 'emergency' words. Write them down, and say them aloud.

16.7

> **(o) passeio (Eur.) / (a) calçada (Br.)**   *pavement*
> **(a) berma (Eur.) / (o) acostamento (Br.)**   *hard shoulder*

16.7.1   You are in Portugal and see this poster by a school promoting road and traffic awareness in children. The child is being addressed in the **tu** verb form.

Caminha pelo lado direito do passeio ou da berma

(i)   What is the written instruction that accompanies the picture?
(ii) Rewrite it for an adult pedestrian.

16.7.2   Nearby there is more written advice. It reads:

> Para atravessar
>
> Pára no passeio
>
> Olha primeiro para a esquerda e depois para a direita para ver se vem algum carro
>
> Se não vier nenhum, atravessa, olhando novamente para a esquerda até ao meio da rua e depois para a direita

(i)   What do these instructions say? (Note that **vier** comes from **vir**)
(ii) Rewrite them for an adult pedestrian.

16.7.3   Rewrite for Brazilian readers the instructions in (i) 16.7.1 and

(ii) 6.7.2 above.

17 | SE OS ACHAREM, TELEFONEM LOGO
If you find them, phone right away

In this unit you will learn how to:

- deal with missing property
- cope with road accident and car breakdown
- and solve a number of other problems

 'Perdidos e achados'

 Heloísa is reporting the loss of some valuables.

Heloísa	Perdi a minha carteira e um saquinho com jóias que eu tinha dentro da bolsa.
Empregado	Sabe onde e quando perdeu essas coisas?
Heloísa	Não, não sei, mas usei a carteira há umas quatro horas quando fui fazer compras. Creio que não foi roubo. A carteira e o saquinho devem ter caído para fora da bolsa.
Empregado	E o que tinham dentro?
Heloísa	A carteira tinha cartões de crédito, notas e moedas e o saquinho tinha um anel de ouro com um brilhante e um pendente de prata em forma de coração. (*depois de ter dado o endereço e o número do telefone do hotel*) Se os acharem, telefonem-me logo para o hotel, por favor.

perdidos e achados *lost and found (items)*	**(o) roubo** *theft*
perder – achar *to lose – to find*	**(o) anel de ouro** *gold ring*
(a) carteira *wallet / purse*	**(o) brilhante** *diamond*
(o) saquinho *small bag*	**em forma de coração** *heart-shaped*
(as) jóias *items of jewellery*	

Numa garagem

 Teresa has taken her car to a garage for some repair work.

Teresa Queria mandar consertar o carro. Está amolgado na frente e riscado no lado. Além disso, às vezes não pega. Eu tenho muita pressa, preciso muito do carro. Para quando é que pode consertá-lo?

Mecânico O carro não pega... Depende da causa. Se o problema não for grande, estará pronto daqui a dois dias, incluindo pintura.

Teresa Obrigada. Pode também verificar o óleo, encher o lavador de pára-brisa e completar o tanque.

Mecânico Estará tudo em ordem quando a senhora vier, mas é melhor telefonar primeiro.

mandar consertar *to have (something) repaired*	**(a) pintura** *paintwork*
amolgado, riscado *dented, scratched*	**encher** *to fill*
	(o) tanque/(o) depósito (Eur.) *tank*
além de *in addition to*	**(o) lavador de pára-brisa/**
pegar *to start (engine)*	**pára-brisas** (Eur.) *windscreen bottle*
ter pressa *to be in a hurry*	**completar** *to fill/top up (tank)*

✓ Exercícios

17.1 Perguntas e respostas

1 O que estava dentro da carteira que Heloísa perdeu?
   (*a*) notas e moedas.   (*b*) dinheiro e bilhetes.
   (*c*) cartões de crédito, notas e moedas.

2 Que jóias é que Heloísa perdeu?
   (*a*) Um anel de ouro e um pendente de prata.
   (*b*) Um anel de prata e um pendente de ouro.

3 Em que forma era o pendente?
   (*a*) Em forma de estrela. (*b*) Em forma de coração.

4 O carro da Teresa precisa de ser consertado. Por quê? / Porquê? (Eur.)
   (*a*) Porque às vezes não pega, está riscado no lado e amolgado na frente.
   (*b*) Porque está amolgado no lado e riscado na frente e às vezes não pega.

5 Além do carro consertado, que mais é que a Teresa quer?
   (*a*) Água no lavador de pára-brisa, gasolina no tanque e mais óleo.
   (*b*) Mais óleo se necessário, o lavador de pára-brisa cheio de água e o
       tanque cheio de gasolina.

Expressões-chave

ser *or* estar? – estar com *or* ter?

As you learned in Unit 3 for **está** and **é**, **estar** (*to be*) is for something that
can change easily in contrast with **ser** (*to be*) which is used to identify or
characterise something or someone.

ser (inherent condition)	**estar** (condition not inherent)
Sou professor. *I am a teacher.*	Hoje está quente. *Today it's hot.*
Ela é bonita. *She is pretty.*	Estou cansado. *I am tired.*
Ele é simpático. *He is nice.*	Ele está constipado (Eur.) /
Eles são ingleses *They are English.*	resfriado (Br.). *He has a cold.*
Sou doente. *I do not enjoy good*	Estou doente *I am ill*
health.	*(currently).*

Estar com or **ter** + noun is used with certain expressions of feeling.

Tenho	sede / fome.	*I'm*	*thirsty/hungry*
(lit. *I have*)	frio / calor.		*cold/hot*
	pressa.		*in a hurry*
Estou com	febre.	*I've got*	*a fever*
(lit. *I am with*)	dor de cabeça.		*a headache*

To express physical pain **dói-me** (lit. *it hurts me*) is, however, of more
versatile application.

   Caí. Dói-me aqui... e aqui... *I fell down. It hurts here... and here...*

how long? / for / ago

Note that **há** can translate all three.

Há quanto tempo está aqui?	*How long have you been here?*
	(verb in the present)
Estou aqui **há** duas horas.	*I have been here for two hours.*
	(verb in the present)
Cheguei **há** duas horas (**atrás**).	*I arrived two hours ago.*
	(verb in the preterite)

In the last example you may wish to add **atrás**, but it is not necessary.

Como funciona

Perfect tenses

The Portuguese compound perfect tenses are formed with the verb **ter** as an auxiliary plus the past participle of the verb you want to express. The latter remains invariable, i.e., does not agree with the subject (in gender or number). The former changes as follows:

Perfect Indicative – (**ter** in the present)

Use for a continuous state or for a continuous or frequently repeated action or event, or series of actions or events, occurring within a period of time which has not yet elapsed.

O tempo **tem** est**ado** bom.	*The weather has been fine.*
Eu **tenho** trabalh**ado** muito ultimamente.	*I have been working hard lately.*

Pluperfect Indicative – (**ter** in the imperfect)

Use for a state which had taken place or for an action or event which had been completed before something else happened in the past or before a set time in the past.

O tempo **tinha** est**ado** bom, antes da trovoada.	*The weather had been fine, before the storm.*
Eu já **tinha** sa**ído** quando ele chegou.	*I had already left when he arrived.*
Ele ainda não **tinha** cheg**ado** quando eu saí.	*He had not yet arrived when I left.*

Meaning the same as the compound pluperfect indicative, there is also a simple, or synthetic, pluperfect indicative.

O tempo est**ivera** bom, antes da trovoada.	*The weather had been fine, before the storm.*

This tense is not used much nowadays other than in literary and formal style, but you will find its endings in the verb tables at the end of the book. In speech it tends to be used only in idiomatic expressions.

Tom**ara** estar em férias.	*I wish I were on holiday.*

The pluperfect (compound or simple) can be said to express the past of the past. The compound format can also be used with other forms of the verb **ter** and express the 'past of the future' as well as other kinds of sequence.

Poderemos falar quando eu **tiver** acab**ado** este trabalho.
We shall be able to talk when I have finished this work.

Espero que você **tenha** consegu**ido** consulta ontem.
I hope that you may have managed to get an appointment yesterday.

Note: You may come across the verb **haver** instead of **ter** as the auxiliary in compound perfect tenses, but this is not used much nowadays: e.g., Eu já hav**ia** sa**ído** quando ele chegou.

Reported speech

As in English, when you report what someone has said or what you have thought, you often use a form of the past of the verb you want to express.

Ele disse que **gosta** de música.   *He has said that he likes music.*
but also
Ele disse que **gostava** de música.   *He has said that he liked music.*
and, similarly,
Pensei que ele **ia falar**.   *I thought that he was going to speak.*

não funciona *or* não está funcionando?

There are some cases in which the Portuguese are happy to use just the present (Unit 7) and the imperfect (Unit 13) while Brazilians tend to prefer the more precise continuous forms of the verb (Unit 14), particularly for the present, e.g. with any device that is out of order.

Não **funciona** (Eur.)   *It is not working* (lit. *it does not work*)

Não **está funcionando** (Br.)   *It is not working*

Superlatives

(i) **muito**   *very*

Peter é **muito** alto
Peter fala português **muito** fluentemente.

muito/muita/muitos/muitas   *much, a lot of*

Peter tem **muita** bagagem.
Peter tem **muitas** malas.

(ii)   **-íssimo/-íssima/-íssimos/-íssimas**   *most, extremely; a very large quantity/number of*; **-issimamente** *extremely*

Peter é alt**íssimo**.
Peter tem muit**íssima** bagagem.
Peter tem muit**íssimas** malas.
Peter fala português fluent**issimamente**.

(iii)   **o mais...** *the -est*,   *the most...*

Peter é o **mais** alto (de todos).
Peter fala português **o mais** fluentemente (de todos).

a maior quantidade de...   *the most, the largest quantity of*

Peter tem **a maior quantidade de** bagagem (de todos).

o maior número de...   *the most, the largest number of*

Peter tem **o maior número de** malas (de todos).

There is also a parallel format for **o menos...** *the least*, but this is not so widely used.

Joseph é **o menos** alto (de todos).

The irregular superlatives for (iii) above are the same as the irregular comparatives you learned in Unit 16. For the superlative in (i) and (ii) above, where no comparison is involved, note the following:

grande **máximo**   pequeno **mínimo**

bom, bem **óptimo**(Eur.)/**ótimo**(Br.); **optimamente**(Eur.)/**otimamente**(Br.)
mau, ruim; mal **péssimo**; **pessimamente**

mais que *or* mais de ?

Use **mais (do) que**, and **menos (do) que**, where the second term of the comparison involves a verb, expressed or implicit (see Unit 13).

Peter é mais alto do que Mary (é).   *Peter is taller than Mary (is).*

Use **mais de**, and **menos de**, before a number or other expression of quantity, where no comparison is implied.

Mais de 60 km por hora.	*More than 60 km per hour.*
Menos de 60 km por hora.	*Less than 60 km per hour.*

Gender

In Portuguese there isn't a neuter form as such, but you have come across the masculine ending **-o** acting as a neuter, e.g. in ist**o** (Unit 11).

Also compare the following:

Ess**a** infracç**ão** (Eur.) / infraç**ão** (Br.) de trânsito é graví**ssima**.
That traffic offence is extremely serious. Feminine endings throughout.

but

É graví**ssimo**. *It is extremely serious.* Ending **-o** acting as a neuter.

✔️ Exercícios

🔑 **17.2 Tive um acidente** *I have had a car crash*

🎧 **17.2.1**

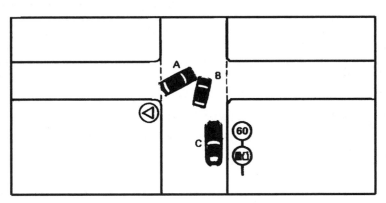

o cruzamento = o ponto de encontro com a estrada transversal

(o) sinal de obrigação de parar/ paragem obrigatória	*stop sign*
(o) sinal de proibição de ultrapassar	*no overtaking sign*
em violação de	*breaking (law)*

Study the following exchange of words between the two drivers who have had an accident, and find out who was driving which car.

Afonso   O senhor não parou no cruzamento, em violação do sinal de paragem obrigatória.

Olavo   O senhor ultrapassou, em violação da proibição de ultrapassar.

17.2.2

(o) ferido	*injured person*	**(o) morto**	*dead person*

Afonso phones the rescue service for help. Study Afonso's words which are written below and listen to the operator's questions on your recording. Then put them together in a dialogue.

– Na estrada de Sagres para Lagos, a mais ou menos 10 km de Sagres.

– Não preciso de ambulância. Não há feridos, nem mortos. Mas preciso de um rebocador. O meu carro não funciona (Eur.)/está funcionando (Br.).

17.2.3

(a) velocidade *speed*	**(o) quilómetro /Eur) /** **quilômetro (Br.)** *kilometre*

When the police arrive...

Match the official's questions with Afonso's replies:

1 O senhor ultrapassou?	(a) Vi...
2 A que velocidade ia?	(b) Hum... ultrapassei.

parecer que	*to appear to, look as if*	**bater em**	*to hit (collide)*
avançar	*to move forwards*		

3 Não viu o outro carro?   (c) Hum... a 60 km por hora.

17.2.4

Write a report on the accident. It is Afonso's version of the story.

Fill in the gaps with the appropriate forms of the verbs in brackets.

Eu _____ (*seguir*) pela estrada a 60 km por hora. À minha frente ___
___ (*seguir*) o carro C, muito lentamente. Eu ____ (*ver*) o carro A, que
parecia que tinha parado no cruzamento. Eu _____ (*ultrapassar*) o
carro C, mas o carro A _____ (*avançar*) e _____ (*bater*) no meu.

17.3

This is a drink-drive warning sign from Portugal.

conduzir (Eur.) = dirigir (Br.)

17.3.1 'If you drive (any time in the
future) do not drink', says the safety
warning. Starting with **Nunca** say in
Portuguese *I never drink when I drive.*

17.3.2 Say the same again but for when
you are in Brazil.

17.4 *Mishaps, complaints and solutions*

17.4.1 Study the following list of mishaps and complaints:

  (i) Penso que me roubaram a carteira e o telefone portátil.
 (ii) Perdi o meu passaporte e o visto.
(iii) Perdi uma lente de contacto (Eur.) / contato (Br.).
 (iv) O quarto é muito barulhento.
  (v) O chuveiro não funciona (Eur.) / está funcionando (Br.).

17.4.2 Can you find below a suggestion or solution for each mishap or
complaint? Match them.

(*a*) Onde é o oculista mais próximo?
(*b*) Por favor, pode mandar consertar o chuveiro?
(*c*) Então deve informar a polícia.
(*d*) Talvez seja melhor pedir para mudar de quarto.
(*e*) Pergunte na secção (Eur.) / seção (Br.) de perdidos e achados

| **fugir** | *to flee (run or drive away)* |

17.5

17.5.1 Emy's pendant may have been stolen. She may have seen the thief running down a nearby road. Help her describe the following in Portuguese:

(i) pendant: (*made of gold and* ★ *shaped*)
(ii) the suspect: Ele fugiu pela rua ali à direita. Ele deve ter uns vinte anos, (*black hair / white T-shirt / blue jeans*)

17.5.2 Ben has been hit by a car and the driver did not stop. Help him describe in Portuguese what he remembers for a police report.

(i) *car:* Não vi bem o número da placa nem de que marca o carro é. O motorista fugiu. Sei apenas que... (*a dark green car*).
(ii) *driver:* Não vi bem. Foi tudo muito rápido, mas penso que ele... (*around 40 / short blond hair / yellow shirt*)

17.6

Can you match the different words of sympathy with the two pieces of bad news below, according to how serious they are?

1 Ontem a minha melhor amiga foi atropelada. Está no hospital em observação.

    (*a*) Não se preocupe. Podia ter sido pior.

2 Caí. Torci o pé direito e feri a mão esquerda. Hoje não posso nadar.

    (*b*) Sinto muito. Estimo rápidas melhoras.

17.7 A multa *The fine*

In Curitiba, capital city of the State of Paraná, Brazil, the local authorities have issued a leaflet showing the penalties incurred for speeding.

		VELOCIDADE	INFRAÇÃO
30 km/h	FISCALIZAÇÃO ELETRÔNICA	*38–52 km/h* *Mais de 52 km/h*	*Grave* *Gravíssima*

*Com suspensão da carteira da habilitação por 2 a 7 meses.

17.7.1   Study this extract and answer the questions which follow.

eletrônica (Br.) = electrónica (Eur.) infração (Br.) = infracção (Eur.)
carteira da habilitação = carteira de motorista (Br.) = carta de condução (Eur.)

(i)   Numa rua de 30 km por hora, 40 km/hr é grave ou gravíssimo?
(ii) A partir de que velocidade é gravíssimo?
(iii) Se fizer mais de 52 km/h que outra penalidade terá além da multa?

17.7.2   The other side of the leaflet shows this picture and text.

CUIDADO COM
O EXCESSO
DE VELOCIDADE.
A PRESSA
E A SEGURANÇA
NUNCA ESTÃO
NA MESMA MÃO.

(i)   What does the first sentence say?
(ii) What does the second sentence say? Do you 'get' the pun?

18 | GOSTARIA MUITO DE VIAJAR MAIS
I'd love to travel more

In this unit you will learn how to:

- express likes and dislikes
- talk about interests, leisure pursuits and sport
- express a condition, a wish or a hope

Falando acerca de lazer e férias

Roberto and Natália are talking about leisure and holidays.

Roberto	O que é que você faz nas horas vagas?
Natália	Tenho poucas horas vagas, mas, quando posso, sento-me diante do televisor, relaxando.
Roberto	E quando está de férias, o que faz? Para onde vai?
Natália	Normalmente não vou longe. Passo o tempo na praia, ao sol. Tomo banho de mar e banho de sol ... e não faço nada. Gostaria muito de viajar mais. Infelizmente agora não posso, mas espero poder num futuro próximo, talvez no ano que vem ou daqui a dois anos.

(as) horas vagas *spare time*
diante de *facing*
relaxando *relaxing*
tomar banho de mar *to bathe, have a swim in the sea*
tomar (banho de) sol *to sunbathe*

(eu) gostaria de *I should/would like to*
gostaria muito de *I'd love to*
viajar mais *to do more travelling* (lit. *travel more*)

Comparando interesses

 Silvana and Alfredo are comparing their interests and leisure pursuits.

Alfredo O que é que você faz no seu tempo livre?

Silvana Leio, principalmente romances históricos, e adoro pintar quadros. Aos fins de semana normalmente vou a uma galeria de arte ou visito um museu. Também gosto muito de música, isto é, música clássica, e às vezes vou a um concerto. Também vou ao teatro, uma ou duas vezes por mês. E você?

Alfredo Eu não gosto muito de ler mas leio revistas e novelas policiais. Gosto de música popular. Faço natação. Jogo futebol, ocasionalmente, mas tenciono jogar mais vezes.

Silvana Eu detesto jogos de bola, principalmente futebol. Nado, mas raramente, e só na piscina; no mar não. Às vezes dou um passeio a pé e uma vez por outra faço uma caminhada.

Alfredo Hum... Temos interesses bastante diferentes.

(o) tempo livre = (as) horas vagas
(o) romance histórico *historical novel*
adoro *I love*
pintar quadros *to do painting*
(a) novela policial *detective novel*
uma vez por outra *once in a while*

natação *swimming (sport)*
jogo futebol *I play soccer*
tenciono *I intend to*
eu detesto *I detest, hate*
(os) jogos de bola *ball games*
dou um passeio a pé *I go for a stroll*
(a) caminhada *walk (long), rambling*

 **Exercícios**

18.1 Perguntas e respostas

1 Quem tem pouco tempo livre?
(*a*) Roberto. (*b*) Natália. (*c*) Alfredo. (*d*) Silvana.

2 Como é que a Natália passa o dia quando está de férias?
(*a*) Toma banho na piscina. (*b*) Nada no mar.
(*c*) Toma banho de mar e sol.

3 O que é que a Silvana gosta mais de fazer nas horas vagas?
(*a*) Pintar quadros. (*b*) Dar passeios.
(*c*) Ler livros e revistas.

4 O que é que a Silvana detesta?
   (*a*) Futebol.   (*b*) Caminhadas.   (*c*) Jogos de bola.

5 Quais são os interesses do Alfredo?
   (*a*) Jogos de bola, caminhadas, natação, e ler romances históricos.
   (*b*) Ir a concertos e ao teatro, e visitar galerias de arte e museus.
   (*c*) Futebol, natação, música popular, e ler revistas e novelas policiais.

Expressões-chave

Intentions

Tencionar (to intend) or **ter a intenção de** (*to have the intention of*) are
ways of expressing one's intention.

Tenciono / tenho a intenção de fazer mais exercício.
I am intending /It's my intention to take more exercise.

Also revise what you have learned about **vou...** (Unit 8) and **hei de...** (Unit
12).

Vou fazer mais exercício.   *I am going to take more exercise.*
Hei de fazer mais exercício.   *I will take more exercise.*

play

Note that the verb *to play* finds a Portuguese translation as follows:

jogar (*to participate in a game*)
   Jogo futebol.   *I play soccer.*

tocar (*to perform on a musical instrument*)
   Toco piano.   *I play the piano.*

brincar (*to engage in children's play*)
   Onde há um parque infantil onde as crianças possam brincar?
   Where is there a children's playground for the children to play?

brincar (*to engage in frivolous play, as, for example, playing with words;*
hence to joke)
   Isso não é a sério, você está a brincar (Eur.) / está brincando (Br.).
   You are not being serious, you are joking (kidding).

passear *and* dar passeios

Passear translates *to stroll* but it also translates *to ride* and *to drive*, when this is a leisurely activity. If you want to specify whether you are walking or using a means of transport, then you add **a pé** or **de carro, a cavalo**, or other.

Vou passear a pé / Vou dar um passeio a pé. *I am going to go for a stroll.*

Vou passear de carro / Vou dar um passeio de carro. *I am going to go for a drive or ride (for pleasure).*

Como funciona

Verbs: the three conjugations – conditional

	I should...	*buy*	*sell*	*leave*
eu		compr**aria**	vend**eria**	part**iria**
tu		compr**arias**	vend**erias**	part**irias**
você, o sr/a sra ele/ela		compr**aria**	vend**eria**	part**iria**
nós		compr**aríamos**	vend**eríamos**	part**iríamos**
vocês, os sres/as sras eles/elas		compr**ariam**	vend**eriam**	part**iriam**

The conditional is formed by attaching endings **-ia, -ias, -ia, -íamos, -iam** to the infinitive of the verb. As with the simple future (Unit 12), the three exceptions are **dizer, fazer, trazer**, where the endings are added to shortened forms of the infinitive: **dir**ia etc., **far**ia etc., **trar**ia etc.

Handy Hints
Note that these endings are the same as the imperfect indicative of **ir**.

Use in the following cases:

1 Where a condition is involved and in English you would say *I should, you would*, etc.

Podemos sair, mas eu gost**aria** de, primeiro, ler o jornal. *We can go out, but I should like to, first, read the paper.*

2 In reported speech or thought for something that had not happened yet when it was talked / thought about (see also Unit 17).

Pensei que ele **iria** falar. *I thought that he would be speaking.*

Note that in speech the conditional is often replaced with the imperfect indicative (Unit 13).

Pensei que ele **ia** falar. *I thought that he was going to speak.*
Pensei em perguntar se você que**reria** (or que**ria**) ir ao cinema.
I thought of asking whether you would like to go to the cinema.

I would like

Eu gosto de jogar golfe means *I like playing golf,* i.e., *I enjoy playing golf.* **Eu gostaria de jogar golfe** translates *I should like to play golf.* It is the expression of a wish rather than a courteous way of asking for something. For this, you find a more appropriate rendering in **Eu queria jogar golfe**, often with **eu** omitted, **Queria jogar golfe**. In fact, **queria** is the imperfect indicative you learned in Unit 13 used in place of the conditional.

Verbs: the three conjugations – imperfect subjunctive

I might/should...	*buy*	*sell*	*leave*
eu	compr**asse**	vend**esse**	part**isse**
tu	compr**asses**	vend**esses**	part**isses**
você, o sr/a sra ele/ela	compr**asse**	vend**esse**	part**isse**
nós	compr**ássemos**	vend**êssemos**	part**íssemos**
vocês, os sres/as sras eles/elas	compr**assem**	vend**essem**	part**issem**

The imperfect subjunctive is formed by dropping the final **-ram** of the third person plural (for **eles/elas**, *they*) of the preterite (see Unit 9) and by adding **-sse, -sses, -sse, -ssemos, -ssem**.

Compare with the present subjunctive (Unit 16) and use for:

1 The expression of a wish or hope (like present subjunctive, note 1) transferred to past time and / or a more remote degree of probability.

   Esperava que a consulta **fosse** hoje.   *I hoped / was hoping that the appointment might be today.*

2 The expression of sorrow or sympathy (like pres. subj., note 2) transferred to a past time.

   Senti muito que ela esti**vesse** doente.   *I was very sorry that she was ill.*

3 An action or event regarded as a possibility (like pres. subj. note 3) but with a greater degree of doubt.

   Ela talvez tom**asse** uma bebida quente.   *She might perhaps have a hot drink.*

4 After a statement that implies influence upon other people or things (like pres. subj., note 4) transferred to a past time.

   A hospedeira (Eur.) / aeromoça (Br.) pediu ao passageiro que aperta**sse** o cinto de segurança.   *The stewardess asked the passenger to fasten his safety belt.*

   Eu pedia a/à (Eur.) Maria que fize**sse** o favor de comprar o jornal.
   I used to ask Mary to be so kind as to buy the paper.

if

Conditional sentences usually consist of two parts:

(*a*) *if*-part   and   (*b*) the conclusion (the main clause)

1 When the *if*-part refers to the present or the past and is not contrary- to-fact, the present indicative is used for both verbs (*a*) + (*b*).

   Normalmente se chove fi**co** em casa, se f**az** bom tempo, **dou** um passeio.
   Usually if it rains, I stay at home, if the weather is fine, I go for a stroll.

2 When the *if*-part expresses an unfulfilled condition, the imperfect subjunctive is used for (*a*) and the conditional (or the imperfect indicative in its place) for (*b*).

Se não chov**esse** / estiv**esse** chovendo (Br.), **daria** (or **dava**) um passeio. *If it were not raining, I would go for a stroll.*

3 When the *if*-part expresses a condition to be fulfilled in the future, the future subjunctive is used for (*a*) and an 'indicative' future for (*b*) (simple / colloquial / emphatic).

If it rains tomorrow,
Se chov**er** amanhã, não d**arei** um passeio. *I shall not go for a walk.*
Se chov**er** amanhã, não **vou** d**ar** um passeio. *I am not going to go for a walk.*
Se chov**er** amanhã, não **hei de** d**ar** um passeio. *I will not go for a walk.*
Some people will also use the present indicative instead of the future subjunctive. Se chov**e** amanhã, não **vou** d**ar** um passeio.

I have taken up photography

You have experienced in this course verbs that sometimes are not used alone but as an auxiliary to other verbs.

E.g., Eu **vou** comprar, *I am going to buy*. (Unit 8); Eu **costumava** ler o jornal regularmente. *I used to read the paper regularly*. (Unit 13).

Note some other such cases which are frequently heard:

começar a..., *to begin/start to...*; **deixar de...**, *to stop doing...*; **voltar a**, *to do... again;* **acabar de...**, *to have just done....* They are all followed by the infinitive of the action or state of being that you want to express.

Eu **costumava** gostar de pintar. Mas agora **deixei de** pintar e **vou começar a** fazer fotografia. **Acabo de** me inscrever para um curso de fotografia. Um dia no futuro talvez **volte a** pintar. *I used to like painting. But now I have given up painting and I am going to take up photography. I have just enrolled on a course in photography. Some time in the future I may go back to painting.*

✓ Exercícios
18.2

 o golfe
golf

 a pesca
fishing

 o mergulho
scuba diving

 o esqui o
aquático
water skiing

 o ténis (Eur.)
/ tênis (Br.)
tennis

 a vela
sailing

 o surfe
surfing

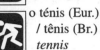 a caça
shooting

 o hipismo
horse racing

18.2.1 Read the following expressed intentions and find the right place for each person.

(i) Quero fazer esqui aquático.
(ii) Tenciono jogar golfe e fazer caça.
(iii) Tenho a intenção de fazer surfe e mergulho.
(iv) Vou fazer vela e pesca.
(v) Hei de jogar ténis (Eur.) / tênis (Br.) e fazer hipismo.

(A)   (B)

18.2.2 Unscramble the words in brackets and help Ian talk, in Portuguese, about his keep-fit routine and his favourite sport.

Every day, I go jogging early in the morning. At the weekend, I practise water skiing, when the weather is fine; and I would practise it more often if I had more time.

> **fazer (o) jogging = fazer (o) cooper (Br.) = fazer o trote (Eur.)**

(Todos os dias, / Aos fins de semana, / quando faz / pratico / praticaria / bom tempo; / mais tempo. / faço jogging/cooper (Br.) / de manhã cedo. / mais vezes, / esqui aquático, / e / se / tivesse)

18.3

The following information has been issued by the local Tourist Office in Funchal, Madeira.

A Madeira é praticamente uma reserva natural, sendo dois terços do território Área Protegida onde abunda fauna e flora raras.

A Madeira foi sempre reconhecida como um paraíso para passeios a pé. Os passeios podem ser tão suaves ou tão desafiadores como desejar. Os que não querem meter-se em grandes aventuras podem apreciar os belos passeios ao longo das "levadas", que circundam toda a ilha, oferecendo as melhores vistas panorâmicas. Para os mais aventureiros há muitos trilhos, bem assinalados com placas, que levam às montanhas.

Mas a Madeira também oferece uma grande variedade de actividades desportivas. Se gosta de golfe, a ilha tem dois campos para campeonatos. E, é claro que, sendo uma ilha, a Madeira é rica em desportos aquáticos. Além disso, a Madeira está a adquirir uma reputação internacional como um destino de primeira classe para a pesca de alto mar, sendo o local certo para pescar espadim azul com mais de 500 kg. Abundam ainda todas as espécies de atum.

Mas o melhor de tudo é que pode praticar o seu desporto favorito durante todo o ano.

---

levadas = pequenos canais de irrigação artificiais

---

desporto (Eur.) = esporte (Br.)
actividades desportivas (Eur.) = atividades esportivas (Br.)
está a adquirir (Eur.) = está adquirindo (Br.)

18.3.1   Study the above information on Madeira.

18.3.2   Keith is contemplating a holiday in Madeira and is enquiring about activities that will suit everyone in the family. Below are his questions. The answers are on your cassette/CD. Listen to the answers, match them with the questions, and write the dialogue.

– A Madeira tem plantas raras? E animais?
– Que passeios a pé tem para pessoas que não estão em boa forma?
– Desculpe. Não compreendo. O que significa "levadas"?
– E que passeios tem para os mais aventureiros?
– O que tem para quem joga golfe?
– Pode fazer-se mergulho e vela?
– Só mais uma pergunta. Seria possível fazer pesca de alto mar?

 18.4

18.4.1 Look at the sports stadium poster and fill in the gaps in the dialogue.

– Ainda tem lugares nas
  bancadas _____?
– Não, não tenho. Já não
  há mais. Só _____.
– Então não quero.

BANCADAS

AO SOL   À SOMBRA

sun seats   *shade seats*

esgotado
sold out

18.4.2 Answer the following questions:

(i)   Esta pessoa comprou ou não comprou uma entrada?
(ii) Por quê? / Porquê? (Eur.)
(iii) Esta pessoa teria comprado uma entrada se ainda houvesse lugares à sombra?

 18.5

> **todo (o) mundo = toda a gente**

Answer the questions on the following chat between Portuguese Filipe and Brazilian Estela. Write in Portuguese. The first answer has been done for you.

1 *É uma pessoa natural do Rio de Janeiro.*

1 What is a *carioca*?
2 What event takes place in the whole of Brazil and above all in Rio, three days before Lent?

3　When do the preparations take place?
4　What name is given to the samba societies?
5　Where does everybody dance?
6　Find the names given to (*a*) the dancers, (*b*) the percussion section, and (*c*) the costumes, in the samba societies parade.

Filipe　Então você é *carioca*, é da capital do Carnaval?

Estela　Eu sou, sou *carioca*. O Brasil inteiro tem Carnaval, mas o Rio de Janeiro é sem dúvida a capital do Carnaval.

Filipe　É verdade que vocês preparam tudo com muita antecedência?

Estela　É. Tem que estar tudo pronto com muita antecedência para os três dias antes da Quaresma. É quando há bailes por toda a parte. Todo mundo vai para a rua.

Filipe　Mas o ponto mais alto da festa é o desfile, não é?

Estela　É, sim, o desfile das *escolas de samba*.

Filipe　E que nome é que vocês dão a esses bailarinos?

Estela　São os *passistas*. E os que tocam o ritmo são a *bateria*. E as *fantasias* são as roupas alegóricas.

Filipe　E quando é o desfile?

Estela　É durante a noite de domingo para 2ª.-feira.

Filipe　Eu gostaria muito de ver o desfile. Se puder, irei vê-lo no próximo ano. Vou começar a pensar nisso a sério.

 18.6

> **arquibancada = bancada grande**
> **números pares**　*even numbers*
> **números ímpares**　*odd numbers*

18.6.1　Your admission ticket for the Rio Carnival parade is number 00303, sector 9 (**o setor** (Br.) / **sector** (Eur.)), row C (**a fila**), seat (**o lugar**) 001. Say, all in words: **É o número ...** Continue on your own.

18.6.2　You are on the northern side of the boulevard trying to get to your seat. You have asked: **Por onde se vai para este lugar?** And you have been told:

Não é por aqui. Deste lado são números pares. Esse lugar fica numa arquibancada no lado sul, do outro lado da Avenida.

(i) Where are you going wrong?　(ii) What have you got to do?

18.7

You have been given this transport voucher for your return journey from the Carnival parade to the hotel where you are staying.

BILHETE DE TRANSPORTE – RIO CARNAVAL

Válido para uma (01) pessoa para transporte do desfile de Carnaval para qualquer Hotel.

Válido somente para 14/fevereiro e 15/fevereiro

---

1 Apologise and say that it looks as if you have lost it.
2 Say you have found it and hand it over to the driver.

19 SE FOSSE UMA COISA DIFERENTE
If it were something different

In this unit you will learn how to:

- explore local cuisine and drink
- explain what a place is like and what is special about it
- give detailed information about your home town and area

Jantando fora

Marília and Gustavo are dining out in a new restaurant tonight. Waiter Joaquim is waiting for them to place their order from the menu card.

Joaquim	Os senhores já escolheram?
Gustavo	Já. Para começar, queremos uma canja e uma sopa de tomate.
Joaquim	E para depois da entrada, o que vão pedir? Peixe, carne, ave, ou um prato vegetariano?
Marília	Para mim um prato de peixe, bacalhau Gomes de Sá.
Gustavo	Para mim bife na brasa.
Joaquim	Prefere mal ou bem passado?
Gustavo	Ao ponto.
Joaquim	E para acompanhar, querem guarnições?
Gustavo	Traga uma salada mista, porção dupla, para os dois.
Joaquim	E para beber?
Gustavo	Uma garrafa do vinho da casa.
Joaquim	Branco ou tinto?
Gustavo	É melhor meia garrafa de branco para beber com o peixe e meia de tinto para a carne.
	(*Depois do prato principal*)
Joaquim	Estava tudo bem?
Gustavo	Estava excelente.
Joaquim	E o que vão querer para sobremesa?
Gustavo	Para mim, fruta... Pode ser uma laranja.

Marília	Ainda não conheço o doce da casa. Eu talvez queira provar, mas primeiro gostaria de saber em que consiste.
Joaquim	É um doce de ovos.
Marília	Não... Se fosse uma coisa diferente.... Não, não quero. Prefiro um sorvete. Que sabores tem?
Joaquim	Chocolate, morango...
Marília	Morango, por favor. (*falando para Gustavo*) Adoro morango.

(a) canja *chicken broth*		**ao ponto** *medium*	
(a) sopa de tomate *tomato soup*		**para acompanhar** *to go with*	
(a) entrada *starter*		**(as) guarnições** *accompaniments*	
peixe, carne, aves *fish, meat, poultry*		**(a) salada mista** *mixed salad*	
prato de peixe *fish dish*		**(o) vinho da casa** *the restaurant's wine, house wine*	
(o) bacalhau (à) Gomes de Sá *dried cod speciality*		**branco ou tinto** *white or red*	
(o) bife na brasa *charcoal grilled steak*		**(a) sobremesa** *dessert*	
bem / mal passado *well done / rare*		**(o) doce** *sweet*	
		em que consiste *what it consists of*	
		adoro *I love*	

☑ Exercícios

19.1 Perguntas e respostas

(o) empregado (de mesa) (Eur.) / (o) garçom *waiter*

1 O Gustavo e a Marília já tinham escolhido quando o empregado (Eur.) / garçom (Br.) perguntou o que eles queriam?
   (*a*) Já.   (*b*) Ainda não.

2 O que é que eles escolheram para entrada?
   (*a*) uma salada e uma sopa.   (*b*) Canja e sopa de tomate.

3 Que comida é que eles escolheram para prato principal?
   (*a*) Um prato de peixe e um vegetariano.   (*b*) Dois pratos de carne.
   (*c*) Um prato de peixe, um de carne e salada mista para dois.

4 E que bebidas pediram?
   (*a*) Uma garrafa de vinho tinto.   (*b*) Uma garrafa de vinho branco.
   (*c*) 1/2 garrafa de vinho tinto e 1/2 de branco.

5 Quais são as sobremesas que eles preferiram?
   (*a*) Doce da casa e fruta   (*b*) Laranja e sorvete de morango.
   (*c*) Sorvete de chocolate e uma laranja.

🔑 Expressões-chave

pedir *or* perguntar ?

Note that both **pedir** and **perguntar** translate *to ask*. For the right choice remember the following:

pedir = t*o ask for, to request*   **perguntar** = *to ask, to enquire*

A cliente **pediu** o sal e a pimenta.   *The client asked for the salt and pepper.*

O cliente **pediu** um prato de carne. *The client asked for a meat dish.*

O empregado (Eur.) / garçom **perguntou** se ele queria a carne bem passada.   *The waiter asked whether he wanted the meat well done.*

que *or* qual?

As with other words, the interrogative pronoun **que** can be used with or without preceding **o**.

O que é isto? = **Que** é isto?   *What is this?*

Also note that **qual** (and its plural **quais**) translates *which* and **que** translates *what*, but sometimes it can be the other way round.

Qual prefere? *Which do you prefer?* which? → **qual/quais**

Que prato prefere? *Which dish do you prefer?* which (+ noun)? → **que**

(O) que é bacalhau "Gomes de Sá"? *What is 'Gomes de Sá' cod?* seeking a definition / description → **(o) que**

Quais são os pratos de bacalhau que prefere? *What are the cod dishes you prefer?* referring to a choice / selection → **qual/quais**

I'd love and I love

To express a strong wish, say **(eu) gostaria muito de**.

Eu **gostaria muito de** viajar mais. *I'd love to travel more*

Also, an emphatic alternative to **(eu) gosto muito de** is found in verb **adorar** (lit. *to adore*), with **detestar** (*to hate, detest*) as its opposite.

Adoro jardinagem e **detesto** cozinhar. *I love gardening and hate cooking.*

Adoro viajar. É o melhor dos meus passatempos predilectos (Eur.) / prediletos (Br.) *I love travelling. It's the best of my favourite pastimes/hobbies.*

Adoro animais. Tenho um cão / cachorro (Br.) e também um gato. *I love animals. I have a dog and also a cat.*

Otherwise English *to love* finds a translation in **amar**.

Amo (os) meus filhos.   *I love my children.*

saber *and* poder

Both **saber** and **poder** translate *can*, but use **saber** for knowledge or ability and **poder** for possibility or permission.

Sei cantar mas hoje não **posso**; perdi a voz. *I can sing but not today; I've lost my voice.*
Você **sabe** falar português? *Can you speak Portuguese?*
Posso falar agora? *May I speak now?*
Eles **souberam** a notícia ontem. *They learned the news yesterday.*
Eu não **pude** ir à festa dela. *I didn't manage to go to her party.*

saber, conhecer *and* encontrar

Both **saber** and **conhecer** translate *can*, but note the difference:

saber = *to know, to know a fact, to be informed about*
conhecer = *to know, to be acquainted with*

Você sabe onde é que essa rua é?   *Do you know where that road is?*
                                        (have you been told where it is?)
Você conhece essa rua?   *Do you know that road?*
                                        (have you been along it?)

Both **conhecer** and **encontrar** translate *to meet*, but note the difference:

conhecer = *to meet, to make acquaintance with*
encontrar = *to meet, arrange to meet*

Vocês já se **conhecem** ? *Have you ever met?*
Muito prazer em **conhecê**-lo. *Delighted to meet you.*
Quando nos **encontramos** outra vez? *When are we meeting again?*

Also note **encontrar** = **achar**

Felizmente **encontrei** (= **achei**) os óculos que tinha perdido.
Fortunately I have found the spectacles I had lost.

nascer, viver, morar, morrer/falecer

Do not translate literally *I was born* or *someone is dead*.

Remember:

to be born is **nascer**   *to die* is **morrer** or **falecer**

O meu bisavô **nasceu** há cem anos e **morreu** (*or* **faleceu**) há vinte.
My great-grandfather was born a hundred years ago and died twenty years ago.

O meu tio-avô **morreu** (*or* **faleceu**). *My great uncle is dead (has died).*

Also remember:

viver means *to live, to be alive*   **morar** means *to live, to be resident*

Nasci em São Tomé e Príncipe mas agora **vivo** em Portugal; **moro** em Lisboa. *I was born in São Tomé e Príncipe but now I live in Portugal; I am resident in Lisbon.*

📖 Como funciona

a mala da senhora

English possessive case – e.g., *the lady's suitcase* – finds its translation in the following construction:

thing possessed	+	**de**	+	possessor
a mala *the suitcase*		da (= de+a) *of the*		senhora *lady*

Similarly, os pais **de** (*or* **do**) João, *John's parents*

Possessives

My, mine; our, ours

Unlike English, the possessive adjective – e.g., my – and the possessive pronoun – e.g., *mine* – have one same word – **meu**. This word agrees in number (singular or plural) and gender (masculine or feminine) with the thing possessed: **meu, meus,** (masc. sing. and pl.) and **minha, minhas** (fem. sing. and pl.).

(O) meu casaco e **(as) minhas** malas   *my coat and my suitcases*
O casaco é **meu**   *the coat is mine*
As malas são **minhas**   *the suitcases are mine*

The same with our and ours: **nosso, nossos** (masc. sing. and pl.) **nossa, nossas** (fem. sing. and pl.).

(Os) nossos casacos   *our coats*
A mala é **nossa**   *the suitcase is ours*
Os casacos e **a** mala são **nossos**   *the coats and the suitcase are ours*

Note: **o/a/os/as** is used mainly in Portugal.

Your, yours

The same applies as above: **seu, seus; sua, suas**.

> **(Os) seus** casacos e **(a) sua** mala = **seus** casacos e mala *Your coats and suitcase*
> **Este** casaco é **seu** ? *Is this coat yours?*

For someone you address as **tu**, just change to **teu, teus; tua, tuas**.

> **(Os) teus** casacos e **(a) tua** mala = **teus** casacos e mala *Your coats and suitcase*
> **Este** casaco é **teu**? *Is this coat yours?*

His; her, hers; its; their, theirs

Historically this is **seu, seus; sua, suas** (as above for *your/s*) and is still widely used in written Portuguese, but colloquially (including informal writing) preference is given to the following format:

thing possessed + **de** contracted with **ele/ela/eles/elas** (the possessor)

> a mala **dela** (lit. *of she*), *her suitcase*
> a mala **deles** (lit. *of they*), *their suitcase*

Note that in this case there is agreement in number and gender with the possessor, not with the thing possessed.

a mala da senhora... *with a difference*

The format explained above for *his//her/s*etc. is also sometimes applied to *your/s*.

> a mala **de você** (= **(a) sua** mala) (lit. *of you*), *your suitcase*

or, for a courteous approach (revise what you learned about you in Unit 7),

> a mala **da senhora** (lit. *of the lady*), *your suitcase*

o, a, os, as *and the possessives*

In general, there is considerable flexibility in the use, or omission, of the definite article (**o/a/os/as**) with the possessive adjectives **meu**, etc., nosso, etc., and seu, etc.. There are some exceptions, as follows:

Omit

- In direct address:
  Minha amiga, como vai?   *My friend, how are you keeping?*

- In Brazil, referring to a relative:
  Meu pai está em casa.   *My father is at home.*

This can be heard in Portugal too, but not to the same extent.

Always use

■ For emphasis:

A mala preta é **a minha**.   *The black suitcase is mine.*
                              (no one else's)

■ Where subject and possessor are the same, in which case you can actually omit the possessive:

Ontem eu fui **no** carro.   *Yesterday I went in the car (my car).*

 # Exercícios

 ## 19.2

| a ementa (Eur.) / o cardápio (Br.)   *menu card* |

You are in a restaurant waiting for the meal you have ordered. There are people talking around you. What they say is on your cassette/CD. Listen to it and rearrange the jumbled up words in brackets so as to match what you hear.

1 (Faz / a ementa / favor, / traga-me / .)
2 (O / favor / cardápio, / por / .)
3 (Queríamos / da porta, / uma mesa / se possível./ para quatro, / longe)
4 (Pode / pão / ? / mais / trazer)
5 (Queria / um prato / experimentar / desta região / . / típico)

19.3

a caneca	o copo	a chávena(Eur.)	a taça	o cálice
mug	*glass/cup*	a xícara (Br.)	*champagne*	*goblet*
	/tumbler	*cup*	*glass*	

Traga-me um copo de coca, por favor.
Please bring me a glass of coke.

Following the above model, ask for the following:

1	glass of water	4	mug of beer
2	cup of tea	5	goblet of port (**(o) porto**)
3	cup of coffee	6	glass of champagne (**(o) champanhe**)

 ## 19.4 festival da pinga, *rum festival*

Pinga is an alternative name Brazilians use for **a cachaça** or **a aguardente de cana de açúcar**, i.e., a sugar-cane spirit.

(a) pinga (Br.)	*sugar-cane spirit*	(colloquialism)
(a) pinga (Eur.)	*alcoholic beverage*	(colloquialism)

The **festival da pinga** is a regular event in the town of **Paraty** – also spelt **Paratii** or **Parati** – on the Brazilian Atlantic coast, between Rio and Santos. The town's name comes from the Tupi Indians who were its first inhabitants.

19.4.1 A leaflet issued by the local tourist office includes the programme for the festival and some background information on the area. Study the following excerpt.

A terra propícia ao cultivo da cana de açúcar e o conhecimento dos produtos de aguardente da região têm sido fatores fundamentais para garantir, durante séculos, a qualidade da pinga produzida em Paraty.

O resultado desta combinação de boa terra para o cultivo e o conhecimento acumulado em séculos de tradição só poderia resultar em pingas artesanais de ótima qualidade. Estão aqui algumas das melhores pingas do Brasil.

fatores (Br.) = factores (Eur.)   ótima (Br.) = óptima (Eur.)

 ## 19.4.2

   agosto
   paraty sempre

This is on the leaflet's cover page and on your cassette/CD. What is the play on words? (If you need help, revise '*You*' in Unit 7.)

19.4.3 Silvestre is planning to go to the festival. Fill in the gaps in what he wants to say.

Vou ao festival da _____ em Paraty. Lá a _____ é propícia ao cultivo da _____ e há _____ que fazem aguardente. Vou beber o que dizem ser uma das _____ do Brasil.

19.4.4 Unforeseen circumstances prevented Silvestre from going to the festival. Complete the gaps and help him talk about the missed event.

Infelizmente eu não pude ir ao festival. Se _____ ido, teria _____ o que dizem ser uma das _____ do Brasil.

19.5   Como é a terra natal do senhor? *What is your homeland like?*

(Eu) sou de	uma aldeia (*village*) uma cidade (*town*)	em Portugal no Brasil / Canadá na Inglaterra / Nova Zelândia

que se chama ......

Fica / é	no	norte sudeste	do país	perto de .... perto da fronteira (*border*) com...

no interior (*inland*)
na costa leste/oeste/sul (*east/west/south coast*)
na margem / foz de um rio (*river bank/mouth*)
numa região | montanhosa/plana (*mountainous/plain region*)

Tem	uma superfície (*area*) de ... km² (*square kilometres*) quilómetros (Eur.) / quilômetros (Br.) quadrados uma população (*population*) de .... (de) habitantes (*inhabitants*) um clima quente (*hot climate*) indústria de .... (... *industry*)

With the help of the sentences in the above box, say the following:
My home town ((a) **minha cidade natal**) ...

1 is on a river bank.
2 is in a mountainous region.
3 is on the north coast of the country.
4 has one million inhabitants.
5 has a cold climate in winter.
6 has a computer industry. ((o) **computador**)

19.6

Some people are explaining where they come from and highlighting a couple of distinctive features in their home town.

Irish Cathy was born in Limerick, a town in southwest Ireland which has several monasteries and has given its name to a famous type of 'lace'.

Study her words below:

Sou irlandesa. Nasci em Limerick, uma cidade no sudoeste da Irlanda. Limerick tem vários mosteiros e um tipo famoso de renda bordada.

Following the same sentence pattern, help the following people talk about their home town.

1 Scottish Stewart: born in Dundee, a town on the east coast of Scotland – large harbour – famous type of cake.
 (**escocês – Escócia – um porto grande – bolo**)

2 Welsh Gareth: born in Caerphilly, a town in south Wales – old castle – famous type of cheese.
 (**galês – País de Gales – um castelo antigo**)

  ## 19.7

You are in a restaurant which specialises in dried cod recipes.

19.7.1   Study the contents of their list of cod dishes.

PRATOS DE BACALHAU

À Moda da Casa ....
(Posta de bacalhau cozido, acompanhada de cebola, batata e couve)

Gomes de Sá ....
(Bacalhau desfiado refogado, acompanhado de ovo cozido, batata e azeitonas)

Tropical ....
(Bacalhau em pedaços frito, acompanhado de cebola, tomate, batata e leite de coco)

19.7.2   Em que consiste? *What does it consist of?*

Three different customers are unfamiliar with the cuisine jargon on the menu card and have asked the waiter what goes into particular dishes. Listen to the waiter's replies and work out what three questions have been asked.

19.7.3   Ângela would rather have a dish without tomato. She says: **Preferia um prato que não tivesse tomate.**

Say that you would rather have a dish that does not have:

(i) onion; (ii) egg; (iii) cabbage; (iv) coconut milk.

20 | AO VOLTARMOS, ABRIREI CONTA BANCÁRIA
On our return, I shall open a bank account

In this unit you will learn how to:

- open and use a bank account
- accept or decline an invitation to a social event
- talk and write about the place where you are staying

No banco, abrindo conta

Alberto Lopes and his family live in England but they may be moving to Portugal. Alberto is at a bank in Lisboa, opening an account.

Alberto	Eu queria abrir uma conta. Que preciso fazer?
Empregada	Trouxe algum documento de identidade? Passaporte... bilhete de identidade(*)?
Alberto	Trouxe, sim. Aqui tem.
Empregada	Então é só preencher e assinar o formulário e fazer a assinatura modelo. O senhor deseja apenas conta corrente com depósito à ordem ou quer também depósito a prazo?
Alberto	Ambos. Agora eu tenho comigo uns cheques que quero depositar à ordem. No próximo mês virá de Londres uma transferência. É uma quantia elevada. É para ser depositada a prazo. Posteriormente virão transferências menores, mensalmente. Essas são para depositar à ordem.
Empregada	Certo, Sr. Lopes, trataremos disso. (*depois de tudo preenchido e assinado*) Pronto. O senhor receberá pelo correio o livro de cheques(**) e um cartão bancário que pode usar no terminal caixa. Regularmente enviaremos para sua casa o extracto(***) de conta e o aviso de lançamento de juros.

(*) = carteira de identidade (Br.) (**) = talão de cheques (Br.)
(***) = extrato (Br.)

(o) formulário form, questionnaire	**(a) quantia elevada** lump sum
(a) assinatura modelo specimen signature	**posteriormente** at a later date
(a) conta corrente or **(o) depósito à ordem** current account, instant access	**trataremos de** we will see to
	(o) livro de cheques cheque book
	(o) cartão bancário banker's card
(o) depósito a prazo deposit / savings account	**(o) terminal caixa** cash-point
	enviaremos we will send
comigo with me, on me	**(o) extracto de conta** statement
(a) transferência transfer	**(o) aviso de lançamento de juros** earned-interest advice note

 Exercícios

20.1 Perguntas e respostas

1 O que é que Alberto precisa fazer para abrir conta bancária?
   (a) Precisa apresentar o passaporte e preencher os documentos.
   (b) Precisa apresentar um documento de identidade, preencher e assinar o formulário e fazer a assinatura modelo.

2 Que tipo de conta é que ele quer?
   (a) Depósito à ordem.
   (b) Depósito à ordem e a prazo.
   (c) Conta corrente e dois depósitos a prazo.

3 Em que depósito é que deve ficar o dinheiro?
   (a) As transferências de Londres à ordem e os cheques a prazo.
   (b) Os cheques à ordem e as transferências de Londres a prazo.
   (c) A quantia elevada a prazo, as transferências menores e os cheques à ordem.

4 O que é que ele vai receber?
   (a) O livro de cheques (Eur.) / talão de cheques (Br.), o cartão bancário e regularmente aviso de lançamento de juros.
   (b) O livro de cheques (Eur.) / talão de cheques (Br.), o cartão bancário, e regularmente extracto (Eur.) / extrato (Br.) de conta e aviso de lançamento de juros.

Expressões-chave

ir – vir *and* levar – trazer

Know whether you are coming or going... **Ir** (*to go*) and **levar** (*to take*) imply motion away from the person who is speaking. **Vir** (*to come*) and **trazer** (*to bring*) imply motion towards the person who is speaking.

– **Venha** cá, por favor.	*Come here, please.*
– Já **vou**.	*I'm coming.* (lit. *I'm going*)

But as an expression of your personal hospitality, you can use **vir** to invite someone to your home even if you are not speaking from home.

Você pode **vir** jantar em nossa casa.	*You can come to dinner at our house/place.*

Also note the different meanings of **levar**, as follows:

O porteiro do hotel **levou** a mala para o elevador.	*The hotel porter took the suitcase to the lift.*
O elevador **levou** pouco tempo a chegar ao décimo andar.	*The lift soon arrived at the 10th floor* (lit. *took little time to arrive*).

faltar

Faltar means *to be missing* (in relation to a desired or expected whole or completion).

Falta alguma coisa?	*Is there anything missing?*
Falta a minha mala. Não estava na correia transportadora de bagagem.	*My suitcase is missing. It wasn't on the baggage conveyor belt.*
Faltam 5 minutos para as 8.	*It is 5 minutes to 8.*

Como funciona

Object pronouns

In Unit 6 you learned the personal pronouns subject, i.e., the words for *I*, *you*, *s/he*, etc. We have also been using some object pronouns, i.e., the words for *me*, *you*, *him/her*, etc.

me as direct object

Ele viu-**me**. Ele **me** viu. (Br.)	*He saw me.*

me as indirect object (the direct object is 'o cheque')

Ele deu-**me** o cheque. Ele **me** deu o cheque. (Br.) *He gave me the cheque.*

me in preposition (such as **para**) + object

Ele falou para **mim**. *He spoke to me.*

The following table puts together the different object pronouns and shows how they relate to their subject counterparts.

subject	object		
	direct	indirect	with preposition
eu	me	me	mim
tu	te	te	ti
você, o sr /a sra	o, a	lhe	si, você, o sr / a sra
ele / ela	o, a	lhe	ele / ela
nós	nos	nos	nós
vocês, os sres /as sras	os, as	lhes	vocês, os sres / as sras
eles / elas	os, as	lhes	eles

With preposition **com** there are some contracted forms: **comigo**, **contigo**, **consigo**, **connosco** (Eur.) / **conosco** (Br.).

Ele veio **comigo**.   *He came with me.*

Verbs: the three conjugations – personal infinitive

I may...	buy	sell	leave
eu	compr**ar**	vend**er**	part**ir**
tu	compr**ares**	vend**eres**	part**ires**
você, o sr / a sra ele / ela	compr**ar**	vend**er**	part**ir**
nós	compr**armos**	vend**ermos**	part**irmos**
vocês, os sres / as sras eles / elas	compr**arem**	vend**erem**	part**irem**

The personal infinitive is an inflected infinitive. It is derived from the 'impersonal' infinitive you learned in Unit 2 and is formed by adding 'personal' endings as shown above. It is regular for all verbs. In verbs that have a regular preterite (Unit 9), the personal infinitive is identical to the future subjunctive (Unit 16), though *in form only*.

The personal infinitive simplifies grammar inasmuch as it can replace other tenses including the subjunctive tenses, because:

(*a*) it gives the verb the uncharacteristic quality of an infinitive, which will enable it to assume the meaning required by its context – indicative or subjunctive (present, past or future);

(*b*) it retains awareness of the person who is the subject of the action or state of being.

In fact, we have been using the personal infinitive throughout this book, right from Unit 2:

Faça o favor de fal**ar** mais devagar.   (i.e., **você** fal**ar**)

Façam o favor de fal**arem** mais devagar.   (i.e., **vocês** fal**arem**)

Note the following:

■ 'Person' is the active element in the personal infinitive. The personal pronoun (expressed or understood) is in the subject form:

para (**ele**) apertar o cinto   *for him to fasten his belt*
                                   (lit. *for he to fasten*)

■ The use of personal endings with the infinitive can range from the need to avoid obscurity to optional emphasis for extra clarity or effect:

Façam o favor de fal**ar(em)** mais devagar.

Façam o favor de apert**ar(em)** os cintos.

Subjunctive or infinitive?

When expressing a wish or hope, use:

■ the subjunctive, if the subject of the second verb is different from that of the first verb.

Desejo que (você) **faça** boa   *I wish that you may have a*
viagem.   *nice journey.*

■ the infinitive, if the subject is the same.

Espero fazer boa viagem.   *I hope to have a nice journey*
                              (that I may have).

Use the subjunctive where there is no preceding conjunction (such as **que**, **quando**, **se**, etc.) or adverbial phrase (**antes de**, etc.).

Eu talvez **prove** o doce da casa.   *I may well try the restaurant's*
                                     dessert speciality.

Personal infinitive and alternative tenses

In the examples below you can see two different ways of saying the same thing, the first using the personal infinitive, the second using a different tense. It does not matter which you choose.

With a request verb (**pedir** or other), however, the personal infinitive is used only colloquially; not in careful speech or writing.

Noun clauses:

A hospedeira (Eur.) / aeromoça (Br.) | para **apertar** o cinto.
pede ao passageiro | que **aperte** o cinto.
                              (compare with present subjunctive, Unit 16)

A hospedeira (Eur.) / aeromoça (Br.) | para **apertarem** o cinto.
pediu aos passageiros | que **apertassem** o cinto.
                       (compare with imperfect subjunctive, Unit 18)

É possível | ela **tomar** uma bebida quente.
          | que ela **tome** uma bebida quente (cf. pres. subj., Unit 16)
          | que ela **tomasse** uma bebida quente (cf. imp. subj., Unit 18)

Time clauses:

Gosto de beber alguma coisa| antes e depois de **comer**.
                        | antes e depois que **coma**. (pres. subj.)
(I like to have something to drink before and after eating.)
Telefonei para a minha amiga | ao **chegar**.
                      | quando **cheguei**.   (preterite)
(I phoned my friend when I arrived.)
Atravessem | ao **chegarem** à esquina.
          | quando **chegarem** à esquina. (future subj.)
(Cross over when you get to the corner.)
Vamos ficar em casa do João | ao **irmos** ao Porto.
Ficaremos em casa do João | quando **formos** ao Porto. (fut. subj.)
(We are going to stay / shall stay at John's when we go to Oporto.)

Causal clauses and clauses of purpose:

Não vamos ao cinema | por **termos jantado** tarde.
                 | porque **jantamos** tarde. (preterite)
(We are not going to the cinema because we had dinner late.)

Comprei-te / Eu te comprei (Br.) um livro │ para o **leres**.
│ para que o **leias**. (pres. subj.)
(I bought you a book for you to read/ so that you may read it.)

Conditional and concessional clauses:

Vocês engordarão │ a **comerem** assim.
│ se **comerem** assim. (fut. subj.)
(You will put on weight if you eat this much.)
Eles não engordam │ apesar de **comerem** muito.
│ embora **comam** muito. (pres. subj.)
(They do not put on weight despite eating a lot.)

✓ Exercícios

20.2 Um cheque preenchido *(a made-out cheque)*

> If you make a mistake, write *Ressalva*, correct and sign again.

Study the above cheque and answer the following questions.
1 À ordem de quem é que João Castro preencheu este cheque?
2 Que quantia é que se paga com este cheque?
3 O cheque está completo ou falta alguma coisa?

20.3

You are at the bank. Rearrange the jumbled up words in brackets so as to say the following:

1 *I would like to cash this cheque.*
   (Queria / cheque. / descontar / este)
2 *Where do you keep the credit slips (paying-in forms)?*
   (Onde / as fichas / estão / de depósito? / é que)
3 *Is this the receipt for my deposit?*
   (Isto / o recibo / de depósito?/ é)
4 *I would like to see my account balance.*
   (Queria / o meu / saldo. / ver)
5 *How much is the pound today? And how much is the commission?*
   (A quanto / a libra / hoje? / está / E quanto / a comissão? / é)

20.4

You have seen these signs at the post office.

1	2	3
CARTAS E ENCOMENDAS **REGISTADAS** *Registered* *letters and parcels*	**IMPRESSOS** **TELEGRAMAS** *Forms* *Telegrams*	**POSTA RESTANTE** **ENTREGAS** *Post box* *Collection point*

registados (Eur.) = registrados (Br.)

20.4.1 Listen to your cassette/CD and you will hear six people – *a* to *f* –
at the post office. At which service hatch is each one of them?

20.4.2 Write down all that you heard the six people say.

20.5 Um convite para a festa *An invitation to the party*

Helena Monteiro
Augusto Monteiro

*têm o prazer de os convidar para uma festa em sua
casa no sábado próximo das 20h00 à meia-noite.*

Respondam por favor

20.5.1 Study the invitation card.

20.5.2 From the sentences below select and put into the appropriate order those you need for the following:

  (i) The text of a reply card, accepting;
  (ii) A message to be left on the Monteiro's answering machine. You are declining the invitation.

(*a*) É com muito prazer que aceitamos.

(*b*) Estaremos fora do país no sábado. Partimos amanhã.

(*c*) Lá estaremos no sábado às oito horas.

(*d*) Agradecemos muito, mas não vamos poder ir.

(*e*) Fala Joyce Brown acerca do convite para a festa.

(*f*) Ao regressarmos, telefonaremos para combinar um encontro.

 # 20.6

This photograph and text are from the admission ticket Phil has bought in Portugal when visiting the Tower of Belém just outside Lisboa.

TORRE DE BELÉM

PORTUGAL

Considerada como "ex-libris" da arquitectura monumental portuguesa, integrada no conjunto de imóveis que fazem parte do Património Mundial, sob a égide da UNESCO, a Torre de Belém apresenta todas as características individualizantes do estilo Manuelino Português (Séc. XVI).

IPPAR / Torre de Belém

arquitectura (Eur.) = arquitetura (Br.)   património (Eur.) = patrimônio (Br.)
arquitectónico (Eur.) = arquitetônico (Br.)

20.6.1 Study the text on page 225 as well as the text below.

(o) imóvel *building*	**(o) cordame** *rigging*
sob a égide *under the aegis*	**(a) esfera armilar** *armillary sphere*
(o) pilar em espiral *spiral-shaped column*	**(a) cruz da Ordem de Cristo** *cross, emblem of the Order of Christ*

O estilo manuelino é um estilo ornamental arquitectónico português. Data do fim do século XV e principalmente do século XVI, parte final da época dos descobrimentos marítimos.

Foi de Belém, hoje parte da Grande Lisboa, que partiram muitos navegadores portugueses. Em 1487 Bartolomeu Dias dobra o Cabo das Tormentas, a partir de então denominado Cabo da Boa Esperança. Esperança... de se descobrir o caminho marítimo para a Índia. Esse sonho é realizado por Vasco da Gama em 1498. Os portugueses navegam este e oeste. Em 1500 Álvares Cabral desembarca no Brasil. Os portugueses vão até terras remotas – Timor, Macau, Japão.

Esta época de grandeza para Portugal coincide com o reinado de Dom Manuel I. Daí o nome "manuelino". O manuelino é inspirado nos descobrimentos marítimos. Inclui pilares em espiral e, entre vários outros elementos, cordame, esferas armilares e a cruz da Ordem de Cristo, a mesma cruz que se vê nas velas das caravelas.

20.6.2 Answer, in Portuguese, the following questions on both texts.

1 What building is said to be an emblem (*ex-libris*) of Portuguese historical architecture?
2 This is a World Heritage listed building. What is the international organisation involved?
3 What is the manueline style?
4 What name was given to the Cape of Torments after having been rounded by Bartolomeu Dias?
5 The Portuguese travelled both East and West. When did Vasco da Gama arrive in India and Álvares Cabral in Brazil?
6 Mention three features that are characteristic of the manueline style.

20.7

Alda comes from Cape Verde and is on her first visit to Portugal. She has been on the triangular tour of Lisboa, Sintra and Estoril.

20.7.1 Study what she wrote on the holiday card she has sent home.

> Olá, Lúcio!
>
> Tudo bem? Aqui faz bom tempo, a comida é boa e eu estou bem. Ontem fui na excursão do triângulo turístico que inclui visita a Lisboa, Sintra e Estoril. Sendo a capital do país, Lisboa tem muita coisa para ver. Em Sintra adorei os palácios. No Estoril tomei banho na praia.
>
> Um beijo da Alda

20.7.2 On Phil's behalf, write a similar postcard to Georgina, but describe his visit to the Tower of Belém instead: **Ontem fui à.......** Say that the tower dates to the 16th century and has all the characteristics that define the manueline style. Explain what this style is and mention four of its distinctive features.

21 | TENCIONO VISITAR ESSE PAÍS
I'm intending to visit your country

This is the first of the four final revision units where you will further consolidate the language structures you learned throughout this course and you will expand your Portuguese vocabulary in a number of ways.

In this unit you will learn more about:

- services, from hairdressing to e-mail
- sightseeing and getting to know the country
- expressing yourself both verbally and in writing

Exercícios

21.1 No cabeleireiro *At the hairdresser's*

21.1.1 Study how Sibélia and Romeu go about their visit to the hairdresser's, on both sides of the Atlantic.

cortar (o) cabelo *hair-cut*	**(o) verniz** (Eur.) /**esmalte** (Br.)
fazer as unhas *to do one's nails*	*nail polish*
lavar a cabeça *to wash one's hair*	**incolor** *colourless*
(head)	**atendê-lo** *serve you*
atender *to see to, serve*	**bem curto** *quite short*
(a) franja *fringe*	**penteado** *combed*

No cabeleireiro de senhoras

Sibélia	Queria cortar o cabelo. Queria também fazer as unhas. Pode atender-me agora ou preciso marcar hora?
Recepcionista	É melhor marcar hora. Quer hoje à tarde às três e meia?
Sibélia	Está bem.

Sibélia   Boa tarde, eu tenho hora marcada para as três e meia para cortar cabelo, e unhas também.

Empregada   A senhora pode vir, eu vou lhe lavar a cabeça. (*lavando a cabelo de Sibélia*) A água está bem assim ou está quente demais?

_____

Cabeleireira Como é que a senhora quer o cabelo?

Sibélia   Eu quero franja, e dos lados e atrás quero cortar só um pouco.

_____

Manicura   De que cor é que a senhora quer o verniz (Eur.) / esmalte (Br.)?

Sibélia   Prefiro incolor.

No cabeleireiro de homens *or* barbeiro

Recepcionista Tem hora marcada?

Romeu   Não, não tenho.

Recepcionista Então faça favor de esperar um pouco. Vamos atendê-lo daqui a dez minutos.

_____

Cabeleireiro   Como é que o senhor quer o cabelo?

Romeu   Bem curto dos lados e atrás e penteado para o lado esquerdo.

21.1.2 Listen to your cassette/CD and you will hear four different people at the hairdresser's. What are they being asked and how do they reply?

21.1.3 Can you ask for your hair to be done as follows:
- (i)   quite short
- (ii) a bit off the sides and back
- (iii) swept back
- (iv) swept right

---

retirar *to pick up*
(o) auscultador (Eur.) / **fone** (Br.)
  receiver
(o) gancho *hook*
aguardar *to wait for*

(o) sinal / tom de digitar
  dialling tone
digitar / marcar (Eur.) *to dial*
(o) sinal / tom de tocar
  ringing tone

21.2

21.2.1 Julie is having problems in making a phone call and someone is trying to help by describing what must be done:

(ter de = ter que)

Você tem de retirar o auscultador (Eur.) / fone (Br.) do gancho e aguardar o sinal de digitar; digitar primeiro estes números e depois o número do telefone desejado; e aguardar o sinal de tocar.

21.2.2 Describe again what she must do, but in the following way:
Você retira o auscultador (Eur.) / fone (Br.) do gancho.....   *Carry on.*

21.2.3 This time use the 'command' form:
Retire o auscultador do gancho.....   *Carry on.*

 21.3

(o) indicativo (Eur.) / **código** (Br.)	*(phone) code*
(o) sinal de ocupado	*engaged tone*
a ligação foi cortada	*it has been cut off*

  quer dizer = significa

21.3.1 Brian wants to ask what the area code is for the phone call he needs to make. Unscramble his words for him:

(A) In Portugal: Qual / o indicativo (Eur.) / ? / é / da região
(B) In Brazil: Qual / o código (Br.) / ? / é / da região

21.3.2 Now he cannot get through. He wants to ask whether the tone he hears means that the line is engaged. Help him:

  Este sinal / ocupado / ? / quer dizer

21.3.3 Now help him say 'I think it has been cut off':

  Penso / foi /. / que / cortada / a ligação

Expressões-chave

Postcards, letters and parcels

As in English, for informal correspondence, some people simply write the addressee's first and last name plus his/her address.

Addressee:

In formal writing as well as for a more courteous approach in general, use the following for, respectively, a male and female adult addressee:

  Exmo(*) Sr / Exma(*) Sra (Eur.) // Ilmo(**) Sr / Ilma(**) Sra (Br.)

Exmo Sr. David Almeida *Mr David Almeida*
Ilma Sra Irene Almeida *Ms / Miss / Mrs Irene Almeida*
(*)   (= Excelentíssimo / Excelentíssima)
(**)   (= Ilustríssimo / Ilustríssima)

In business and commercial letters, **Ilmos Sres** corresponds to English *Messrs.* on both sides of the Atlantic.

Address:

You are likely to see more than one set of numbers in the address you are given.

Road and building:
The front door number (after the road) + floor + some additional information (for a private apartment or a business office sharing a section of a floor).

Rua Duque de Palmela, 37, 2° esq.

This is the apartment / office *on the left hand side* section of the *2nd floor* at *number 37*, Duque de Palmela *Road*.

(**dto** abbreviates **direito**; **fte**, **frente**; **esq**, **esquerdo**; **tras**, **traseira**; **ctro**, **centro**)

In large apartment blocks you may see the abbreviation **apto**, for **apartamento**, followed by the respective number.

Town and part of the country:
This will be preceded by the post code (**o código postal**). In Brazil, also remember to enter the acronym for the State:

1250-093 Lisboa   **01417-020 - São Paulo - SP**
Portugal   **Brasil**

Letter writing

Below is a list of forms of greetings – the words you open your letter with such as *Dear...* – and their matching forms of endings – the words you close your letter with such as *Yours...* – before signing.

Form of greeting:

(a) For a very close friend: **Querido / Querida** + *first name*

(b) For a friend or acquaintance:
      Caro / Cara or **Prezado / Prezada** + *first name*

or, not so informal,
Caro / Cara or **Prezado / Prezada** + **Sr / Sra** + *surname*

(c) **Caro Senhor / Cara Senhora** or **Prezado Senhor / Prezada Senhora**
Dear Sir / Madam

(d) **Exmo Senhor / Exma Senhora** (Eur.) // **Ilmo Senhor / Ilma Senhora** (Br.) *Dear Sir / Madam*
or **Exmos Senhores** (Eur.) // **Ilmos Senhores** (Br.) *Dear Sirs*

Form of ending:

(a) **Um beijo** (*kiss*) or **beijinhos** (lit. *little kisses*) or **Um abraço** (*embrace, hug*) where in English you would have written *Love*. Also **Saudades** (*missing you*).

(b) **Um abraço** and/or **Saudades** or, not so informal, **Cumprimentos**

(c) **Cumprimentos** or, not so informal, **Cordialmente**

(d) **Subscrevo-me de V. Exa(*) atenciosamente** or just **Atenciosamente**
Subscrevo-me de Vs. Exas(*) atenciosamente or just **Atenciosamente**
or **De Vs. Sras.(**) atenciosamente / Atenciosamente** (*commercial*)
(*) (= Vossa/s Excelência/s)   (**) (= Vossas Senhorias)

⬛ Como funciona

me, te, *etc.*: *where do they go?*

There is a certain amount of flexibility as to the position of the object pronouns in the sentence. Word-order follows the same fundamental rules you learned in Unit 8 for the reflexives. In fact, the reflexive pronouns themselves are a type of personal object pronouns.

The general tendency is to bring the object pronouns to the first part of the sentence or clause. **Pode me dizer onde é a saída?** (*Can you tell me where the exit is?*) is more widely heard than **Pode dizer-me onde é a saída?**

This 'pull' towards the beginning of a sentence or clause is stronger in Brazil. This is linked to the fact that Brazilians give a stronger pronunciation to final **e**, such as in **me** and **te**. If the object pronoun is more audible then it can stand better on its own at the beginning of what you want to say. As with the reflexives, a careful speaker will not make **me**, **te**, etc. the very first word in the sentence, but in colloquial speech e.g. for *Give me that*, **Me dê isso** is often heard in Brazil in preference to **Dê-me isso**.

Some preferences in personal pronouns

In the sense of *for me* many Brazilians will prefer the more literal **para mim**, etc. while Portuguese will rather use **me**, etc.

> Pode **me** chamar um táxi? (Eur.) Pode chamar um táxi **para mim**? (Br.)
> *Can you send for a taxi for me?*

As you learned in Unit 7, Brazilians in general do not use subject pronoun **tu** but they use widely its object forms, often in combination with subject pronoun **você**. They also often use the **tu** approach for the verb but without saying the word **tu**.

> **Você** estava no aeroporto?   *Were you at the airport?*
> Eu não **te** vi lá.   *I didn't see you there.*
> **Me dá** isso. *or* **Dá** isso para mim.   *Give me that.*

o, a and -lo, -la

You have come across instances in which the object pronoun **o/a/os/as** appears to 'have gone missing'. Particularly in speech, this pronoun tends to be omitted wherever context provides enough information.

> Aqui tem. *for* Aqui **a** tem (**a**: a chave do quarto). *Here you are (your room key)*
> Eu talvez prove. *for* Eu talvez **o** prove. (**o**: o doce da casa) *I may try it (the restaurant's speciality dessert)*

When expressed, **o/a/os/as** become **lo/la/los/las** after a verbal form ending in **r**, **s** or **z**, in which case these final letters are dropped.

> comprá-**los** (=comprar+os) *to buy them*
> vendê-**los** (vender+os) *to sell them*
> comprá-**lo**-á (i.e., comprará + o) *s/he will buy it*
> comprá-**lo**-ia (i.e., compraria + a) *s/he would buy it*

(Note the addition of an accent in the infinitive of **-ar** and **-er** verbs.)

Hence,

> Muito prazer em conhecê-lo *Delighted to meet you. (... a man)*
> Muito prazer em conhecê-la *Delighted to meet you.. (... a woman)*

This construction can be avoided by changing the word order

> Tive muito prazer em o conhecer. *It has been a pleasure to meet you.*

✓ Exercícios

21.4 Trem do Corcovado *Corcovado Mountain Railway*

Study the following contents of a leaflet issued by the Brazilian organisation who runs the cog-railway service to the top of the Corcovado mountain. At the top of this rocky peak stands the statue of Christ the Redeemer overlooking the city of Rio de Janeiro.

O trenzinho do Corcovado é um passeio obrigatório para o turista que vem ao Rio de Janeiro e quer conhecer o Cristo Redentor, o principal ponto turístico da Cidade Maravilhosa. Mais de 250 mil pessoas por ano fazem esse passeio inesquecível. Na viagem, o passageiro aprecia uma das mais lindas paisagens do Rio. Mas a vista é apenas uma das atrações: passear no trem é fazer uma viagem pela história do Brasil.

atrações (Br.) = atracções(Eur.)

21.4.1 Answer in Portuguese the following questions on the text:

(i) What does 'trenzinho' mean?
(ii) What is the main tourist spot in Rio?
(iii) What attraction is there in addition to enjoying a beautiful view?

21.4.2 Using the form of greeting and ending *(a)* you learned earlier in this unit, write a holiday postcard to your friend Simão saying the following:

The weather is fine, food good, and you are well. Yesterday you went to the Corcovado by cog-railway. This tourist spot is visited by more than 250 thousand people each year. On the journey you enjoy (the passenger enjoys) a beautiful view.

21.5 O endereço do e-mail *The e-mail address*

Graham is asking Marisa how to say in Portuguese the @ in an e-mail address.

Graham Como é que se diz "@" em português?
Marisa "Arroba".

Fill in the gaps in his next question.

Graham Como é que _____ "dot" em _____ ?
Marisa "Ponto".

21.6 Pedindo informação por escrito
Writing for information

| Tenciono | visitar Portugal / o Brasil em Março do ano que vem |
| | passar duas semanas nesse país, do dia ... ao dia ... |

Estou especialmente interessado/a | no norte do país
| num hotel perto de uma praia

Peço que	faça(m) o favor	de	me enviar(em)...
	tenha(m) a gentileza		me dizer(em) ....
	(lit., *kindness*)		informar(em) ....
.... lista dos hotéis / transportes públicos na região
.... folhetos de informação acerca da região

Fico aguardando resposta e desde já agradeço.

21.6.1 Select and combine words and phrases from the above box as the basis for an e-mail or letter to a tourist office in a Portuguese-speaking country, asking for the following:
(i)   list of hotels in the area
       (*one week in the country / interested in a hotel near a beach /list of
       hotels, please / looking forward to their reply and thank-you*)
(ii) list of campsites in the area
       (*two months / facilities for children / looking forward to their reply
       and thank you*)
(iii) list of hostels in the area
       (*one month / facilities for physically impaired / tourist information
       leaflet/ looking forward to their reply and thank-you*)

21.6.2 What would you be using for (i) form of greeting and (ii) form of ending in these e-mails or letters?

22 | TOMARA QUE ELES TELEFONEM
I wish they would phone

In this revision unit you will learn about:
- replying to an advertisement
- writing your CV and applying for a job
- looking for property on the market, to let or for sale

Exercícios

22.1 Um emprego *A job*

22.1.1 Study the advertisement for the post of translator and interpreter.

Tradutor/a - Intérprete

Pretendemos candidato/a com o seguinte perfil:
* diploma profissional
* bom domínio do inglês falado e escrito
* bons conhecimentos de informática
* elevado grau de autonomia e professionalismo

Oferecemos:
* flexibilidade horária
* bom ambiente de trabalho
* remuneração adequada ao exercício da função

Os interessados deverão enviar, num prazo máximo de 5 dias úteis após publicação, carta de candidatura, manuscrita, C.V. e fotografia tipo passe para o nº 201955 deste Jornal.

22.1.2 Kevin is applying for the post. What form will he be using for the verbs in brackets in the draft for his letter of application below?

Em resposta ao anúncio nº 201955 desse Jornal, venho apresentar a minha candidatura ao cargo de tradutor e intérprete. Eu (*reunir*) todos os requisitos enumerados, e, embora tenha aprendido português como língua estrangeira, (*possuir*) um excelente domínio do idioma, falado e escrito.

Juntamente envio (Eur.) / estou enviando (Br.) o meu currículo e fotografia tipo passe, como pretendido. Fico aguardando resposta com grande interesse e espero que (*poder*) conceder-me uma entrevista.

22.1.3 What would Kevin say at the interview concerning his profile as a candidate if asked about the following:
  (i) professional qualifications;
 (ii) competence in information technology;
(iii) his level of self-management and professionalism.

 ## 22.2

Caso seja devolvido ao remetente *If it is returned to sender*

A letter you had posted was sent back to you. On the back you found the following:

CASO NÃO SEJA ENTREGUE AO DESTINATÁRIO, É FAVOR ASSINALAR A RAZÃO COM "X":
  ☒ ENDEREÇO INSUFICIENTE
  ☐ DESCONHECIDO

What is the reason why your letter wasn't delivered to its addressee?

 ## 22.3 O currículo ou o "curriculum vitae"

Ana Magalhães (you first heard about in Unit 3) completed her general education at Colégio Bom Sucesso and has a "licenciatura" degree in Medicine by the Portuguese University of Coimbra. Ana has not done any post-graduate studies or published any work. She works as a general practitioner at Clínica Boa Saúde, her first job, and is a member of the Associação dos Médicos.

22.3.1 Study Ana's CV below.

Curriculum Vitae

1. Informação geral

   1.1 Nome completo *Ana Isabel Vieira Gama Magalhães*

   1.2 Nome do pai *José Luís Cabral Gama*

        Nome da mãe *Maria Feliciana Miranda Vieira Gama*

   1.3 Data de nascimento *29 de Março*

   1.4 Naturalidade *Guimarães*

   1.5 Nacionalidade *Portuguesa*

   1.6 Estado civil *Casada*

   1.7 Endereço residencial *Faro*

   1.8 Documento de identidade *BI 8170771*

2. Formação educacional

   2.1 Geral *Colégio Bom Sucesso*

   2.2 Superior *Licenciatura em Medicina, Coimbra*

   2.3 Pós-graduação ————

3. Carreira profissional

   3.1 Emprego actual (Eur.) / atual (Br.) *Clínica Boa Saúde*

   3.2 Empregos anteriores ————

4. Informação suplementar

   4.1 Sociedades culturais *Associação dos Médicos*

   4.2 Trabalhos publicados ————

22.3.2 What would Ana's answers be to the following questions.

(Give brief answers.)

  (i)   Onde é que a senhora nasceu?

 (ii) Qual é o seu nome de solteira?

(iii) A senhora é professora?

(iv) Onde se formou?

 (v) Fez estudos de pós-graduação?

(vi) Trabalha num hospital?

🔑 Expressões-chave

estar *or* ficar ?

Use **ficar** in preference to **estar** for the inception of a state or situation.

Hoje eu **estou** cansada. *Today I am (feeling) tired.* but
Eu **fiquei** cansada depois daquele trabalho todo. *I was tired after all that work.*
Eu **estou** no Hotel Central. *I am (staying) at Hotel Central.* but
Quando eu venho, **fico** sempre no Hotel Central. *When I come, I always stay at Hotel Central.*

I think, in my opinion...

Pensar, *to think,* and **achar**, *to find,* can both be used to express one's opinion, with basically the same meaning.

Penso/Acho que ele tem razão. *I think that he is right.*

For an alternative with less conviction, use **parecer** or **na minha opinião**.

Parece-me que ele tem razão. *It seems to me that he is right.*
Na minha opinião, ele tem razão. *In my opinion, he is right.*

Also note that *I think so* and *I don't think so* are rendered by **penso que sim** and **penso que não**.

I am sure... I am right... all right?

Use **ter a certeza** (Eur.) / **ter certeza** (Br.) for *to be sure* and **ter razão** for *to be right (to have made the right judgment).*

Tem a certeza? (Eur.) / **Tem certeza**? (Br.)	*Are you sure?*
Tenho a certeza (Eur.) de que **tenho razão**.	*I am sure I am right.*
Tenho certeza (Br.) de que **tenho razão**.	*I am sure I am right.*
Você **não tem razão**.	*You are wrong.*

You can also use **estar certo** (*to be certain*) for *to be sure.*

Ela **não está certa** de que ele chegue hoje.	*She is not sure that he will/may arrive today.*

In addition, **certo** is used to seek, or give, assent.

(**está certo = está bem**)

– **Está bem?**	– **Certo?**	– *Is it all right / okay?*
– **Está.**	– **Certo.**	– *Yes / Okay.*

Another way of requesting assent is the question-tag **não é?** (*isn't it?*).
Unlike English, this does not change with the verb in the sentence.

– Você vai à festa, **não é?**	*You are going to the party, aren't you?*
– É.	*Yes, I am.*
– Você gosta de música, **não é?**	*You like music, don't you?*
– É.	*Yes, I do.*

🪗 Como funciona

a – de – em – para – por

Make the right choices!

- **Para** points towards a specific purpose or goal (including time or place)

Levantar **para** abrir.	*Lift to open* (lit. *for + to open*)
A cerveja é **para** mim.	*The beer is for me.*

- **Para** versus **por**:

Para translates English *for* where the latter means *movement towards*.

Ele partiu **para** África.	*He set out for Africa.*

Por is wider in its meaning while **para** is more specific inasmuch as it points towards a specific purpose or goal.

Tem um quarto **para** duas pessoas?	*Have you got a room for two?*
Quanto custa **por** noite?	*How much does it cost for a night (per night)?*

For length of time you can just leave *for* out.

Vou ficar aqui (**por**) dois meses.	*I am going to stay here for two months.*

- **Para** versus **de**:

um copo **de** vinho	*a glass of wine*

This will mean, depending on context, *a glass measure of wine* or *a glass meant to contain wine*. Should there be ambiguity, the latter meaning can be expressed by the alternative

um copo **para** vinho   *a wine glass*

- **A** can (i) be static or (ii) imply movement towards something or someone.
  (i) Quem está **à** (= **a**+ a) porta?   *Who is at the door?*
  (ii) Vou **ao** clube.   *I am going to the club.*

- **A** versus **para**:
With verbs of motion, both **a** and **para** frequently translate English *to*, but there is a difference.

Ele vai **a** África.   *He is going to Africa.* (only temporarily)

Ele vai **para** África.   *He is going to Africa.* (to settle there)

Eu vou **a** casa.   *I am going home.* (only in and out)

Eu vou **para** casa.   *I am going home.* (staying in... for the night)

Aonde é que você vai? /   *Where are you going?*
   Para onde é que você vai?

- **Para** and **pára**:
The latter is not a preposition but a form of the verb **parar** and is often spelt without the accent. So watch out!

- **A** and **em**:
Em is used for a position of rest or for movement into or on to something.
    Meti a máquina fotográfica **na** (= **em** + a) mala, que estava **no** (**em** + o) balcão da Alfândega. *I put the camera into the case, which was on the Customs desk.*
Brazilians use **em** with verbs of arrival.
    Cheguei **em** casa. (Br.)   Otherwise
    Cheguei **a** casa. *I arrived home.*

logo – já – já não – ainda não

Both **logo** and **já** refer to time but they don't always have the same English translation. **Logo** can be an alternative to **imediatamente** (*right away*), **em breve** (*soon*) or **mais tarde** (*later*).

| Ele telefonou **logo**. | *He phoned right away.* |
| Até **logo**. | *See you later.* |

Já can refer to a point in time either in the future or in the past, translating *straight away*, *already* or *ever*. It varies with its context.

Verb in the present:

| Volto **já**. | *I'm coming back in a moment.* |
| **Já** está! | *It's done.* (*already done*) |

Verb in the preterite:

| **Já** foi ao Algarve? | *Have you ever been to the Algarve?* |

Reply: Sim, **já**. *Yes, I have.* or Não, **ainda não**. *No, not yet.*

Ainda can also translate *still* (verb in the present):

| **Ainda** mora em Edimburgo? | *Do you still live in Edinburgh?* |

Reply: **Ainda**. *Yes.* or **Já não**. *No longer.*

Exercícios

22.4

Um ramo de flores e... a aliança de casamento
A bunch of flowers and... the wedding ring

This is Geraldo's horoscope for next week.

> Faça um esforço. Instale um sorriso nessa cara sofrida. A sua vida vai mudar completamente. É tempo de amar e ser amado. O futuro é hoje e a hora é agora.

Taking the horoscope seriously, select the two best pieces of advice to give Geraldo:

1 Eu penso que já é tempo de você deixar de ser solteiro e fazer planos para o casamento.
2 Eu acho que um ramo de flores está certo, mas ainda é muito cedo para pensar na aliança.
3 Casar... Se você não tem a certeza (Eur.) / certeza (Br.), o melhor é esperar.

4 Na minha opinião, você deve perguntar muito em breve se ela quer ir escolher a aliança.

 22.5

A viagem de lua-de-mel
The honeymoon trip

Help Bill and Mel write an e-mail or letter booking a hotel apartment for their honeymoon. This is their first draft. Complete their unfinished sentences for them.

Tencionamos visitar esse país (*June this coming year*). Precisamos de um apartamento (*for a couple*). Preferíamos (*the first week of the month*).

Se o hotel não tiver vagas (*on those days*), pedimos que façam o favor de informarem para quando podem fazer a reserva (*in our name, Sanders. We look forward to hearing from you.*)

22.6 Um apartamento mobilado *A furnished flat*

22.6.1 Study the plan of a flat and its furniture (**os móveis**).

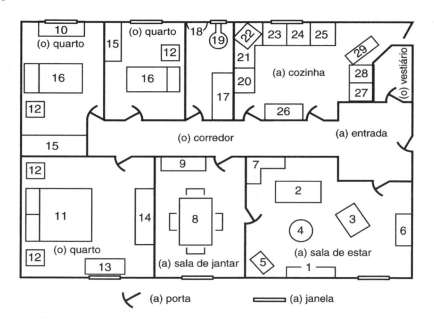

1 **a lareira** *fireplace*
2 **o sofá** *settee*
3 **a poltrona** *armchair*
4 **a mesinha de centro** *coffee table*
5 **o televisor** *television set*
6 **o aparelho de som** *hi-fi, stereo set*
7 **a estante de canto** *corner shelf unit*
8 **a mesa e as cadeiras** *table and chairs*
9 **o aparador** *sideboard*
10 **a mesa para (o) computador e (a) impressora** *work station for computer and printer*
11 **a cama de casal** *double bed*
12 **a mesa de cabeceira** *bedside table*
13 **o toucador** (Eur.) / **a penteadeira** (Br.) *dressing table*
14 **o guarda-roupa** *wardrobe*
15 **o armário** *cupboard, storage unit*

16 **a cama de solteiro** *single bed*
17 **a banheira** *bathtub*
18 **o lavatório/a pia** (Br.) *washbasin*
19 **a bacia/a retrete** (Eur.) *toilet*
20 **o fogão** *stove, cooker*
21 **o balcão** (Eur.) / **a bancada** (Br.) *work surface*
22 **o forno micro ondas** *microwave oven*
23 **o lava louça / a máquina de lavar louça** (Eur.) *dishwasher*
24 **a pia** *sink*
25 **o frigorífico** (Eur.) / **o refrigerador** *or* **a geladeira** (Br.) **e o congelador** *refrigerator and freezer unit*
26 **o armário** *cupboard*
27 **a máquina de lavar roupa** (Eur.) / **a lavadora** (Br.) *washing machine*
28 **a secadora de roupa** *clothes dryer*
29 **a tábua de passar roupa** *ironing board*

Where context makes the meaning clear, some words are omitted, e.g., **a tábua de passar.**

22.6.2 Listen to your cassette/CD. You will hear the lady who lives in this flat talk about what the apartment is like. Make a note of what she says.

 22.7 Aluga-se e vende-se *To let and for sale*

22.7.1 Study these two newspaper advertisements.

(i)

aluga-se
apartamento

mobilado
3 quartos de dormir
com ar condicionado
2º andar, elevador
serviço de limpeza (opcional)
Resposta ao número 27894

(ii)

vende-se
casa

6 quartos de dormir
cozinha equipada
aquecimento central
jardim e piscina
garagem
Resposta ao número 27036

22.7.2 Sharon is interested in advert (i). Help her write the text of her reply to the paper by entering the verbs in brackets in the correct form.

Em resposta ao anúncio nº 27894 desse jornal, tenho o prazer de comunicar que estou interessada em alugar um apartamento e esse talvez me (*convir*). Fico aguardando que (*fazer*) o favor de informar quando o (*poder*) ver.

22.7.3 Reply to the following question, in Portuguese:

Quem poderá estar interessado no anúncio (ii), uma pessoa que queira alugar ou uma pessoa que queira comprar?

22.7.4 Now write a reply to advert (ii).

23 | IREI, SE PUDER
I shall join in, if I can

In this revision unit you will learn about:

- local culture and shows
- family celebrations and parties
- domestic work and a food recipe

☑ Exercícios

23.1

Indo ao teatro, ao cinema, à ópera ou a um concerto
A visit to the theatre, cinema, opera or a concert

a galeria	*gallery (balcony)*
o 2º balcão (Eur.) **/ balcão simples** (Br.)	*upper circle*
o 1º balcão (Eur.) **/ balcão nobre** (Br.)	*dress circle*
os camarotes	*boxes*
a plateia (Eur.) **/ platéia** (Br.)	*stalls*
a orquestra	*orchestra*
o palco	*stage*

o ingresso = a entrada = o bilhete (Eur.)

There are no tickets left for the gallery, upper circle and back stalls. Which of the following questions could be answered with **ainda** and which with **já não há mais**?

1 Ainda há entradas para a galeria?
2 Queria um camarote. Ainda tem?
3 Ainda tem lugares na plateia perto do palco?
4 Queria quatro ingressos para a plateia, nas filas atrás. Ainda há?
5 Ainda tem lugares no segundo balcão?
6 Queria dois lugares no primeiro balcão, no centro. Ainda tem?

23.2

Venha ouvir os melhores fadistas
na casa de fado

a guitarra e a viola

aberta
das 21 às 4 da madrugada

Peça a carta de vinhos

(a) guitarra	*Portuguese lute*
(a) viola (in Brazil **(o) violão**)	*guitar*
(o) instrumento dedilhado	*plucked stringed instrument*

Unscramble the words in brackets and find out about fado singing.

Margarida	Já foi a uma casa de fados?
Charles	Não, nunca fui. O que é uma "casa de fados"?
Margarida	(É / onde / restaurante, / o fado. / um lugar, um / se canta)
Charles	Mas o que significa "fado"?
Margarida	(É / acerca da / experiência da vida. / uma canção / é / portuguesa / mas há / de temas. / O "amor" / um tema frequente, / uma grande variedade)
Charles	E o que são a guitarra e a viola?
Margarida	(São / o fadista ou a fadista. / a pessoa que canta o fado, / os dois instrumentos dedilhados / que normalmente acompanham)
Charles	As casas de fado estão abertas até muito tarde?
Margarida	Estão, até de madrugada. "Madrugada" quer dizer "as primeiras horas do dia".

Expressões-chave

I believe, I agree

Crer and **acreditar em** translate *to believe*, but the latter is better left for trust in veracity rather than for conviction.

Creio que ele tem razão.   *I believe that he is right.*
Acredito nas palavras dele.   *I believe his words.*

Concordar com or **estar de acordo com** will translate *to agree with.*

Não concordo!   *I disagree!*
Concordo com o senhor. / **Estou**   *I agree with you.*
  de acordo com o senhor.

leaving

Note the different renderings for *to leave* and *leave.*

ir-se embora *to leave, go away*
  Fique. Não se vá embora.   *Stay. Don't go.*

despedir-se *to take one's leave*
  Já é tarde. Tenho que me ir   *Time is getting on. I have to be*
    embora. Vou-me despedir.   *going. I am going to say*
                                          goodbye.

partir / sair *to leave, depart*
  O comboio (Eur.) / trem (Br.)   *The train is going to leave at*
    vai partir / sair às 8h35.   *8.35 hrs.*

I miss...

To miss in the sense of *to fail to* corresponds to **perder**.

  Perdi o avião. *I have missed the plane.*

To miss in the sense of *to feel the lack of* corresponds to **sentir a falta de**.

  Sinto a falta de um aparelho de vídeo. *I lack a video.*

To miss in the sense of *to notice with regret the absence or loss of*
corresponds to **ter saudades de** or **estar com saudades de**.
  Tenho saudades da Inglaterra. **Estou com saudades d**a Inglaterra.
  I miss home (home being England).

Sorry and frightened?

For emotions you can use the same format you learned in Unit 17 for
expressions of feeling (pain. etc.) – **estar com** or **ter** + noun:

Tenho	pena (*sorrow, pity*) de	*I'm (feeling)*	*sorry for*
	inveja (*envy*) de		*envious of*
Estou com	ciúme (*jealousy*) de		*jealous of*
	medo (*fear*) de		*afraid of*

O bebé (Eur.) / bebê (Br.) **tem medo d**as ondas do mar. *The baby is afraid of the waves.*

🖐 Como funciona

bem – todo – mesmo – próprio

You have come across certain words which sometimes appear to lose their literal meaning and are used as an intensifier instead. This is the case with **bem** (*well*), **todo** (*all*), **mesmo** (*same*) and **próprio** (*own*).

Quer os ovos **bem** cozidos?	*Do you want the eggs hard boiled?*
Ele está **todo** molhado.	*He is soaking wet.*
Ela ficou **toda** contente quando o viu.	*She was extremely happy when she saw you.*
É isso **mesmo**.	*It's exactly that (what you said).*

Also **eu mesmo**, etc. or **eu próprio**, etc. can translate *I myself, etc.* However, you are more likely to hear **Sou eu quem...** , etc.

Sou eu quem paga.	*I am paying myself. (I am s/he who is paying)*

tudo *ou todo?*

Tudo translates *everything, all.* It usually functions as a pronoun and the neuter form of **todo**.

Quanto é **tudo**?	*How much does it come to? (all the items)*

Todo contains the notion of *whole.*

Quanto é **ao todo**?	*How much does it come to? (in all, altogether)*
Ontem estudei o dia **todo** *or* **todo** o dia.	*Yesterday I studied all day.*
Estudo um pouco **todos** os dias.	*I study a bit every day.*

Toda a gente (Eur.) / **todo** (o) mundo (Br.) dança. *Everyone / everybody dances.*

Who does what?

■ 'No-person' verbs:

You have come across some verbs that have no subject, expressed or implicit. It is so with the weather and other cases.

Chove. *(It) rains.* **Dói.** *(It) hurts.*

■ Different subject:

Note that different meanings can be obtained by changing the subject of the verb.

Não me **lembro**; esqueci-me. *I cannot remember; I have forgotten.*

Lembre-me. *Remind me.*

■ Undefined subject:

When you wish to refer to an action without mentioning who actually does, or did, that action, use the third person of the verb (singular or plural) and no expressed subject.

Disseram-me que a "Baixa" em Lisboa é em forma de rectângulo.
I was told that Lisbon downtown is in the shape of a rectangle.
(lit. *(they) told me...*)

que *or* quê – porque, por que *or* por quê – por causa de

Quê is the strong form of **que**. The following dialogue will help you distinguish between the different forms.

Por que (*) comprou esse lenço? *Why have you bought that scarf?*
Por causa da (**) cor. *Because of its colour.*
Por quê!? *or* **Porquê!?** (Eur.) (***) *Why!?*
Por causa da cor. **Porque** (****) *Because of its colour.*
gosto da cor. *Because I like its colour.*

(*) *Why,* when you can also say **por que motivo** or **por que razão,** *for what reason.*
(**) *Because,* where followed by a noun, *because of.*
(***) *Why,* on its own.
(****) *Because,* other than (**)

Exercícios

23.3

pôr a mesa *to lay the table*	**limpar** *to clean, wipe clean*
tirar a mesa *to clear the table*	**passar o aspirador em/**
preparar *to cook (food, meal)*	**aspirar** (Eur.) *to vacuum*
fazer a cama *to make the bed*	**passar a ferro** *to iron*

23.3.1 Listen to your cassette/CD. The domestic help (**a empregada doméstica**) is being told her tasks for today. Make a note of what you hear.

23.3.2 Reword the instructions you heard in 23.3.1 but present them in a different way, starting with **Hoje precisa...**

23.4 Uma receita para a festa *A recipe for the party*

Ovos com recheio de anchova   *Eggs with anchovy stuffing*

23.4.1 Os ingredientes *The ingredients*

Find on the right a translation for the ingredients on the left.

1 meia dúzia de ovos
2 uma lata pequena de anchova em filete
3 sumo (Eur.) / suco (Br.) de meio limão
4 um boião (Eur.) / vidro (Br.) pequeno de azeitonas recheadas
5 um boião pequeno de maionese
6 uma alface

(a) a lettuce
(b) a small jar of stuffed olives
(c) half a dozen eggs
(d) a small can of anchovy fillets
(e) juice of half a lemon
(f) a small jar of mayonnaise

23.4.2 O procedimento *The method*

Now work out what to do.

Cozer bem os ovos. Descascá-los. Com uma faca, abri-los ao meio ao comprido. Com uma colher, tirar a gema para fora. Cortar a enchova em bocadinhos. Num prato grande, misturá-la com as gemas e o limão, usando um garfo. Encher as claras com a mistura. Por cima colocar um pouco de maionese e uma azeitona no meio. Cobrir o fundo de uma travessa com a alface cortada em tirinhas. Colocar os ovos recheados no leito de alface.

23.4.3 Beginning with **Cozi bem os ovos,** explain to your friend how you have prepared the ingredients.

23.5 Palavras para a festa *Words for the party*

Fill in the gaps in the 'party talk' below with words from the box.
In some cases you have more than one choice. Use all the options.

1 (i) *Someone is going to a party. Tell him/her to have a good time.*
        Divirta-se! *or* _____
   (ii) *Tell a group of people that you hope they'll have a good time at the
        party:*
        Desejo que _____ na festa.
2 (i) *You want to make a guest feel particularly welcome to your party.
        When your special guest arrives say 'It's good to see you':*
        É bom _____ *or* _____ *or* _____ .
   (ii) *You want to stress your appreciation for a present a guest brought
        you:*
        Gosto muito do seu presente. _____ muito contente.
3 (i) *You are going to a party and are buying something to give your
        host or hostess. In the shop ask to have the item gift-wrapped:*
        Pode _____ embrulhar para presente?
   (ii) *You arrive at the party with your gift and say:*
        Isto é para _____ *or* _____ *or* _____ .
4 *Join in the party toast:*
   - Saúde!   - Saúde!   - _____   - Saúde!

Diverte-te!	ver você		Fiquei
ti	você	ver-te	si	Saúde!
se divirtam	vê-lo / vê-la		fazer o favor de

 23.6 Quando é o seu aniversário? *When is your birthday?*

> o dia de anos (Eur.) = o aniversário

– Quando é o seu aniversário?
– No dia 3 de dezembro. E o seu?
– O meu é hoje.
– Então parabéns! Quantos anos é que você faz?
– Faço vinte anos.
– Tenho de ir comprar um presente para você/para si (Eur.).
– Não, não se incomode.

Rewrite the above dialogue in the **tu** approach throughout, starting with
Quando é o dia dos teus anos (Eur.)?

24 GOSTARIA DE PRATICAR MAIS
I should like to practise further

This last revision unit gives you advice for your continued success in Portuguese in the future.

24.1 Português como Língua Estrangeira (PLE)
Portuguese as a Foreign Language (PFL)

Jenny is a very successful student of Portuguese as a foreign language. She has been interviewed for a radio broadcast. Below you will find Jenny's replies to Luísa's questions. The latter are on your cassette/CD. Listen to the recording and put questions and replies together in a dialogue.

Jenny:

– Aprendi principalmente ensinando a mim própria como autodidacta (Eur.) / autodidata (Br.). Mas sentia a falta de pessoas com quem pudesse falar. Então resolvi passar um tempo em Portugal, dois meses, a praticar e estudar a língua.

– Frequentei (Eur.) / freqüentei (Br.) um curso de PLE na Universidade Nova de Lisboa. Tínhamos aulas de língua todos os dias e de cultura três vezes por semana. No fim do curso submeti-me a um exame. Passei com distinção. Fiquei muito contente.

– Obrigada. E aproveitei todas as oportunidades para falar, nas lojas, nos restaurantes, em todo o lado. Gostei muito de Portugal e da sua capital, das pessoas... de tudo. Tive muita pena de me vir embora.

– Vou... vou voltar para um país de língua portuguesa, mas vai ser outro. Quero ir ao Brasil, quero passar dois ou três meses lá.

– Ainda não sei, mas gostaria de visitar Brasília.

– Não sei bem... Talvez porque é a capital federal. Talvez (*rindo*) também porque me disseram que Brasília foi construída em forma de avião. Não sei se acredite ou não. O melhor é ir ver.

– Ir ao Brasil é também uma boa oportunidade para ouvir outro sotaque e outras expressões.

– Hei de ir, mas quando ainda não sei.

✓ 24.2 **Procure e descubra** *Look for and find out*

For your continued success after completing this course, always try to 'think Portuguese' when you want to speak Portuguese. This is a golden rule.

Imagine that you are being shown several brands of **vinho tinto** at a wine shop. You make your choice and use the verb **ter** meaning to say *I'll have that one*. To your surprise, though, the assistant puts the bottle away. He thinks you are trying to say that you *already have* that one. As we saw earlier, **Quero esse** or **Levo esse** would have conveyed the right meaning.

The key lies in remaining aware of the boundary line in the area of meaning covered by a word. One English word may cover the main area of meaning of more than one Portuguese word, and vice-versa.

24.2.1 Find one single English word that will translate the different Portuguese words in each set.

(i) Vou ⎸ perguntar ⎸ onde ele está.
   Vou ⎸ pedir ⎸ um copo de água.

(ii) ⎸ Aprendi ⎸ português numa escola.
   ⎸ Ele soube ⎸ a notícia pelo jornal.

(iii) Tenho de ⎸ procurar ⎸ um apartamento.
   Ela vai ⎸ olhar ⎸ pelas crianças.

(iv) ⎸ Diga ⎸ o que aconteceu, por favor.
   ⎸ Conte ⎸ como isso aconteceu, por favor.

(v) Você quer a luz ⎸ acesa ⎸ ou ⎸ apagada?
   Você quer o vídeo ⎸ ligado ⎸ ou ⎸ desligado?
   Você quer o casaco ⎸ vestido ⎸ ou ⎸ despido?

24.2.2 Now find the words that go into the 'question mark' boxes in the sentences below (one for each set). They are hidden in the word search grid on page 256.

(i)   Fez bom   [**?**]   e muito sol.
     Quanto   vamos esperar?

(ii)   Agora vou para   [**?**]   .
     Ele mora numa   ou num apartamento?

(iii)   Esta senhora   [**?**]   o telefone portátil.
     A filha dele   o avião das 9 horas.

(iv)   Ele vai se   [**?**]   no hospital.
     Se puder, vou   disso amanhã.
     Posso   o João por "tu"?.

(v)   Você não me   [**?**]   esse dinheiro.
     O Nuno   chegar em breve.
     O senhor   reservar lugar.

(vi)   A que horas é que   [**?**]   o jantar?
     Para que é que   isto?
     Este casaco não me   . Está apertado.

(vii)   [**?**]   20 para as 8.
          duas pessoas no grupo.
          os guardanapos na mesa.

(viii)   Você já   [**?**]   a Teresa?
     Ela não   ninguém aqui.
     Peter não   Belém.

(ix)   Peter   [**?**]   onde fica Belém.
     O senhor   falar português?
     Você   se ela chegou bem?

(x)   Onde   [**?**]   o seu apartamento?
     Quem   em casa e quem vai sair?
     Ela   contente quando o vê.

C	O	N	H	E	C	E	R	A
O	C	A	S	D	E	V	A	S
F	A	T	T	E	M	P	O	S
A	O	R	E	V	I	E	R	E
L	P	A	M	E	D	R	O	R
T	I	T	O	V	Z	D	E	V
A	C	A	S	A	G	E	M	E
M	O	R	U	H	L	U	M	J
S	A	B	E	U	F	I	C	A

✓ 24.3 Desvenda o mistério *Solve the mystery*

You will come across Portuguese words which will suggest English words. They may sound, look or even both sound and look alike, but the meaning will be different, sometimes 'dangerously' so.

Imagine that, on heading towards a door, you hear your friend say to you **Puxe**, which will sound very much like English *Push*. But (as you have learned in this course) pushing is exactly what you must not do – pull instead!

Other 'false friends' have been unmasked for you throughout this course, such as *cup* – **copo** and *parent* – **parente**. Some more are in the box below. Study them.

	'false friend'	meaning (*)	
P	(a) marmelada	*quince cheese*	E
E	*marmalade*	(a) geleia (Eur.) / geléia (Br.) de laranja	P
P	preocupado	*worried*	E
E	*preoccupied*	absorto	P
P	pretender	*to go for, to intend*	E
E	*to pretend*	fingir	P
P	sensível	*sensitive*	E
E	*sensible*	sensato	P

(*) not necessarily the only one

Now read the following and find out who stole the quince 'cheese' from the local food store that morning, leaving an empty box on the shelf (!!)

10h00. D. Rosa, uma das empregadas, colocou as caixas de marmelada nas duas primeiras prateleiras a contar de baixo.

10h10. D. Berta entrou com Joãozinho, o filho de dois anos, que chorava porque queria descalçar as luvas mas a mãe não deixava; é uma criança muito sensível. D. Maria, a empregada da caixa, diz que D. Berta não comprou nada e parecia preocupada ao sair.

10h15. D. Zulmira, senhora de sesssenta anos, entrou com o seu cachorro Piloto. Conversou durante uns cinco minutos com D. Rosa junto às prateleiras da marmelada.

10h20. Sr. Olavo, homem de ar absorto, entrou na loja. Ele parecia pretender alguma coisa especial. Encontraram-se as suas impressões digitais na caixa vazia.

10h30. Sr. José, o gerente, notou que uma das caixas de marmelada não tinha nada dentro, estava vazia. A marmelada tinha desaparecido mas a caixa estava na prateleira.

24.4 Não ao pé da letra... *Not literally...*

Similarly to what happens with some English words, throughout this course you have come across Portuguese words which sometimes lose their literal meaning in order to be used some other way. This includes verbs such as **andar**, **voltar**, **deixar**, **começar**, **acabar** and others.

Below you have two sets of sentences. Pair up the sentences in (1) to (5) with another way of saying the same in (*a*) to (*e*).

1 Eu **comecei a** estudar português há seis meses.
2 Mas em breve **deixei de** estudar português por falta de tempo.
3 Depois de um intervalo **voltei a** estudar português.
4 E **ando a estudar** (Eur.) / **ando estudando** muito.
5 **Acabo de** fazer o penúltimo exercício deste curso.

(*a*) Depois de um intervalo estudei português novamente.
(*b*) Fiz agora mesmo o penúltimo exercício deste curso.
(*c*) Eu estudei português pela primeira vez há seis meses.
(*d*) E tenho estudado muito ultimamente.
(*e*) Mas em breve parei de estudar por falta de tempo.

24.5 A cultura do país *The country's culture*

24.5.1 Study the information shown below. It appeared in a leaflet from the Arts Centre of a Brazilian University – Centro de Artes da Universidade Federal Fluminense.

24.5.2 Reply to the following questions, in Portuguese:

(i)   Qual é o tema geral deste curso da UFF?
(ii) Quem são os organizadores?
(iii) Onde é que se vai realizar?
(iv) Quando é que se vai realizar?

24.5.3 Write to UFF:

(You are intending to spend 6 months in Brazil this coming year, July to December / Interested in an introductory course on Brazilian culture / Would like to take part in UFF's course / Applying and enclosing CV / Looking forward to a reply and hoping to be granted a place.)

KEY TO THE EXERCISES

Introductory Unit

A.3: (*a*) Boa noite. (*b*) Bom dia. (*c*) Boa tarde. A.6: (*a*) Boa tarde, Dona/dona Laura. (*b*) Olá! *or* Oi! (Br.) C.2: 2 (*d*) (f); 3 (*c*) (*e*); 4 (*a*) (*g*). C.4: (*a*) Bom dia. (*b*) Boa tarde. (*c*) Até logo. *You can add*: Adeus / Tchau! (*d*) Tchau, até logo.

Unit 1

1.1 certo (2) (3), errado (1).
1.2 (1) (*b*). (2) (*a*). (3) (*b*).
1.3.1 (ii) A+C, (iii) B+C, (iv) B+C, (v) A+B.
1.3.2 (i) Faz favor, pode me dizer onde é a recolha de bagagem? A recolha de bagagem é à direita, em frente do controle de passaporte. Obrigada. (ii) Onde são as informações, por favor? As informações são lá em cima, à direita. Obrigado. (iii) Desculpe, onde são os sanitários para senhoras? Os sanitários para senhoras são à esquerda, a seguir aos sanitários para homens. Muito obrigada. (iv) Faz favor, pode me dizer onde é o aluguer de carros? O aluguer de carros é a seguir às informações e ao ao ponto de encontro. Muito obrigado. (v) Por favor, onde é a praça de táxis? A praça de táxis é lá em baixo (Eur.) / lá embaixo (Br.), em frente. Muito agradecida.
1.4.1 Por favor / Faz favor / Desculpe, (*a*) pode me dizer onde é a farmácia? *or simply* onde é a farmácia? (*b*) (pode me dizer) onde é o banco? (*c*) (pode me dizer) onde são as informações? (*d*) (pode me dizer) onde são os sanitários para homens?
1.4.2 Como? / Como? Mais devagar, por favor / faz favor (Eur.).

1.4.3 (Muito) obrigado / obrigada. *Your reply is also right if you said* (Muito) agradecido / agradecida.
1.5 (i) À esquerda (ii) Em frente.
1.6 Por favor, pode me dizer onde é o câmbio?

Unit 2

2.1 certo (1) (2), errado (3).
2.2 (1) (*a*). (2) (*a*). (3) (*c*).
2.3 (1) closed, (2) closed, (3) engaged (occupied), (4) Non-smokers, (5) Wait in the queue (*as an instruction*), (6) No stopping or parking (*as a prohibition*), (7) No camping (*as a prohibition*), (8) No smoking, please (*as a polite request rather than an instruction or prohibition*). (9) A reminder that litter should be disposed of in the litter-bin, not on the floor, lit., 'litter on the floor, no, in here, yes'.
2.4.1 (i) 2, (ii) 1, (iii) 5, 6, (iv) 10, (v) 3, 4 (vi) 8, (vii) 7, (viii) 9.
2.4.2 (i) Faz favor(Eur.), queria um mapa. (ii) Queria dois cafés. (iii) Por favor, quatro sandes. / Por favor, quatro sanduíches. (iv) Por favor, queria papel de carta e uma caneta. (v) Queria um penso adesivo (Eur.) / Queria um esparadrapo (Br.). (vi) Faça o favor de me dar alguma coisa para dor de cabeça. (vii) Pode me dar alguma coisa para indigestão? (viii) Faça o favor de me dar alguma coisa para queimadura de sol.
2.5.1 (i) três - ida, (ii) quatro - ida e volta, (iii) dez - ida e volta, (iv) oito - simples, (v) seis - ida e volta, (vi) cinco - ida, (vii) nove - ida e volta, (viii) sete - ida.
2.5.2 (i) Queria três bilhetes de ida para Faro. (ii) Quatro de ida e volta para o Porto,

faça favor. (iii) Dez de ida e volta para Cacilhas, por favor. (iv) Faz favor, oito simples para o Estoril. (v) Queria seis passagens de ida e volta para Manaus. (vi) Por favor, cinco de ida para Belo Horizonte. (vii) Nove para o Rio, ida e volta, por favor. (viii) Por favor, queria sete para Salvador, somente ida.

2.5.3 Queria ... (i) duas passagens de ida para Belo Horizonte. (ii) dois bilhetes de ida e volta para Faro. (iii) quatro passagens de ida para Manaus. (iv) oito bilhetes de ida e volta para Cacilhas. *Your answer will also be correct if you have worded it in any of the following ways*: (i) (Queria) duas (passagens) de ida para Belo Horizonte. / Duas (passagens) para Belo Horizonte, (somente) ida. (ii) (Queria) dois (bilhetes) de ida e volta para Faro. / Dois (bilhetes) para Faro, ida e volta. (iii) (Queria) quatro (passagens) de ida para Manaus. / Quatro (passagens) para Manaus, (somente) ida. (iv) (Queria) oito (bilhetes) de ida e volta para Cacilhas. / Oito (bilhetes) para Cacilhas, ida e volta. (*Adding* por favor / faz favor / faça favor *at the beginning or end*).

2.6.1 (i) Pode me dar a lista dos telefones? (ii) Pode me ligar para este número?

2.6.2 (i) cabine 5. (ii) caixa 7.

Unit 3

3.1 certo (2) (3), errado (1).

3.2 (1) (*b*). (2) (*c*). (3) (*b*).

3.3.1 (i) 2; (ii) 4; (iv) 3; (v) 5.

3.3.2 Queria (i) um apartamento simples, com chuveiro, para cinco noites. (ii) dois quartos individuais, com banheira, para oito noites. (iii) um quarto duplo, com banheira, para nove noites. (iv) dois apartamentos duplos com chuveiro e banheira, para dez noites. (v) um quarto de casal e dois quartos simples, com chuveiro, para sete noites.

3.4 Queria (*a*) um quarto simples / individual, com chuveiro, para uma noite. (*b*) um quarto duplo / de casal, com banheira, para duas noites. (*c*) um quarto duplo / de casal e um quarto simples / individual, com chuveiro e banheira, para sete noites. (*d*) um quarto duplo / de casal, com chuveiro, para cinco noites. Queria duas camas.

3.5.2 Stewart é o nome de baptismo (Eur.) / batismo (Br.) *or* Stewart é o nome próprio (Eur.) / prenome (Br.) e Martin é o nome de família *or* Martin é o apelido (Eur.) / sobrenome (Br.).

3.6.1 supermercado, 1; restaurante, 2; museu, 3; igreja, 4; praia, 5; bombas de gasolina, 6; passagem subterrânea, 7; Hotel Sol-Mar, 8; parada de ônibus, 9; paragem de autocarros, 10; o turismo, 11; Estrada do Aeroporto, 12.

3.6.2 (i) Por favor, pode me dizer onde é o supermercado? (ii) Faz favor, pode me dizer onde é o restaurante? (iii) Faz favor, onde fica o museu? (iv) Desculpe, pode me dizer onde é a igreja? (v) Por favor, onde é a praia? (vi) Por favor, onde ficam as bombas de gasolina? (vii) Faz favor, onde é a passagem subterrânea? (viii) Faz favor, pode me dizer onde fica o Hotel Sol-Mar? (ix) Por favor, onde é a parada de ônibus? (x) Faz favor, onde é a paragem de autocarros? (xi) Desculpe, onde fica o turismo? (xii) Faz favor, onde é a Estrada do Aeroporto?

3.6.3 Por favor/Faz favor, pode me dizer onde (i) é a Estrada do Aeroporto? (ii) fica a praia? (iii) é a passagem subterrânea? (iv) fica o museu? (v) fica o supermercado? (vi) é a paragem de autocarros / a parada de ônibus / o ponto de ônibus? (vii) são as bombas de gasolina? (viii) fica o Hotel Sol-Mar?

Unit 4

4.1 certo (1), errado (2) (3).

4.2 (1) (*b*). (2) (*b*). (3) (*a*).

4.3.1 Desculpe, tem pão e leite?

4.3.2 Queria (i) duas garrafas de leite, (ii) dois pães, (iii) duas bananas (iv) e duas maçãs.

4.4.1 (i) de sexta-feira a domingo. (ii) sete dias por semana. (iii) dez minutos a pé. (iv) dez minutos de carro.

4.4.2 Há um parque de campismo (Eur.) / um camping (Br.) perto daqui com (ii) loja, chuveiro frio e quente e sala de televisão? (iii) tomada de corrente, frigorífico (Eur.) / geladeira (Br.) e sala de televisão? (iv) chuveiro frio e quente, lavandaria (Eur.) / lavanderia (Br.) e gás para campistas? *Your* *answer will also be correct if, instead of* perto de aqui *you used* aqui perto *or* por aqui.

4.4.3 Tem vaga para (i) um trailer, isto é, carro de moradia rebocado, e uma barraca? (ii) uma caravana, isto é, carro de moradia rebocado, e duas tendas? (iii) um carro-cama, isto é, carro de moradia motorizado, um reboque pequeno e uma tenda? (iv) um carro de moradia motorizado, um reboque pequeno, uma rulote, isto é, um carro de moradia rebocado, e uma barraca?

4.4.4 Tem vaga para (ii) um carro-cama, isto é, carro de moradia motorizado, e uma tenda? (iii) uma caravana / rulote / trailer, isto é, carro de moradia rebocado, e uma barraca? (iv) dois reboques pequenos e duas tendas?

4.5 1 Queria uma garrafa de vinho. 2 Tem um saca-rolhas? 3 Tem óculos de sol? 4 Queria uma escova de dentes e pasta de dentes. *Saying simply* Queria escova e pasta de dentes *would also be correct.*

4.6.1 Queria fazer uma chamada a cobrar para o Canadá.

4.6.2 (i) Tem cartões credifone? (ii) Tem fichas telefônicas? (Br.)

Unit 5

5.1.3 Faça o favor de (i) repetir, mais devagar. (ii) escrever aqui quanto é. (iii) escrever aqui o nome, (o) endereço e (o) número do telefone. (iv) escrever aqui essa(s) palavra(s). (v) me mostrar essa palavra no dicionário *or* me mostrar no dicionário essa palavra. (vi) me mostrar no mapa onde fica. (vii) me mostrar no mapa onde estou. (viii) me mostrar as horas.

5.2 Não, não tenho nada a declarar.

5.3.1 (i) o meu (ii) a minha (iii) meu (iv) minha

5.3.2 Aqui tem (i) o meu passaporte. (ii) a minha carta de condução. (iii) meu passaporte. (iv) minha carteira de motorista.

5.4.2 (i) Pode me mostrar a lista dos modelos e preços? (ii) Quanto é por semana? (iii) Quanto é por dia? (iv) Quanto é por quilómetro rodado? (v) Quanto é por quilômetro rodado? (vi) Quanto é a caução? (vii) Quanto é o seguro contra todos os riscos? (viii) Queria este carro, pagando por semana. (ix) Queria este carro, pagando por dia. (x) Queria o carro sem motorista. (xi) Queria o carro com motorista. (xii) Queria o carro para cinco dias. (xiii) Pode me dar os documentos do carro? (xiv) Pode me dar um recibo?

5.4.3 (i) Pode me mostrar a lista dos models e preços? (ii) Quanto é por dia? (iii) Quanto é o seguro? E a caução? (iv) Queria este carro, pagando por dia. (v) Queria o carro para dois dias, sem motorista. (vi) Pode me dar um recibo? (vii) Pode me dar os documentos do carro?

5.5 (1) (*b*), (2) (*a*), (3) (*c*), (4) (*e*), (5) (*d*).

5.6.2 (2) A câmara municipal fica à esquerda. (3) Os bombeiros ficam à esquerda. (4) O centro de saúde fica à direita. *Your replies will still be correct if instead of* fica-ficam *you used* é-são.

5.7.1 (i) três (ii) cais; um (iii) plataforma; cinco (iv) o trem; plataforma.

5.7.2 (i) Do cais três. (ii) Do cais número um. (iii) Da plataforma cinco. (iv) Da segunda plataforma.

5.7.3 (i) De que cais parte o comboio para o Porto? (ii) De que cais parte o comboio para Braga? (iii) De que plataforma parte o trem para o Rio? (iv) De que plataforma parte o trem para Campinas?

5.8.1 (i) 4, (ii) 5, (iii) 2, (iv) 3, (v) 1.

5.8.2 (i) Tem varanda? (ii) Tem vista para o mar? (iii) Queria um apartamento com ar condicionado. (iv) Tem aparelho de televisão? (v) Queria um apartamento sem barulho.

5.8.3 Tem (i) ar condicionado? (ii) aparelho de televisão? (iii) varanda e vista para o mar?

5.8.4 Queria um quarto / apartamento sem barulho.

5.9.1 Por favor, pode me trazer mais (ii) um lençol. (iii) um edredão (Eur.) /edredom (Br.). (iv) um cobertor. (v) uma toalha. (vi) um sabonete. (vii) um rolo de papel higiénico (Eur.)/higiênico (Br.). (viii) um cabide.

5.9.2 Por favor, pode me trazer mais (i) duas almofadas (Eur.)/dois travesseiros (Br.). (ii) dois lençóis. (iii) dois edredões (Eur.) /edredons (Br.). (iv) dois cobertores. (v)

duas toalhas. (vi) dois sabonetes. (vii) dois rolos de papel higiénico (Eur.) /higiênico (Br.). (viii) dois cabides.
5.9.3 Por favor, pode me trazer mais quatro cabides e (mais) dois cobertores. Obrigado/a.
5.10.1 (*a*) (i) Não, não há. (ii) Há. (iii) Há. (iv) Não, não há. (*b*) Não há um mecânico perto daqui. Não há um médico aqui perto, mas há um enfermeiro. Há um dentista muito perto, na primeira rua à direita.
5.10.2 Pode chamar (i) um médico (ii) um enfermeiro (iii) um mecânico (iv) um táxi para mim?
5.11 (*a*) desculpar, (*d*) fazer, (*e*) ficar, (*g*) partir, (*h*) poder.
5.12 Por favor, queria três pães, meia dúzia de maçãs, uma garrafa pequena de leite e uma garrafa grande de água.
5.14 Across: 1 Não tem importância. 2 Com licença. 3 Desculpe. 4 Agradecido/a. 5 De nada. 6 Muito obrigado/a. Down: 1 Não tem de quê. 2 Obrigado/a. 3 De nada. 4 Por favor.

Unit 6

6.1 certo (2), errado (1) (3).
6.2 (1) (*b*). (2) (*b*). (3) (*c*).
6.3 Este é (o) Nuno, essa é (a) Rosa e aquela é (a) Mariana.
6.4.1 (ii) Natal, Rio Grande do Norte; 34 anos, professora; noiva, não tem filhos. (iii) Porto Alegre, Rio Grande do Sul; 75 anos, homem de negócios aposentado; viúvo, tem um filho e uma neta. (iv) Funchal, Madeira; 41 anos, dona de casa; casada, tem um filho e uma filha.
6.4.2 (i) O meu nome é José Fontes. Sou de Faro, no Algarve. Tenho vinte e dois anos e sou estudante. Não tenho filhos. Sou solteiro. (ii) Eu me chamo Glória Fonseca e sou de Natal, no Rio Grande do Norte. Tenho trinta e quatro anos de idade. Sou professora. Não tenho filhos. Não sou casada, mas estou noiva. (iii) Me chamo Osvaldo Medeiros e sou de Porto Alegre, no Rio Grande do Sul. Tenho muitos anos, setenta e cinco. Sou homem de negócios aposentado. Sou viúvo, mas tenho um filho e uma neta. (iv) Chamo-me Amélia Sarmento. Sou do Funchal, na Madeira. Tenho quarenta e um anos de idade. Sou

dona de casa. Sou casada e tenho um filho e uma filha.
6.5 Não, não sou. Sou inglês. // (Eu) chamo-me Matthew Smith (Eur.) / (Eu) me chamo (Br.) Matthew Smith (Eur.). (Eu) sou de Manchester. *Your answer is equally right if you have said* O meu nome é Matthew Smith (Eur.) / Meu nome é Matthew Smith (Br.) // (Eu) estou sozinho e vou ficar oito dias, de férias. // Aqui está. *or* Aqui tem. *You can also say* Aqui está *or* tem a minha carta de condução (Eur.) / Aqui está *or* tem minha carteira de motorista (Br.).

Unit 7

7.1 certo (1) (2), errado (3) (4).
7.2 (1) (*b*). (2) (*c*).
7.3 domingo, segunda-feira, terça-feira, quarta-feira, quinta-feira, sexta-feira, sábado.
7.4.1 (i) abre (ii) fecha (iii) começa (iv) parte (v) chega (vi) parte (vii) chega (viii) passa.
7.4.2 (ii) À meia-noite. (iii) Ao meio-dia. (iv) Às duas e um quarto (*or* quinze) da tarde. (v) Às dez e meia (*or* trinta) da noite. (vi) À uma da tarde. (vii) Às dez e vinte da manhã. (viii) Às quatro da tarde menos um quarto *or* A um quarto para as quatro da tarde. *Your answers are also right if you have used the words* hora(s) *and* minutos *throughout, e.g., for* (viii) Às quatro horas da tarde menos quinze minutos *or* Aos quinze minutos para as quatro horas da tarde.
7.5.2 Tenho (1) cabelo louro, ondulado, comprido, tenho olhos verdes e pele clara. (2) cabelo loiro, liso, curto, tenho olhos castanhos e pele clara. (3) cabelo castanho, ondulado, comprido, tenho olhos azuis e pele morena. (4) cabelo grisalho, frisado, curto, tenho olhos castanhos e pele morena. (5) cabelo preto, crespo, curto, tenho olhos pretos e pele morena. (6) cabelo ruivo, liso, comprido, tenho olhos azuis e pele clara.
7.5.3 (i) Ela tem cabelo louro (*or* loiro), muito liso e comprido, tem olhos azuis e pele clara. (ii) Ele tem cabelo grisalho, ondulado e curto, tem olhos pretos, e pele muito morena. (iii) Ele tem cabelo castanho,

frisado/crespo e muito curto, tem olhos castanhos, e pele morena. (iv) Ela tem cabelo ruivo, ondulado e muito comprido, tem olhos verdes e pele clara.

Unit 8

8.1 certo (3), errado (1), (2).
8.2 (1) (*a*). (2) (*c*). (3) (*b*).
8.3.1 Naquela esquina ali, a do semáforo, você vira à esquerda, depois segue em frente, na terceira transversal vira à direita e depois toma a primeira rua à esquerda. A piscina é aí, à esquerda.
8.3.2 Naquela esquina ali, a do semáforo, a senhora vira à esquerda, depois segue em frente... (*as above*).
8.4.2 (1) Vou vestir terno marrom claro. (2) Vou estar vestida de saia e jaqueta cinza e blusa vermelha. (3) Vou vestir casaco laranja escuro, calças verdes e camiseta branca. (4) Vou estar vestido de blusão preto, calças de ganga azuis e camisa amarela.
8.4.3 Para viajar normalmente visto (2) (uma) saia e jaqueta e (uma) blusa. (3) (um) casaco, (umas) calças e (uma) camiseta. (4) (um) blusão, (umas) calças de ganga e (uma) camisa.
8.4.4 *Numbers* 1 and 2 (terno marrom, saia e jaqueta cinza).
8.4.5 (i) É aquela senhora de blusa cor-de-rosa e saia verde. (ii) É aquele senhor de camisa branca e calças castanhas (Eur.)/ calça marrom (Br.). *Your reply would also have been correct if you had said* com (um/a) *throughout:* É aquela senhora com blusa, etc. *or* É aquela senhora com uma blusa, etc.
8.5 (1) O senhor, por favor, como se chama? (2) Eu? Chamo-me Valdemar Nascimento. (3) Por favor! Esta é a pessoa que se chama Mauro de Sá. (4) Aquele senhor? Eu penso que ele se chama Fernando Camargo. (5) Desculpe a pergunta, a senhora chama-se Flávia Couto? (6) Não, não me chamo Flávia Couto. Chamo-me Rute Bento.

Unit 9

9.1 certo (1), errado (2) (3).
9.2 (1) (*c*). (2) (*b*). (3) (*c*).

9.3 Onde eles moram faz vento no outono, neva no inverno, chove na primavera e faz (muito) sol e calor / está (muito) quente no verão.
9.4.1 (ii) junho, julho; mau tempo (iii) agosto; muito calor (iv) março, abril; chove muito (v) dezembro, janeiro, fevereiro; muito quente (vi) setembro, outubro, novembro; sol, um pouco frio. (*for the names of the months you can use upper or lower case*)
9.4.2 (i) Na minha terra maio é na primavera e faz bom tempo. (ii) Na terra do meu marido em junho e julho é inverno e faz mau tempo. (iii) Na terra da minha esposa agosto é um mês de verão e faz muito calor. (iv) Na terra dos meus avós é outono em março e abril e chove muito. (v) Aquele rapaz é de uma terra onde em dezembro, janeiro e fevereiro é verão e está muito quente. (vi) Estas crianças são de uma terra onde em setembro, outubro e novembro é primavera e faz sol mas está um pouco frio.
9.4.3 Fez mau tempo. Esteve/fez frio, fez vento, choveu, houve nevoeiro e não fez sol.
9.5.1 Normalmente eu levanto-me / me levanto (Br.) às sete (horas), saio de casa às oito, volto para casa às oito e meia da noite e deito-me às onze (da noite).
9.5.2 Ontem eu levantei-me / me levantei (Br.) às oito (horas), saí de casa às nove, voltei para casa às dez da noite e deitei-me à meia noite.
9.5.3 Normalmente ele levanta-se / se levanta (Br.) às sete (horas), sai de casa às oito, volta para casa às oito e meia da noite e deita-se às onze (da noite).
9.5.4 Ontem ele levantou-se / se levantou (Br.) às oito (horas), saiu de casa às nove, voltou para casa às dez da noite e deitou-se à meia noite.

Unit 10

10.1.1 (i) norte. (ii) sul. (iii) este. (iv) leste. (v) oeste. (vi) nordeste. (vii) sudeste. (viii) noroeste. (ix) sudoeste.
10.1.2 (Fica/É) no + *cardinal point as above.*
10.2.1 (i) (*d*); (ii) (*c*); (iii) (*f*); (iv) (*e*); (v) (*b*); (vi) (*a*).
10.2.2 (i) fez sol a sul do Rio Tejo; (ii) fez

vento nordeste-sudoeste; (iii) choveu a norte do Rio Tejo; (iv) esteve muito nublado a norte do Rio Douro; (v) estiveram vinte e seis graus centígrados em Lisboa; (vi) estiveram vinte e quatro graus centígrados no Porto.

10.2.3 (i) Fez mais calor em Lisboa. (ii) A temperatura esteve mais baixa no Porto. (iii) Fez bom tempo no sul. (iv) A norte do Rio Douro esteve muito nublado. (v) Fez (sim), fez vento de nordeste. (vi) Choveu a norte do Rio Tejo.

10.3.1 Queria fazer uma reserva para Curitiba para amanhã à noite.// À noite tem o Executivo.// A que horas parte?// Às vinte e duas e quarenta e cinco.// Está bem. Queria "não fumante", somente ida.// O ônibus é todo "não fumante". É proibido fumar.// Certo.// Aqui está a passagem da senhora. Poltrona quinze no Executivo das dez e quarenta e cinco amanhã à noite. O ônibus sai da primeira plataforma.

10.3.2 Queria fazer uma reserva para Lisboa para amanhã de manhã.// De manhã tem o Intercidades.// A que horas parte?// Às dez e vinte e cinco.// Está bem.// "Fumador" ou "não fumador"?// "Não fumador", somente ida.// Quer lugar junto à janela?// Quero, sim. Obrigada.// Aqui está o bilhete da senhora. Lugar vinte e dois na carruagem vinte e um do Intercidades das dez e vinte e cinco amanhã de manhã. O comboio sai da linha número dois.

10.4.2 a de água, l de longe, p de praia e h de homem.

10.5.1 (i) Onde é que o senhor mora? (ii) Onde é que tu moras?

10.5.2 (ii) Moro na Rua da Aldeia Norte número 42.

10.6.1 (i) Pode me levar para este endereço? (ii) Can you take me to this address? (iii) (a) Pode me levar para a Rua do Atlântico número cem? (b) Faça o favor de me levar para a Rua do Atlântico número cem.

10.7.1 (i) B; (ii) A; (iii) C.

10.7.2 (i) Esta rua é perpendicular à rua do jardim. Você segue em frente até chegar lá. (ii) Você toma a primeira rua à direita, depois (você) vira à esquerda e continua nessa rua. O jardim fica em frente. (iii) Você vai em frente. Na primeira transversal

(você) vira à esquerda. O jardim fica nessa rua, mas antes de chegar lá (você) tem que passar duas ruas à direita.

10.7.3 With o senhor / a senhora (no other changes).

10.8.1 (i) A minha filha é aquela senhora de biquíni cor-de-rosa. (ii) Minha irmã é aquela senhora de maiô laranja e cabelo loiro comprido. (iii) O meu pai é aquele senhor de calções de banho pretos e muito moreno.

10.8.2 (i) A minha neta é aquela senhora que está sentada. (ii) A minha mãe é aquela senhora que está deitada. (iii) Meu avô é aquele senhor que está em pé.

10.8.3 (i) A minha (Eur.) / Minha (Br.) amiga é aquela senhora de biquíni vermelho, muito morena, que está em pé *or* de pé. (ii) O meu (Eur.) / Meu (Br.) amigo é aquele senhor de calções de banho verdes (Eur.) / calção de banho verde (Br.) e cabelo preto, que está deitado. *Alternative:* de tanga (Eur.) / sunga (Br.) verde.

10.9.1 (i) Chamo-me Álvaro Maia. (ii) Sou de Maputo, em Moçambique. (iii) Tenho dezoito anos. (iv) Moro aqui na África do Sul. (v) Moro aqui há dois anos. (vi) Vou sair daqui no próximo ano. (vii) Moro com os meus pais, a minha irmã e o meu irmão. (viii) A terra dos meus pais é Portugal. (ix) No próximo ano vou para o norte de Portugal. (x) Quero ser médico. (xi) Vou estudar na Universidade do Porto.

10.9.2 (ii) De onde é que tu és? (iii) Quantos anos é que tu tens? (iv) Onde é que tu moras? (v) Há quanto tempo é que moras aqui? (vi) Quando é que vais sair daqui? (vii) Com quem é que tu moras? (viii) Qual é que é a terra dos teus pais? (ix) Para onde é que tu vais no próximo ano? (x) O que é que tu queres ser profissionalmente? (xi) Em que universidade é que tu vais estudar?

10.11 Parabéns no seu vigésimo quinto aniversário. Muitas felicidades.

10.12 Feliz Natal e Feliz Ano Novo *or* e Próspero Ano Novo *or* e Próspero e Feliz Ano Novo *or* e Boas entradas.

Unit 11

11.1 (1) (*b*). (2) (*a*). (3) (*b*). (4) (*a*). (5) (*c*).

11.2.2 (ii) A senhora tem que introduzir as

moedas, pressionar a tecla onde diz "açúcar", esperar um pouco e depois retirar o troco e o café.

11.2.3 (ii) A senhora introduz as moedas, pressiona a tecla onde diz "açúcar", espera um pouco e depois retira o troco e o café.

11.2.4 (ii) Introduza as moedas, pressione a tecla onde diz "açúcar", espere um pouco e depois retire o troco e o café.

11.2.5 The machine is out of order.

11.3 (1) Queria... (2) Quanto é? / custa? (3) Prefiro... (4) Um pouco mais / menos, por favor / faz favor (Eur.). (5) Está bem / certo. (6) Só isso, obrigado/a *or* É tudo, obrigado/a (7) Quanto é tudo? / custa tudo? *or* Quanto é / custa ao todo? (8) Pode me dar um saco / uma sacola (Br.)?

11.4 Queria (i) isso que está à sua frente. (ii) esta lata de cerveja. (iii) quatro fatias daquele fiambre (Eur.) / presunto (Br.). (iv) mais ou menos meio quilo destas maçãs. (v) uma garrafa de vinho, uma dessas de litro. (vi) duzentos e cinquenta (Eur.) / duzentos e cinqüenta (Br.) gramas daquele queijo, o terceiro a contar da esquerda.

11.5.1 Stand on the right, walk on the left.

11.5.2 Mantenham-se à direita, caminhem pela esquerda.

11.5.2 Mantém-te à direita, caminha pela esquerda.

Unit 12

12.1 (1) (c). (2) (c). (3) (b). (4) (a). (5) (a).

12.2.1 (i) 0 (ii) 4, 6 (iii) 0, 2 (iv) 3, 5, 7 (v) 4, 5, 9 (vi) 5, 3, 47.

12.2.2 (i) Custa nove mil e oitocentos. (ii) Vai custar quarenta e quatro mil, quinhentos e sessenta. (iii) Vai custar setecentos mil, cento e vinte e dois. (iv) Custará talvez treze milhões, seiscentos e trinta e cinco mil, setecentos e setenta e um. (v) Não sei se custará quarenta e oito milhões, quinhentos e sete mil, novecentos e seis. (vi) Há de custar menos de noventa e cinco milhões, trezentos e trinta mil, oitocentos e quarenta e sete.

12.2.3 (ii) Noventa e nove reais. (iii) Quinhentos reais. (iv) Dois mil e vinte e cinco reais. (v) Trinta e um euros e meio. (vi) Quarenta e sete euros. (vii) Duzentos euros. (viii) Dois mil e setenta euros.

12.3.2 *The following items in this or other order:* Três sandes (Eur.) / sanduíches de fiambre, uma sandes (Eur.) /sanduíche de queijo, um iogurte de banana, duas cervejas, um café com leite e sem açúcar, um café sem leite e com açúcar e uma água mineral.

12.3.4 Teremos que esperar muito tempo?

12.3.5 A água mineral e o iogurte são para a senhora de camiseta / T-shirt vermelha e o café com leite e uma das sandes (Eur.) / sanduíches de fiambre são para o senhor de camisa verde.

12.3.6 A conta, por favor.

12.3.7 Pode ficar com o troco.

12.4.1 (i) É favor não incomodar. (ii) Não incomode, por favor.

12.4.2 (i) Agora pode arrumar o quarto, por favor. (ii) Quando é que o quarto estará pronto?

12.5.1 (i) Será possível ter os roupões prontos antes de 5ª.-feira? Obrigada. (ii) Será possível ter o pijama pronto antes de 6ª.-feira? Obrigada.

Unit 13

13.1 (1) (c). (2) (i) (c), (ii) (b). (3) (c). (4) (b). (5) (b).

13.2.2 Comprei esta quando estava no Algarve e esta quando estava na Serra da Estrela.

13.2.3 *In the preterite* (comprei) *and the imperfect* (estava), *for a point in time* (comprei) *within the period of time of her stay* (estava).

13.2.4 Estive lá no ano passado. Fui em Março e voltei dois meses depois, em Maio.

13.2.5 (i) Quando é que você esteve lá? (ii) Quando é que (tu) estiveste lá?

13.3.1 (i) Este vestido está muito curto. Tem outro mais comprido do que este? (ii) Este vestido está muito apertado. Tem outro mais folgado do que este?

13.3.2 (i) Este vestido está muito comprido. Tem outro menos comprido do que este? (ii) Este vestido está muito folgado. Tem outro menos folgado do que este?

13.4.1 (b), (g), (d), (c), (f), (a), (e).

13.4.2 – No meu país calço nº 5 mas aqui não sei que número é.// Cinco... isso será número 37 ou 38. Eu trago três ténis (Eur.) /

ténis (Br.), um em 37, um em 38 e um em 39.// (*experimentando o n° 37*) Este ténis (Eur.) / ténis (Br.) está muito apertado.// Então quer experimentar o n° 38?// (*experimentando o n° 38*) Este está menos apertado do que o 37, mas está um pouco apertado. // Talvez o número acima, o 39.// (*experimentando o n° 39*) Este está bem, obrigada. Levo este par.

13.4.3 estava *throughout*.

13.5.1 Por favor, queria (ii) uns sapatos (iii) um vestido (iv) uma gravata (v) uma saia.

13.5.2 *As 13.5.1 plus* de (ii) pelica (iii) linho (iv) seda (v) fibra sintética.

13.5.3 *As 13.5.2 plus* (ii) lisos (iii) estampado (iv) listrada / às riscas (Eur.) (v) xadrez.

13.5.4 *As 13.5.3 plus* em (ii) azul escuro (iii) amarelo e verde (iv) preto e vermelho (v) duas ou três cores diferentes.

13.5.5 (i) Comprei estes sapatos na semana passada. (ii) Comprei esta camisa na 2ª.-feira passada e esta gravata na 4ª.-feira passada. (iii) Quando é que (tu) compraste esses sapatos / essa camisa e essa gravata?

Unit 14

14.1 (1) (*b*). (2) (*c*). (3) (*b*). (4) (*c*). (5) (*b*). (6) (*b*).

14.2.1 (i) Não, não vai. (ii) (Ela) vai a cavalo.

14.2.2 (i) Gosto de andar a cavalo. (ii) Ando a cavalo todos os sábados. (iii) Andei a cavalo no sábado passado.

14.2.3 Eu encontrei o Raul quando (eu) estava a andar a cavalo (Eur.) / estava andando a cavalo (Br.) no sábado passado. Ele também estava a andar (Eur.) / estava andando (Br.) a cavalo.

14.2.4 I met Raul when I was horse riding last Saturday. He was also horse riding *or* riding a horse. (*Sally met Raul when she was riding, and they were both riding at the same time.*)

14.3.1 (*a*), (*f*), (*c*), (*b*), (*e*), (*d*).

14.3.2 Tu falas português muito bem. / Obrigado. Tu és muito amável. Eu ainda faço muitos erros. Corrige-me, está bem? / Está. Há quanto tempo aprendes português? / Há dois meses. / Há só dois meses!? Como

consegues aprender tão rapidamente? / Estudando um pouco todos os dias.

14.4.1 Do you accept this credit card? / Yes, we do.

14.4.2 (i) Aceitamos. (ii) Pode. (iii) Não, não tem.

14.5.2 (i) O clube abre às oito horas da noite. (ii) O jantar começa às oito horas e trinta (da noite). (iii) O museu está aberto até às dezasseis (Eur.) / as dezesseis (Br.) horas. (iv) A primeira matiné começa às quinze horas. (v) Há futebol no domingo. (vi) Não, não está. (Fecha às seis horas). (vii) A piscina está aberta a partir das oito horas da manhã. (viii) A biblioteca fecha às nove horas da noite. (ix) Pode. (A partir das nove horas.) (x) Não, não está. (Está aberta toda a noite.) (xi) O horário de atendimento do médico de clínica geral é das dezassete (Eur.) / dezessete (Br.) às vinte horas. (xii) Sim, ainda. (A terceira tiragem (Eur.) / coleta (Br.) é às vinte e uma horas.)

14.5.3 (i) Não, começa às nove e meia. (ii) Está aberta toda a noite. (iii) Não, só a partir das dezassete (Eur.) / dezessete (Br.). (iv) Às onze horas.

14.5.4 (i) A soiré começa antes das nove horas? (ii) Até que horas é que a farmácia está aberta? (iii) No médico, há consultas de manhã? (iv) A que horas abre a galeria de arte?

14.5.5 (i) A que horas é que o restaurante abre? (ii) A que horas é que a soiré começa? (iii) Até que horas é que a farmácia está aberta hoje à noite / esta noite? (iv) A que horas é que o museu fecha?

Unit 15

15.1 1 (*b*), 2 (*a*), 3 (*d*), 4 (*c*), 6 (*e*), 7 (*f*).

15.2 (1) Amanhã, sábado, trabalho. (2) Amanhã vou trabalhar. (3) Provavelmente trabalharei amanhã *or* amanhã trabalharei. (4) Amanhã hei de trabalhar. (5) Agora não posso. Estou a trabalhar. (Eur.) / Agora não posso. Estou trabalhando. (Br.) (6) Trabalhei ontem, sábado. (7) Hugo telefonou ontem quando eu estava a trabalhar (Eur.) / Hugo telefonou ontem quando eu estava trabalhando (Br.) (8) Eu trabalhava aos sábados, mas agora não trabalho. *or* Eu

costumava trabalhar aos sábados, mas agora não trabalho.
15.3.1 (i) Está atrasado. (ii) Está adiantado.
15.3.2 (i) Bernardo. (ii) Gonçalo.
15.4.1 Esta conta está errada. Três mil, trezentos e sessenta de bolos e bebidas mais trezentos e trinta e cinco de serviço não são três mil, setessentos e noventa e cinco. São três mil, seiscentos e noventa e cinco.
15.4.2 três mais três igual a seis, não igual a sete *or* três mais três são seis, não são sete.
15.5 1 Façam o favor de falar mais baixo. 2 Por favor, queiram falar mais baixo. 3 Querem falar mais baixo, por favor? 4 Falem mais baixo!
15.6.1 (i) carregue. (ii) Press to open. (iii) To obtain 'green' press here. Thank-you. (iv) Carregar para abrir. Para obter verde carregar aqui. (Eur.)
15.6.2 (i) Carregue para abrir. (ii) Tem que carregar para abrir. (iii) Quer carregar para abrir? (iv) Queira carregar para abrir. (v) Faça o favor de carregar para abrir. (Eur.)
15.6.3 (i) Carregue para obter verde. (ii) Tem que carregar para obter verde. (iii) Quer carregar para obter verde? (iv) Queira carregar para obter verde. (v) Faça o favor de carregar para obter verde. (Eur.)
15.6.4 (*a*) Aperte para abrir. (*b*) Para obter verde aperte aqui. Obrigado. (Br.)
15.6.5 Apertar para abrir. Para obter verde apertar aqui. (Br.)
15.6.6 (i) Aperte para abrir. (ii) Tem que apertar para abrir. (iii) Quer apertar para abrir? (iv) Queira apertar para abrir. (v) Faça o favor de apertar para abrir. (Br.)
15.6.7 (i) Aperte para obter verde. (ii) Tem que apertar para obter verde. (iii) Quer apertar para obter verde? (iv) Queira apertar para obter verde. (v) Faça o favor de apertar para obter verde. (Br.)
15.7.1 a pé.
15.7.2 Ontem fui a pé.
15.7.3 Amanhã vou a pé.
15.7.4 Como é que tu vais para as aulas de português? *or* Como é que vais para as aulas de português? *or* Como vais para as aulas de português?
15.8 (a) Pode me dar o horário dos comboios? (b) Pode me dar a tabela de horário dos trens? *or* Pode me dar o horário

dos trens?
15.9.1 Tem um vôo para Brasília amanhã de manhã sem escala?// Não, o voo faz escala no Rio.
15.9.2 Tem um voo para Lisboa amanhã de manhã sem escala?// Não, o vôo faz escala no Rio.
15.10 1 (i) O comboio das 15.25 para Tomar é directo ou tem transbordo?// É directo. (ii) O comboio das 15.25 para a Guarda é directo ou tem transbordo?// É directo. 2 trem.
15.11 1 (*b*), 1 (*d*), 1 (*e*). 2 (*a*), 3 (*c*).
15.12.2 (*a*) 1 trabalho; metro; 20 minutos. 2 colégio; trem; 1/2 hora. 3 biblioteca; autocarro; 1/4 hora. 4 estádio; comboio; 3/4 hora. 5 cinema; ônibus; 10 minutos. (*b*) 1 Normalmente vou para o trabalho de metro. Levo vinte minutos. 2 Eu vou para o colégio de trem(Br.). Levo meia hora. 3 Vou para a biblioteca de autocarro(Eur.). Levo um quarto de hora. 4 Eu vou para o estádio de comboio(Eur.). Levo três quartos de hora. 5 Eu vou para o cinema de ônibus(Br.). Levo dez minutos. 6 Eu vou para a praia de bicicleta. Levo cinco minutos mais ou menos.
15.12.3 (ii) Agora normalmente vou de autocarro mas costumava ir de metro. (Eur.) / Agora normalmente vou de ônibus mas costumava ir de metrô. (Br.) (iii) Agora normalmente vou de comboio mas costumava ir de carro. (Eur.) / Agora normalmente vou de trem mas costumava ir de carro. (Br.) (iv) Agora normalmente vou de autocarro mas costuma ir de bicicleta. (Eur.) / Agora normalmente vou de ônibus mas costumava ir de bicicleta. (Br.)
15.13 1 Aquela menina de cabelo louro (*or* loiro) comprido e vestido vermelho e branco. 2 Aquele rapaz que está em pé (*or* de pé) junto da (*or* à) venda automática de café. *Your reply is equally correct if you have said* máquina de venda automática de café. 3 Aquela senhora de biquíni preto que está a falar (Eur.) / falando (Br.) junto do (*or* ao) carro amarelo. 4 Aquele senhor de cabelo preto curto e camisa às/com riscas (Eur.) / listrada (Br.) que está sentado a ler (Eur.) / lendo (Br.) o jornal.
15.14.2 1 Para a cave. 2 Para o segundo. 3

Para o rés-do-chão.

15.14.3 (i) Por favor, pode me dar a chave do quarto (*or* do apartamento, *depending on type of hotel*) número quatro - três - nove. (ii) Por favor, pode me dar a chave do quarto (*or* do apartamento) número quatrocentos e trinta e nove.

15.15.1 *Boxes ticked for:* 08.00-08.30; torradas; geleia; manteiga; laranja; café; leite; ovos cozidos; presunto. *Special requirements:* ovo bem cozido; leite magro (Eur.); pão integral.

15.15.2 Before going to bed, please hang your breakfast order form on the outside handle of your door. (*lit.* Before going to bed, could you please hang (this form) on the outside door handle.)

15.15.3 Bom dia. Esqueci-me de pendurar na maçaneta da porta o cartão para pedir o pequeno almoço (Eur.) (café da manhã (Br.) *if you were in Brazil*). Ainda posso pedir? // Pode, sim. O que deseja? // Queria ovo cozido, torradas, presunto, manteiga, geleia, sumo (Eur) de laranja, café e leite.// Prefere o ovo bem ou mal cozido? // Bem cozido. E só mais duas coisa, desculpe. Prefiro leite magro (Eur.) e pão integral. Terei que esperar muito tempo? // Não, meia hora mais ou menos.

15.16 1 (*c*), 2 (*a*), 3 (*d*), 4 (*n*), 5 (*g*), 6 (*b*), 7 (*j*), 8 (*m*), 9 (*e*), 10 (*f*), 11 (*h*), 12 (*k*), 13 (*i*), 14 (*l*).

15.17.1 (i) The word 'alimentação', food store. (ii) The shop window. (iii) In the centre. (iv) Shelves. (v) The door to the back.

15.17.2 (ii) (a) A caixa que *A* quer está em cima do balcão. (b) A caixa que *B* quer está perto da montra (Eur.) / vitrine (Br.). (c) A caixa que *D* quer está dentro do balcão. (d) A pessoa que prefere uma das caixas pequenas em volta da caixa grande é *D*. (e) Quem quer uma caixa que está na segunda prateleira a contar de baixo, atrás do balcão, é *C*.

15.18.1 Estou só a ver (Eur.) / Estou só olhando (Br.).

15.18.2 Onde posso encontrar uma loja que vende guarda-sóis? *or* Onde é que posso encontrar uma loja que venda guarda-sóis?

15.18.3 Pay at the cash desk and take the voucher / receipt stub back to the assistant who has been serving you.

15.19.1 (i) Às oito (horas) e quarenta e três (minutos).(ii) Às vinte e cinquenta (Eur.) / cinqüenta (Br.) e cinco. (iii) Às duas e cinquenta (Eur.) / cinqüenta (Br.). (iv) Às quinze e quinze.

15.19.2 (i) Estará, sim. *or* Está, sim. (*no doubt*). (ii) Estará, sim *or* Está, sim.

15.20.1 Pode me dizer onde é o aluguer (Eur.) / aluguel (Br.) de toldos e barracas (de praia). *Alternative:* Pode me dizer onde se alugam toldos e barracas? *or* Pode me dizer onde posso alugar um toldo ou uma barraca?

15.20.2 (i) Queria alugar uma barraca por um dia. (ii) Queria alugar um toldo por meio dia.

15.20.3 (i) Quanto é a barraca por um dia? *or* Quanto custa a barraca por um dia? (ii) Quanto é o toldo por meio dia? *or* Quanto custa o toldo por meio dia?

Unit 16

16.1 (1) (*c*). (2) (*b*). (3) (*b*). (4) (*b*). (5) (*b*).

16.2.1 (i) Quer deitar-se? (ii) Quer levantar-se e sentar-se? (iii) Quer levantar-se?

16.2.2 Faça favor de (i) sentar-se (ii) deitar-se (iii) levantar-se.

16.2.3 Queira (i) sentar-se (ii) deitar-se (iii) levantar-se.

16.2.4 Sente-se (ii) Deite-se (iii) Levante-se.

16.2.5 (ii) Deitem-se (iii) Levantem-se.

16.2.6 (ii) Deita-te (iii) Levanta-te.

16.2.7 (i) Sentem-se (ii) Deitem-se (iii) Levantem-se.

16.3 Queira (i) despir *or* tirar o seu casaco. (ii) descalçar *or* tirar as suas botas. (iii) tirar o seu chapéu.

16.4.1 Dói-me (i) muito a garganta desde domingo passado. (ii) um dente há dois dias. (iii) muito o ouvido direito desde ontem à noite. (iv) um pouco aqui desde quarta-feira passada.

16.4.2 Já me despi.

16.4.3 (i) every 6 hours. (ii) twice a day. (iii) every other day.

16.5 (1) Sim, sou. (2) Sofro do coração. (3) (Sou), sim, sou alérgica a penicilina. (4) Não, não tomei. (5) Deve informar meu marido, Óscar Campos. O número do

telefone é quatro três oito, um zero, dois dois.
16.6 (1) Cuidado! (2) Tem perigo! (3) Depressa! (4) É perigoso! (5) Aqui há perigo! (6) Fogo! (7) Socorro!
16.7.1 (i) Walk on the right-hand side of a pavement or hard shoulder. (ii) Caminhe pelo lado direito do passeios ou da berma.
16.7.2 (i) To cross the road (cross over) / - Stop on the pavement / - Look first left and then right to see whether there is a car coming / - If no car is coming, cross over, but keep looking, left the first half of the road and then right.   (ii) Para atravessar / Pare no passeio / Olhe primeiro para a esquerda e depois para a direita para ver se vem algum carro / Se não vier nenhum, atravesse, olhando novamente para a esquerda até ao meio da rua e depois para a direita.
16.7.3 (i) Caminhe pelo lado direito da calçada ou do acostamento. (ii) Para atravessar / Pare na calçada / Olhe primeiro para a esquerda e depois para a direita para ver se vem algum carro / Se não vier nenhum, atravesse, olhando novamente para a esquerda até o meio da rua e depois para a direita.

Unit 17

17.1 (1) (c). (2) (a). (3) (b). (4) (a). (5) (b).
17.2.1 Afonso, car B; Olavo, car A.
17.2.2 Onde é que o senhor está? // Na estrada de Sagres para Lagos, a mais ou menos 10 km de Sagres. // Precisa de ambulância ou de rebocador? // Não preciso de ambulância. Não há feridos, nem mortos. Mas preciso de um rebocador. O meu carro não funciona (Eur.)/está funcionando (Br.).
17.2.3 1 (b), 2 (c), 3 (a).
17.2.4 Eu seguia / estava seguindo (Br.) pela estrada a 60 km por hora. À minha frente seguia / estava seguindo (Br.) o carro C, muito lentamente. Eu vi o carro A, que parecia que tinha parado no cruzamento. Eu ultrapassei o carro C, mas o carro A avançou e bateu no meu.
17.3.1 Nunca bebo quando conduzo.
17.3.2 Nunca bebo quando dirijo / estou dirigindo.

17.4.2 (i) (c), (ii) (e), (iii) (a), (iv) (d), (v) (b).
17.5.1 (i) um pendente (feito) de ouro e em forma de estrela. (ii) tem cabelo preto e está vestido de camiseta / T-shirt branca e calças de ganga azuis (Eur) / calça de zuarte azul (Br.). *Your answer would also be correct in the past tense (he might have changed his clothes or dyed his hair a different colour in the meantime)* tinha cabelo preto e estava vestido de camiseta / T-shirt branca e calças de ganga azuis (Eur) / calça de zuarte azul (Br.).
17.5.2 (i) é/era um carro verde escuro. *or* o carro é/era verde escuro. (ii) tem (*or* deve ter) uns quarenta anos (*or* mais ou menos quarenta anos), tem/tinha cabelo louro curto e está/estava vestido de camisa amarela.
17.6 1 (b), 2 (a).
17.7.1 (i) É grave. (ii) A partir de 53 km/hr. (iii) Suspensão da carteira da habilitação (Br.) / carteira de motorista (Br.) / carta de condução (Eur.) por 2 a 7 meses.
17.7.2 (i) Watch out if you speed / Beware of speeding. (ii) Rushing and safety never go well together (lit. never go the same way), *play on the different meanings of the word* mão: hand *and* flow of traffic.

Unit 18

18.1 (1) (b). (2) (c). (3) (a). (4) (c). (5) (c).
18.2.1 (i) (B), (ii) (A), (iii) (B), (iv) (B), (v) (A).
18.2.2 Todos os dias, faço jogging / cooper (Br.) de manhã cedo. Aos fins de semana, pratico esqui aquático, quando faz bom tempo; e praticaria mais vezes, se tivesse mais tempo.
18.3.2 A Madeira tem plantas raras? E animais?// Sim, tem. A Madeira é praticamente uma reserva natural, sendo dois terços do território Área Protegida onde abunda fauna e flora raras. // Que passeios a pé tem para pessoas que não estão em boa forma? // Tem passeios suaves. Para os que não se querem meter em grandes aventuras, tem os belos passeios ao longo das "levadas". // Desculpe. Não compreendo. O que significa "levadas"? // "Levadas" significa pequenos canais de irrigação

artificiais. // E que passeios tem para os mais aventureiros? // Para os mais aventureiros tem muitos trilhos, que estão bem assinalados com placas e que levam às montanhas. // O que tem para quem joga golfe? // Para quem joga golfe tem muita coisa, incluindo dois campos para campeonatos. // Pode fazer-se mergulho e vela? // Pode, sim. A Madeira, sendo uma ilha, é rica em desportos aquáticos. // Só mais uma pergunta. Seria possível fazer pesca de alto mar? // É, sim. E é possível pescar espadim azul com mais de 500 kg.
18.4.1 à sombra. ao sol.
18.4.2 (i) Não comprou. (ii) Porque já não havia mais lugares nas bancadas à sombra. (iii) Teria. *or* Teria, sim.
18.5 (2) O Carnaval. (3) Com muita antecedência. (4) Escolas de samba. (5) Por toda a parte. Na rua. (6) (a) os passistas, (b) a bateria, (c) as fantasias.
18.6.1 trezentos e três (*or* zero zero três, zero três), setor (Br.) / sector (Eur.) nove, fila C, lugar um (*or* primeiro *or* número um *or* zero zero um).
18.6.2 (i) You have an odd number but are on the even-number side. (ii) Go to the southern side, the other side of the boulevard.
18.7 (1) Desculpe. Parece que perdi o bilhete de transporte. (2) Achei o bilhete de transporte. Aqui tem. *or* Aqui está.

Unit 19

19.1 (1) (*a*). (2) (*b*). (3) (*c*). (4) (*c*). (5) (*b*).
19.2 (1) Faz favor, traga-me a ementa. (2) O cardápio, por favor. (3) Queríamos uma mesa para quatro, longe da porta, se possível. (4) Pode trazer mais pão? (5) Queria experimentar um prato típico desta região.
19.3 Traga-me (1) um copo de água, por favor. (2) uma chávena (Eur.) / xícara (Br.) de chá, por favor. (3) uma chávena (Eur.) / xícara (Br.) de café, por favor. (4) uma caneca de cerveja, por favor. (5) um cálice de porto, por favor. (6) uma taça de champanhe, por favor.
19.4.2 Paraty ↔ para ti: Paraty in August is for you (para ti), always.

19.4.3 Vou ao festival da pinga em Paraty. Lá a terra é propícia ao cultivo da cana de açúcar e há séculos que fazem aguardente. Vou beber o que dizem ser uma das melhores pingas do Brasil.
19.4.4 Infelizmente eu não pude ir ao festival. Se tivesse ido, teria bebido o que dizem ser uma das melhores pingas do Brasil.
19.5 A minha / minha (Br.) cidade natal fica (*or* é) (1) na margem de um rio. (2) numa região montanhosa. (3) na costa norte do país. A minha / minha (Br.) cidade natal tem (4) um milhão de habitantes. (5) um clima frio no inverno. (6) indústria de computadores.
19.6 (1) Sou escocês. Nasci em Dundee, uma cidade na costa leste da Escócia. Dundee tem um porto grande e um tipo famoso de bolo. (2) Sou galês. Nasci em Caerphilly, uma cidade no sul do País de Gales. Caerphilly tem um castelo antigo e um tipo famoso de queijo.
19.7.2 (i) Em que consiste o bacalhau gomes de sá? (ii) Em que consiste o bacalhau tropical? (iii) Em que consiste o bacalhau à moda da casa?
19.7.3 (i) Preferia um prato que não tivesse cebola. (ii) Preferia um prato que não tivesse ovo. (iii) Preferia um prato que não tivesse couve. (iv) Preferia um prato que não tivesse leite de coco.

Unit 20

20.1 (1) (*b*). (2) (*b*). (3) (*c*). (4) (*b*).
20.2 (1) À ordem de Fernando Costa Machado. (2) Sessenta mil escudos. (3) Falta o ano na data.
20.3 (1) Queria descontar este cheque. (2) Onde é que estão as fichas de depósito? (3) Isto é o recibo de depósito? (4) Queria ver o mcu saldo. (5) A quanto está a libra hoje? E quanto é a comissão?
20.4.1 *At service hatch 1*: b, e, f. *At service hatch 2*: no one. *At service hatch 3*: a, c, d.
20.4.2 (*a*) Que preciso fazer para ter uma posta restante? (*b*) Faz favor, queria enviar esta carta registada (*c*) Tem algumas cartas para Donald Cooper? (*d*) Tem alguma coisa em nome de Alison Davies? (*e*) Quanto

custa enviar isto para os Estados Unidos, registado? (*f*) Quanto custa enviar este pacote para Inglaterra, por via aérea, registrado?
20.5.2 (i) (*a*), (*c*). (ii) (*e*), (*d*), (*b*), (*f*).
20.6.2 (1) A Torre de Belém. (2) A UNESCO (3) O estilo manuelino é um estilo ornamental arquitectónico (Eur.) / arquitetônico (Br.) português. (Data do fim do século quinze e princípio do século dezasseis (Eur.) / dezesseis (Br.), época de grandeza para Portugal que coincide com o reinado de Dom Manuel; daí o nome "manuelino".) (4) Cabo da Boa Esperança. (5) Vasco da Gama chegou à Índia em 1498 e Álvares Cabral chegou ao Brasil em 1500. (6) *Three out of* pilares em espiral, cordame, esferas armilares e a cruz da Ordem de Cristo.
20.7.2 Olá, Georgina! / Tudo bem? Aqui faz bom tempo, a comida é boa e eu estou bem. Ontem fui à Torre de Belém. Data do século XVI e tem (*or* apresenta) todas as características individualizantes do estilo manuelino. O estilo manuelino é um estilo ornamental arquitectónico (Eur.) / arquitetônico (Br.) português. Inclui pilares em espiral, cordame, esferas armilares e a cruz da Ordem de Cristo. / Um beijo do Phil.

Unit 21

21.1.2 (i) Como é que a senhora quer o cabelo? // Eu quero uma franja bem curta, e dos lados e atrás quero cortar só um pouco. (ii) Como é que o senhor quer o cabelo? // Quero bem curto atrás e penteado para trás. (iii) Como é que a senhora quer as unhas? // Quero cortar só um pouco e quero esmalte incolor. (iv) De que cor é que a senhora quer o verniz?// Vermelho escuro.
21.1.3 Quero (i) bem curto. (ii) cortar só um pouco dos lados e atrás. (iii) penteado para trás. (iv) penteado para o lado direito.
21.2.2 Você retira o auscultador (Eur.) / fone (Br.) do gancho e aguarda o sinal de digitar; digita primeiro estes números e depois o número do telefone desejado; e aguarda o sinal de tocar.
21.2.3 Retire o auscultador (Eur.) / fone

(Br.) do gancho e aguarde o sinal de digitar; digite primeiro estes números e depois o número do telefone desejado; e aguarde o sinal de tocar.
21.3.1 (A) Qual é o indicativo (Eur.) da região? (B) Qual é o código (Br.) da região?
21.3.2 Este sinal quer dizer ocupado?
21.3.3 Penso que a ligação foi cortada.
21.4.1 (i) "Trenzinho" significa "pequeno trem" ou "trem pequeno" *or* "Trenzinho" quer dizer "pequeno trem" ou "trem pequeno". (ii) O Cristo Redentor é o principal ponto turístico do Rio. (iii) Passear no trem é fazer uma viagem pela história do Brasil.
21.4.2 Querido Simão // (Aqui) faz bom tempo, a comida é boa e eu estou bem. Ontem fui ao Corcovado de trenzinho. Este ponto turístico é visitado por mais de 250 mil pessoas por ano. Na viagem aprecia-se (o passageiro aprecia) uma linda vista. / Um beijo do + *your name* (*if you are male*) // Um beijo da + *your name* (if you are female) *Alternatives:* Saudades e beijinhos / Saudades. Um abraço.
21.5 Como é que se diz "dot" em português?
21.6.1 (i) (Eu) tenciono passar uma semana nesse país. Estou especialmente interessado (*if you are male*) / interessada (*female*) num hotel perto de uma praia. Peço que façam o favor (*or* tenham a gentileza) de me enviarem a lista dos hotéis perto de uma praia. Fico aguardando resposta e desde já agradeço. (ii) (Eu) tenciono passar dois meses nesse país. Estou especialmente interessado (*if you are male*) / interessada (*female*) num parque de campismo (Eur.) / camping (Br.) com facilidades / instalações para crianças. Peço que façam o favor (*or* tenham a gentileza) de me enviarem a lista dos parques de campismo (Eur.) / campings (Br.) com facilidades para crianças. Fico aguardando resposta e desde já agradeço. (iii) (Eu) tenciono passar um mês nesse país. Estou especialmente interessado (*if you are male*) / interessada (*female*) num albergue da juventude com facilidades / instalações para deficientes físicos. Peço que façam o favor (*or* tenham a gentileza) de me enviarem a lista dos albergues da juventude

com facilidades / instalações para deficientes físicos. Fico aguardando resposta e desde já agradeço.
21.6.2 (i) Caros Senhores *or* Prezados Senhores. (ii) Cordialmente.

Unit 22

22.1.2 reuno; possuo; possam.
22.1.3 Tenho / Possuo (i) um diploma profissional. (ii) bons conhecimentos de informática. (iii) um elevado grau de autonomia e professionalismo.
22.2 Incomplete address, not providing enough information.
22.3.2 (i) Em Guimarães. (ii) Ana Isabel Vieira Gama. (iii) Não, sou médica. (iv) Na Universidade de Coimbra. (v) Não, não fiz. (vi) Não, trabalho numa clínica.
22.4 (1) and (4).
22.5 Tencionamos visitar esse país em junho do ano que vem. Precisamos de um apartamento para casal. Preferíamos a primeira semana do mês. / Se o hotel não tiver vagas nesses dias, pedimos que façam o favor de informarem para quando podem fazer a reserva em nosso nome, Sanders. Ficamos aguardando resposta (com grande interesse).
22.6.2 O apartamento tem três quartos de dormir, um sendo de casal. A sala de estar fica à esquerda de quem entra e, a seguir, fica a sala de jantar. A cozinha fica mais ou menos em frente da sala de estar e tem uma porta perto da sala de jantar. A cozinha tem fogão, micro ondas, lava louça..., tudo o que precisamos. A sala de estar tem uma lareira, para os dias frios. Claro que tem sofá, poltrona, mesinha de centro e televisor. Tem também uma estante e aparelho de som. O apartamento não é muito grande mas é bom.
22.7.2 convenha; façam; poderei *or* vou poder *or* posso.
22.7.3 Uma pessoa que queira comprar.
22.7.4 Em resposta ao anúncio nº 27036 desse jornal, tenho o prazer de comunicar que estou interessada em comprar uma casa e essa talvez me convenha. Fico aguardando que façam o favor de informar quando a poderei ver. (*or* vou poder *or* posso)

Unit 23

23.1 já não há mais (1), (4), (5); ainda (2), (3), (6).
23.2 É um lugar, um restaurante, onde se canta o fado. // É uma canção portuguesa acerca da experiência da vida. O "amor" é um tema frequente, mas há uma grande variedade de temas. // São os dois instrumentos dedilhados que normalmente acompanham a pessoa que canta o fado, o fadista ou a fadista.
23.3.1 (i) Faça as camas todas. (ii) Limpe a casa de banho (Eur.) / o banheiro (Br.). (iii) Arrume a sala de estar. (iv) Passe o aspirador na sala de estar e na sala de jantar. (v) Passe a ferro a roupa que foi lavada ontem. (vi) Prepare o jantar. (vii) Ponha a mesa para o jantar. (viii) Depois do jantar, tire a mesa e lave a louça. (ix) Leve o lixo lá para baixo. (x) Dê de comer ao gato.
23.3.2 Hoje precisa (de) (i) fazer as camas todas. (ii) limpar a casa de banho (Eur.) / o banheiro (Br.). (iii) arrumar a sala de estar. (iv) passar o aspirador na sala de estar e na sala de jantar. (v) passar a ferro a roupa que foi lavada ontem. (vi) preparar o jantar. (vii) pôr a mesa para o jantar. (viii) depois do jantar, tirar a mesa e lavar a louça. (ix) levar o lixo lá para baixo. (x) dar de comer ao gato.
23.4.1 (1) (*c*); (2) (*d*); (3) (*e*); (4) (*b*); (5) (*f*); (6) (*a*).
23.4.2 Hard-boil the eggs. Shell them. With a knife, cut them in half lengthways. With a spoon, take out the yolk. Cut the anchovy fillets into small pieces. On a large plate, mix the cut-up anchovy fillets with the egg-yolks and the lemon juice, using a fork. Fill the egg-whites with the mixture. Over the eggs put a bit of mayonnaise and a stuffed olive in the middle. Shred the lettuce and use it to cover the bottom of a serving dish. Place the stuffed eggs on the bed of shredded lettuce.
23.4.3 Descasquei-os. Com uma faca, abri-os ao meio ao comprido. Com uma colher, tirei a gema para fora. Cortei a enchova em bocadinhos. Num prato grande, misturei-a com as gemas e o limão, usando um garfo. Enchi as claras com a mistura. Por cima

coloquei um pouco de maionese e uma azeitona no meio. Cobri o fundo de uma travessa com a alface cortada em tirinhas. Coloquei os ovos recheados no leito de alface.
23.5 (1) (i) Diverte-te! (ii) se divirtam (2) (i) vê-lo/la / ver você / ver-te (ii) Fiquei (3) (i) fazer o favor de (ii) si / você / ti (4) Saúde!
23.6 No dia 3 de dezembro. E o teu? / O meu é hoje. / Então parabéns! Quantos anos é que tu fazes? / Faço vinte anos. / Tenho de ir comprar um presente para ti. / Não, não te incomodes.

Unit 24

24.1
– Você sabe falar português muito bem. Onde aprendeu?
– Aprendi principalmente ensinando a mim própria como autodidacta (Eur.) / autodidata (Br.). Mas sentia a falta de pessoas com quem pudesse falar. Então resolvi passar um tempo em Portugal, dois meses, a praticar e estudar a língua.
– E em Portugal, como estudou?
– Frequentei (Eur.) / freqüentei (Br.) um curso de PLE na Universidade Nova de Lisboa. Tínhamos aulas de língua todos os dias e de cultura três vezes por semana. No fim do curso submeti-me a um exame. Passei com distinção. Fiquei muito contente.
– Muitos parabéns!
– Obrigada. E aproveitei todas as oportunidades para falar, nas lojas, nos restaurantes, em todo o lado. Gostei muito de Portugal e da sua capital, das pessoas... de tudo. Tive muita pena de me vir embora.
– Então vai voltar?
– Vou... vou voltar para um país de língua portuguesa, mas vai ser outro. Quero ir ao Brasil, quero passar dois ou três meses lá.
– E no Brasil, onde vai ficar?
– Ainda não sei, mas gostaria de visitar Brasília.

– Brasília? Por quê?/Porquê? (Eur.)
– Não sei bem... Talvez porque é a capital federal. Talvez (*rindo*) também porque me disseram que Brasília foi construída em forma de avião. Não sei se acredite ou não. O melhor é ir ver.
– (*rindo*) Tem razão. O melhor é ver.
– Ir ao Brasil é também uma boa oportunidade para ouvir outro sotaque e outras expressões.
– Concordo. Acho que faz muito bem. E irá também a alguns países de África onde se fala português?
– Hei de ir, mas quando ainda não sei.
– Muito obrigada pela entrevista. E muitos parabéns por saber falar português tão bem, fluentissimamente... e sem erros. Boa sorte para o futuro!
24.2.1 i) ask (for). (ii) learned. (iii) look (for/after). (iv) tell. (v) on; off.
24.2.2 (i) tempo. (ii) casa. (iii) perdeu. (iv) tratar. (v) deve. (vi) serve. (vii) faltam. (viii) conhece. (ix) sabe. (x) fica.
24.3 The quince 'cheese' was stolen by the dog. Johnny took the lid off the box. Piloto knocked the box off the shelf and ate its contents. Absent-minded Sr. Olavo placed the box back on the shelf.
24.4 (1) (*c*); (2) (*e*); (3) (*a*); (4) (*d*); (5) (*b*).
24.5.2 (i) A cultura brasileira. (ii) A Secretaria de Cultura de Niterói. (iii) No Teatro da UFF. (iv) De 3 de agosto a 10 de dezembro.
24.5.3 Ilmos Senhores, // Tenciono passar seis meses no Brasil no ano que vem, de julho a dezembro. Estou interessado/a num curso de introdução à cultura brasileira; e gostaria de participar no curso da UFF. Venho apresentar a minha candidatura e juntamente envio (Eur.) / estou enviando (Br.) o meu currículo. Fico aguardando resposta (com grande interesse) e espero que possam conceder-me lugar no curso. // Atenciosamente, (*signature*).

GLOSSARY OF GRAMMATICAL TERMS

ADJECTIVE – describes or qualifies a noun. The hotel is *good*. **O hotel é bom**.

ADVERB – gives information about a verb. He speaks Portuguese *fluently*. **Ele fala português *fluentemente*** (Portuguese **-mente** corresponding to English *-ly*). She went *there*. **Ela foi *lá***. I can't *now*. **Não posso *agora***. Some adverbs can also give information about an adjective. *Very* good. *Muito* **bom**.

ARTICLE – see **DEFINITE ARTICLE** and **INDEFINITE ARTICLE**.

CLAUSE – is a group of words with a verb that makes sense on its own, as a sentence or as part of a sentence. In a two-clause sentence, one of the clauses is often more important. This is the **main clause**. The other is the **subordinate clause**. *I shall phone, when he arrives.* ***Eu telefonarei, quando ele chegar***. (*when he arrives* / ***quando ele chegar*** is the subordinate clause).

CONJUGATION – the different endings and forms given to a verb. I *phone*. **Eu *telefono***. He *phones*. **Ele *telefona***. He *phoned*. **Ele *telefonou***.

CONJUNCTION – joins two **clauses** together. I shall phone *when* he arrives. **Telefonarei *quando* ele chegar**.

CONSONANT – a speech-sound such as that represented by the letter **t**, **b** or **m** in which the breath is at least in part obstructed at some point in your mouth or lips. Consonants combine with vowels to form syllables.

DEFINITE ARTICLE – in English *the*, precedes a noun which is presented as a specific item. *The* hotel is good. *O* **hotel é bom**.

DEMONSTRATIVE – determines which noun you mean (more precisely than *the*) and it may stand for a noun as a pronoun. *This* hotel is good. *Este* **hotel é bom**. *This* is new. *Isto* **é novo**.

DIRECT SPEECH – is when you report what someone has said using the person's exact words. He said, *'I have a puncture'*. **Ele disse: *"Estou com um pneu furado"***.

GENDER − nouns (adjectives, adjective-like words and some pronouns) may be **masculine** or **feminine** even if they do not refer to a sexed being − *car*, *carro* is masculine in Portuguese. Some nouns are **common**, i.e., the same for male and female − *dentist*, *dentista*. There are also **neuter** words − *this (thing)*, *isto* (the Portuguese word has a masculine ending, -*o*, but acts as a neuter).

INDEFINITE − refers to the noun you mean (more selectively than *a/an*) and it may stand for a noun as a pronoun. I am going to visit *some* of these museums. **Eu vou visitar *alguns* destes museus.**

INDEFINITE ARTICLE − in English *a/an*, precedes a noun which is presented in an unspecified manner. I am going to visit *a* museum. **Eu vou visitar *um* museu**.

INDICATIVE − is a set of verb forms mainly for statements of fact. I *live* here. **Eu *moro* aqui**. It *is* cold. ***Está* frio**.

INDIRECT SPEECH − is when you report what someone has said without using the person's exact words, hence also known as **reported speech**. He said *that he had a puncture*. **Ele disse *que estava com um pneu furado*.** Also see DIRECT SPEECH.

INFINITIVE − the basic form of the verb. It is in this form that you should look up a verb in a dictionary. Portuguese infinitives end in **-ar**, **-er**, **-ir** and **-or**.

INTERROGATIVE WORD − it often starts a question and may belong to different categories of words, such as a pronoun (*Who* is it? *Quem* **é?**) or an adverb (*Where* is it? *Onde* **é?**).

NOUN − is a naming word − *car*, *carro*; *beach*, *praia*; *John*, *João*.

OBJECT − is what receives the action expressed by the verb. He ate *the apple*. **Ele comeu *a maçã*.**

PERSON − is the subject of an action or state of being. For example, **1st person** is the person speaking; **2nd person** the person spoken to; and **3rd person** the person spoken of. *She* is nice. ***Ela* é simpática**. (*she / ela* = 3rd person).

PERSONAL PRONOUN − the words for *I*, **eu**, *me*, **me** or **mim**, etc.

PHRASE − is a group of words which is part of a clause or sentence but does not make sense on its own − *by him*, *por ele*.

POSSESSIVE − shows ownership or belonging. This car is *hers*. **Este carro é *dela*.**

PREPOSITION – shows the relationship of one thing to another. I have come *from* the beach. **Eu vim *da* praia**. The book is *on top of* the table. **O livro está *em cima d*a mesa**.

PRONOUN – stands in place of a noun. *I*, *eu* (says John talking about himself; where pronoun *I* = noun *John*).

REFLEXIVE – where subject and object are the same. *Eu* **lavo-*me***. *I wash myself*.

RELATIVE PRONOUN – it both stands for a noun and joins two sentences together like a conjunction. This is the dish *which* I am going to order. **Este é o prato *que* eu vou pedir** (*which* / *que* relates to *dish* / *prato* and links the two clauses).

REPORTED SPEECH – see INDIRECT SPEECH.

SENTENCE – is a group of words complete in itself. It may consist of one or more clauses. *I shall phone*. **Eu telefonarei**.

SUBJECT – is what does the action or bears the state of being expressed by the verb. It is often referred to as PERSON.

SUBJUNCTIVE – is a set of verb forms mainly for what is imagined or wished for. If I *were* a millionaire. **Se eu *fosse* milionário**.

SUBORDINATE – see **clause**.

SYLLABLE – is a short uninterrupted unit of pronunciation. The word **ca-fé** has two syllables and the word **con-cer-to** three.

TENSE – MEANS the verb changes to express 'present', 'past' and 'future'. I *write* / *wrote* / *shall write*. **Eu *escrevo* / *escrevi* / *escreverei***.

VERB – is a doing or being word.

VOWEL – is a speech-sound such as that represented by the letter **a** or **o** where the vibration of the vocal cords is the main characteristic. It is more open than a consonant and in some cases may stand on its own as a syllable.

VOICE – is the relationship between the verb and the subject. It is **active** when the subject does the action. It is **passive** when the subject has the action done to it: *The apple was eaten by him*. **A maçã foi comida por ele**.

PRONUNCIATION

Stress and Accentuation

Portuguese words in general are stressed on the penultimate syllable:
    passa'porte (*passport*)

The chief constituent, or centre, of the syllable is a vowel element:
    passa'porte

In words which do not end in a single **a**, **e**, or **o**, the stress usually falls on the last syllable:
    ho'tel (*hotel*)   **esta'ção** (*station*)

Words which are an exception to the above stress rules usually bear a written accent:
    al'fândega (*customs*)

In Portugal, contrast between stressed and unstressed syllables is sharp. There is a tendency to linger on the stressed syllable and glide over the intermediate sounds. As a result, unstressed vowels become 'neutralised' and final **e** tends to disappear. Brazilian stress is more evenly spaced out, and a secondary stress often emerges in a single word:
    humani'dade (Eur.) (*humankind*)
    hum'ani'dade (Br.)

Portuguese Sounds

The chart on pages 279–84 will give you a detailed description of the Portuguese sounds. Differences between European and Brazilian practice are highlighted with the abbreviations (Eur.) and (Br.).

In the first column you will see a letter or group of letters as used in normal spelling. The sound that letter (or group of letters) stands for is represented in the second column by a phonetic symbol from the International Phonetic Alphabet. You needn't worry if you are not familiar with phonetic symbols. Just move on to the third column. It compares the Portuguese sound with an English sound. In some cases a French sound-alike is given too. The fourth column tells you the position of the sound in the word. In the last column you will be able to see an example of a Portuguese word including the respective sound.

Liaison and Elision

In the flow of speech, consecutive words are often linked together and the faster a person speaks the more this happens. E.g., **dois endereços** (*two addresses*) [doizẽde'reso∫] (Eur.) /[doizẽde'resos] (Br.). The final **s** in **dois** is now between vowels (see chart of sounds, page 284).

A word ending in a vowel tends to be run together with a word beginning with a vowel. E.g., **De onde é?** (*Where do you come from?*) ['dõ'dɛ] (Eur.) / ['dõ'dji'ɛ] (Br.). (A careful speaker, though, will pronounce the unstressed vowel element as a semi-vowel.)

Elision of vowels often occurs in relaxed speech, as shown in some unconventional spellings. E.g., **p'ra** or **pra** instead of **para** (*to*) ['prɐ]. Also, this tendency is sometimes taken to extremes.

> **n'é** or **né** instead of **não é** ? (*in't it?*)
>
> **t'obrigado** or **tobrigado** instead of **muito obrigado** (*thank you very much*)

Metropolitan and American Spelling

A difference in spelling stands out when you put side by side a Portuguese text written on the eastern side of the Atlantic and one written on the western side of the same ocean. There is a Metropolitan tendency to retain etymological spelling, some letters from the Latin (or other) origin of the word. In contrast, Brazilians act under the principle that what you don't pronounce you don't spell. E.g., **excepto** (Eur.) / **exceto** (Br.) (*except*). This is a situation in some respects comparable to e.g. Metropolitan English *through* and American English *thru*.

Another recognisable difference is found in some written accents. E.g., **quilómetro** (Eur.) / **quilômetro** (Br.) (*kilometre*). This reflects a different value given to the vowel. To a point, a parallel can be drawn with Metropolitan English *harbour* as compared with American *harbor*.

For further information, please refer to the chart of sounds on pages 279–84.

Vowel Sounds

spell-ing	IPA symbol	sound-alikes	position	examples
a	[a]	more open than English a, approaching ah	stressed	falo (I speak); fala (you speak); mapa (map); mala (suitcase)
a	[ɐ]	resembling a as in among but longer	stressed, before m or n starting a new syllable	cama (bed); ano (year); falamos (we speak)
a	[ɑ]	between a and ah, as above, but pronounced further back in the mouth	before l or u in the same syllable	hospital (hospital); mau (bad); carnaval (carnival)
á, à	[a]	between a and ah, as above	stressed	há (there is); lá (there)
â	[ɐ]	resembling a as in among, as above	stressed	câmara (council)
a	[ɐ]	resembling a as in among	unstressed, at the end of word, and elsewhere	mala (suitcase); cama (bed); falamos (we speak)
e	[ɛ]	resembling e in tell	stressed	zero (zero); ela (she)
e	[e]	like ey in they but without the final glide (like the French word et)	stressed and unstressed depending on the origin of the word and/or its surrounding sounds	mesa (table); caneta (pen); esteve (it was); ele (he); comer (to eat)
é	[ɛ]	resembling e in tell	stressed	café (coffee); pé (foot)
ê	[e]	like ey, as above	stressed	você (you); mês (month)
e	[ɪ]	resembling i in cigarette	unstressed, particularly before a vowel or at the beginning of syllable	compreendo (I understand); está (it is); exame (exam)
e	[ə]	like e in butter, or disappears (Eur.)	at the end of word	noite (night); vinte (twenty); nome (name); me (me); envelope (envelope)
	[ɪ]	resembling i in cigarette (Br.)		
i	[i]	like ee in meet but usually shorter	stressed	dizer (to say); aquí (here)

			unstressed	cigarro (*cigarette*)
i	[I]	resembling *i* in *cigarette*		
i	[I]	like *i* in *pill*	before **l** or **u** in the same syllable	**mil** (*thousand*); **partiu** (*s/he left*)
í	[i]	like *ee* in *meet* but usually shorter	stressed	**saí** (*I got out*)
i	[j]	like *y* in *yet*	before another vowel other than **u**	**fazia** (*s/he used to do*)
o	[ɔ]	resembling *o* in *jolly*	stressed	**ovos** (*eggs*); **come** (*you eat*)
o	[o]	a bit like *o* in *note* (like French *au* in *chaud*)	stressed and unstressed depending on the origin of the word and/or its surrounding sounds	**ovo** (*egg*); **bolo** (*cake*); **fogo** (*fire*); **porto** (*port*); **como** (*I eat*); **como** (*how; as*); **todo** (*all*)
ó	[ɔ]	resembling *o* in *jolly*	stressed	**avó** (*grandmother*); **próximo** (*next*)
ô	[o]	a bit like *o* in *note*, as above	stressed	**avô** (*grandfather*); **pôr** (*to put*)
o	[u]	resembling *u* in *put*	unstressed, at end of word	**ovo**, **ovos** (*egg/s*)
u	[u]	resembling *oo* in *soon* (like French *ou* in *où*)	stressed	**tudo** (*everything*); **uva** (*grape*); **aluno** (*pupil, student*)
ú	[u]	a bit like *oo* in *soon*, as above	stressed	**número** (*number*)
u	[ʷu]	like *ou* in *could*	before **l** in the same syllable	**azul** (*blue*); **sul** (*south*)
u	[w]	like *w* in *water*	after **g** or **q** and before **a** or **o**	**quando** (*when*); **quanto** (*how much*); **água** (*water*)
u	[ ]	silent	after **g** or **q** and before **e** or **i**, in general	**aqui** (*here*); **quero** (*I want*); **seguir** (*to follow*)
u	[w]	like *w* in *water*	after **g** or **q** and before **e** or **i**, in some cases (European spelling)	**cinquenta** (*fifty*) (Eur.); **aguentar** (*to stand, bear*) (Eur.)
ü	[w]	like *w* in *water*	after **g** or **q** and before **e** or **i**, in some cases (Brazilian spelling)	**cinqüenta** (*fifty*) (Br.); **agüentar** (*to stand, bear*) (Br.)
ai	[aj]	like *y* in *my*	any position	**pai** (*father*); **mais** (*more*)

au	[au]	resembling *ow* in *how*	any position	**mau** (*bad*)
ei	[ɐj]	resembling *ay* in *pay* (Eur.)	any position	di**rei**ta (*right*); **lei**te (*milk*); **sei** (*I know*)
	[ej]	resembling *ey* in *they* (Br.)		
eu	[eu]	a bit like *ey* in *they* plus *oo* in *soon* (like the French word *et* plus the French spelling *ou*)	any position	**eu** (*I*); **meu** (*my*); **seu** (*your*); **Eu**ropa (*Europe*)
oi	[oj]	a bit like *o* in *note* (like French *au* in *chaud*) plus *y* in *yet*	any position	c**oi**sa (*thing*); d**oi**s (*two*)
ou	[o]	a bit like *o* in *note* (French *au* in *chaud*) (Eur.)		s**ou** (*I am*); v**ou** (*I go*); **ou**tro (*other*)
	[ou]	resembling *o* in *note* (Br.)	any position	
ui	[uj]	a bit like *oo* in *soon* plus *y* in *yet*	in general, but in the word **muito** (*much; very*) it is often pronounced like *ui* in *ruin*	**fui** (*I went*)

Nasal Vowel Sounds

ã, am, an	[ɐ̃]	a bit like *an* in *anchor*	any position as one syllable (spelling **am** before **p** or **b**)	aman**hã** (*tomorrow*); **am**bos (*both*); b**an**co (*bank*)
am, ão	[ɐ̃ũ]	like *ow* in *how* but nasalised, i.e., pronounced through your nose	any position (spelling **am** in unstressed 3rd-person verbal endings)	fal**am** (*they speak*); n**ão** (*no*); p**ão** (*bread*); irm**ão** (*brother*)
em, ãe	[ɐ̃j]	like *ay* in *pay* but nasalised (Eur.)	end of word	**em** (*in, on*); b**em** (*well*); hom**em** (*man*); m**ãe** (*mother*); p**ães** (*loaves*)
	[ẽj]	like *ey* in *they* but nasalised (Br.)		
êm	[ɐ̃j]	(Eur.) the same as for the spelling **em** above but the sound should be repeated	end of word (3rd -p. plural verb ending)	t**êm** (*they have*)
	[ẽj]	(Br.)		

em, en	[ẽ]	like *ey* in *they* but without the final glide and nasalised	any position (but not end of word)	**em**prego (*job, employment*); **en**tre (*enter; come/go in*)
im, in	[ĩ]	like *ee* in *meet* but nasalised	any position	s**im** (*yes*); c**in**co (*five*)
om, on	[õ]	like *o* in *note* but nasalised	any position	b**om** (*good*); c**on**ta (*bill*)
õe	[õj]	like *o* in *note* plus *y* in *yet* but nasalised	any position	liç**õe**s (*lessons*); p**õe** (*s/he puts*)
um, un	[ũ]	like *oo* in *soon* but nasalised	any position	**um** (*one*); j**un**tos (*together*)

Consonants

b	[b]	as in English, but softer	any position	**b**elo (*beautiful*)
c	[s]	as English *s*	before **e** or **i**	**c**em (*a hundred*); **c**inco (*five*)
c	[ ] *or* [k]	silent or like *c* in *cat*	in words with original -ct- (Eur.)	fa**c**to (*fact*); a**c**to (*act*)
c	[k]	like *c* in *cat*	elsewhere	**c**arro (*car*); **c**om (*with*)
ç	[s]	as English *s*	any position	informa**ç**ão (*information*)
ch	[ʃ]	like *sh* in *show*	any position	**ch**ave (*key*); a**ch**ar (*to find*)
d	[d]	as in English, but with tip of tongue against teeth, not gum ridge	any position (Eur.) in general (Br.)	**d**ar (*to give*); tar**d**e (*late*); universida**d**e (*university*)
d	[dj]	the same as explained for **d** above, plus *y* in *yet*	before sound [i], in some parts of Brazil	tar**d**e (*late*); universi**d**ade (*university*)
f	[f]	as in English	any position	**f**ácil (*easy*)
g	[ʒ]	like *s* in *pleasure*	before **e** or **i**	**g**ente (*people*)
g	[g]	like *g* in *good*	elsewhere	**g**rande (*large*); garra**f**a (*bottle*)
h	[ ]	silent	in general	**h**otel (*hotel*); **h**omem (*man*)
j	[ʒ]	like *s* in *pleasure*	any position	lo**j**a (*shop*); ho**j**e (*today*)

l	[ɬ]	as in English, but drawing your tongue back	at the end of syllable	sol (*sun*); mil (*thousand*); almoço (*lunch*)
l	[l]	as in English	elsewhere	lanche (*snack*); falar (*to speak*)
lh	[ʎ]	resembling *lli* in *million*	any position	filho (*son*); trabalho (*work*)
m	[m]	as in English	at beginning of syllable	mãe (*mother*); mesa (*table*)
n	[n]	as in English	at beginning of syllable	nome (*name*); nada (*nothing*)
nh	[ɲ]	resembling *ni* in *onion*	any position	vinho (*wine*); senhora (*lady*)
p	[p]	as in English, but softer	any position	pai (*father*); perto (*near*)
p	[ ]	silent	in words with original -pt- (Eur.)	excepto (*except*)
q	[k]	like *c* in *cat*	any position	quatro (*four*); quente (*hot*)
r	[rr] or [ʀ]	like the rolled Scottish *r*, with multiple trill, or like *ch* in *loch* or a very heavy English *h*	at the beginning of word and generally at the beginning of syllable	rua (*road*); rio (*river*); refeição (*meal*); repetir (*to repeat*)
r	[ɾ] or [ɹ]	like the *r* in *baker*, or 'swallowed'	at end of word and generally at the end of syllable	jantar (*dinner*); fazer (*to do*); porta (*door*); norte (*north*)
r	[ɾ]	like the *r* in *bakery*	elsewhere	caro (*dear*); barato (*cheap*)
rr	[rr] or [ʀ]	as explained above for spelling **r** at the beginning of word and generally at the beginning of syllable	between vowels	carro (*car*)
s	[s]	like *s* in *so*	at the beginning of word or after a consonant	sol (*sun*); semana (*week*); observar (*to watch*)
s	[ʃ]	like *s* in *push* (Eur.) and (Br.) Rio de Janeiro	at the end of word or syllable	dois (*two*); homens (*men*); esquerda (*left*); nascer (*to be born*)
s	[s]	like *s* in *so* (Br.) but not in Rio de Janeiro		

s	[ʒ]	like s in *pleasure* (Eur.) and (Br.) Rio de Janeiro		mesmo (*same*); desde (*since*); desfazer (*to undo*)
	[z]	like English z (Br.) but not in Rio de Janeiro	before a voiced consonant	
s	[z]	like English z	between vowels	casa (*house, home*)
ss	[s]	like s in *so*	between vowels	passaporte (*passport*)
t	[t]	as in English, but with tip of tongue against teeth, not gum ridge	in general	tudo (*everything*); tive (*I had*); noite (*night*)
t	[tj]	the same as explained for **t** above, plus y in *yet*	before sound [i], in some parts of Brazil	tive (*I had*); noite (*night*)
v	[v]	as in English	any position	vago (*vacant*)
x	[ʃ]	like *sh* in *show*	at the beginning of word or syllable and in some cases between vowels	xarope (*syrup*); xícara (*cup*); xadrez (*checked*); caixa (*check-out*); puxar (*to pull*)
x	[z]	like English z	where **ex** comes before a vowel	exame (*exam*)
x	[ks]	like x in *taxi*	in some words	táxi (*taxi*); fixo (*fixed*)
x	[s]	like s in *so*	between vowels, other than above	próximo (*next*); trouxe (*I brought*)
x	[ʃ]	like *sh* in *push* (Eur.) and (Br.) Rio de Janeiro		extra (*extra*); sexta-feira (*Friday*)
	[s]	like s in *so* (Br.) but not in Rio de Janeiro	before a consonant	
z	[z]	like English z	at the beginning of a word and between vowels	zero (*zero*); fazer (*to do*)
z	[ʃ]	like *sh* in *push*	at end of word	luz (*light*); feliz (*happy*)
z	[ʒ]	like s in *pleasure*		Feliz Natal (*Happy Christmas*)
	[z]	like English z (Br.) but not in Rio de Janeiro	before a voiced consonant	

VERB GUIDE

Verbs follow general conjugation patterns for present, past and future, as well as for other meanings they may express. However, there is a certain range of variation in the degree to which each verb conforms to the general pattern. This section explains the relevant differences in Portuguese verbs. It also contains a quick-reference table of the regular conjugation endings (for more detail see *conjugations* in the cross-section Grammar index) and tables of verbs with anomalous features.

Regular verbs

Regular verbs simply follow the standard pattern for their conjugation, like the three model verbs used in this course, namely **comprar**, **vender** and **partir**.

Special verbs

(i) *Orthography-changing verbs:* those which change their spelling in order to preserve the same pronunciation.

– Conhe**ce** o Rio?	*Do you know Rio?*
– Sim, conhe**ço**.	*Yes, I do* (verb **conhecer**)

(ii) *Radical-changing verbs:* those which change their stem vowel under certain conditions, as, for example, when the stress falls on the stem or through the influence of a nearby vowel.

– Prefere chá ou café?	*Do you prefer tea or coffee?*
– Pref**i**ro chá.	*I prefer tea.* (verb **preferir**)

(iii) *Irregular verbs:* those which do not conform to the model endings for the three conjugations **-ar**, **-er**, **-ir**.

Onde **é** o hotel?	*Where is the hotel?*	(verb **ser**)
Vou amanhã.	*I am going tomorrow.*	(verb **ir**)

One single verb may display features from more than one group above ((i)/(ii)/(iii)).

Quando eu **segu**ia pela estrada. *When I was going along the road.*
Siga em frente. *Go straight on.* (verb **seguir** (i)+(ii))

Regular Verbs (endings only)

Infinitive	Present Indicative	Preterite Indicative	Imperfect Indicative	Pluperfect Indicative	Future Indicative	'Commands' (Imperative)
-ar	-o	-ei	-ava	-ara	-arei	—
	-as	-aste	-avas	-aras	-arás	-a
	-a	-ou	-ava	-ara	-ará	-e
	-a	-ou	-ava	-ara	-ará	—
	-amos	-ámos	-ávamos	-áramos	-aremos	-emos
	(-ais)	(-astes)	(-áveis)	(-áreis)	(-areis)	(-ai)
	-am	-aram	-avam	-aram	-arão	-em
	-am	-aram	-avam	-aram	-arão	—
-er	-o	-i	-ia	-era	-erei	—
	-es	-este	-ias	-eras	-erás	-e
	-e	-eu	-ia	-era	-erá	-a
	-e	-eu	-ia	-era	-erá	—
	-emos	-emos	-íamos	-êramos	-eremos	-amos
	(-eis)	(-estes)	(-íeis)	(-êreis)	(-ereis)	(-ei)
	-em	-eram	-iam	-eram	-erão	-am
	-em	-eram	-iam	-eram	-erão	—
-ir	-o	-i	-ia	-ira	-irei	—
	-es	-iste	-ias	-iras	-irás	-e
	-e	-iu	-ia	-ira	-irá	-a
	-e	-iu	-ia	-ira	-irá	—
	-imos	-imos	-íamos	-íramos	-iremos	-amos
	(-is)	(-istes)	(-íeis)	(-íreis)	(-ireis)	(-i)
	-em	-iram	-iam	-iram	-irão	-am
	-em	-iram	-iam	-iram	-irão	—

Present Subjunctive	Imperfect Subjunctive	Future Subjunctive	Conditional	Personal Infinitive	Present Participle	Past Participle
-e	-asse	-ar	-aria	-ar	-ando	-ado
-es	-asses	-ares	-arias	-ares		
-e	-asse	-ar	-aria	-ar		
-e	-asse	-ar	-aria	-ar		
-emos	-ássemos	-armos	-aríamos	-armos		
(-eis)	(-ásseis)	(-ardes)	(-aríeis)	(-ardes)		
-em	-assem	-arem	-ariam	-arem		
-em	-assem	-arem	-ariam	-arem		
-a	-esse	-er	-eria	-er	-endo	-ido
-as	-esses	-eres	-erias	-eres		
-a	-esse	-er	-eria	-er		
-a	-esse	-er	-eria	-er		
-amos	-êssemos	-ermos	-eríamos	-ermos		
(-ais)	(-êsseis)	(-erdes)	(-eríeis)	(-erdes)		
-am	-essem	-erem	-eriam	-erem		
-am	-essem	-erem	-eriam	-erem		
-a	-isse	-ir	-iria	-ir	-indo	-ido
-as	-isses	-ires	-irias	-ires		
-a	-isse	-ir	-iria	-ir		
-a	-isse	-ir	-iria	-ir		
-amos	-íssemos	-irmos	-iríamos	-irmos		
(-ais)	(-ísseis)	(-irdes)	(-iríeis)	(-irdes)		
-am	-issem	-irem	-iriam	-irem		
-am	-issem	-irem	-iriam	-irem		

Note: The verbal forms corresponding to 'vós' have been entered in brackets in view of their limited use.

Orthography-changing verbs

The following chart shows the required changes.

-ca	-çar	-gar	-cer	-ger -gir	-guer -guir
↓	↓	↓	↓	↓	↓
-qu	-c	-gu	-ç	-j	-g
before *e*			before *a* or *o*		

ficar (*to stay*)	→ fiquei; fique
começar (*to begin*)	→ comecei; comece
pagar (*to pay*)	→ paguei; pague
conhecer (*to know*)	→ conheço; conheça
proteger (*to protect*)	→ protejo; proteja
dirigir (*to drive*)	→ dirijo; dirijam
erguer (*to lift*)	→ ergo; erga
seguir (*to follow, go*)	→ sigo; sigam

Verbs whose infinitive ends in **o+er** have a spelling change in the 3rd person of the present indicative (the *it, s/he* form), where the end vowel is written **-i**. Also note the written accent in the example below.

doer – dói aqui (*it hurts here*)

Radical-changing verbs

Please refer to the following chart for the required changes.

e	o	u
↓	↓	↓
i	u	o
*Present indicative, 1st person (**eu** form) *Present subjunctive *Command forms from present subjunctive		*Present indicative, 2nd and 3rd persons and respective plurals (**tu**, **você(s)**, **ele(s)** forms) *Command form for **tu**

repetir (*to repeat, to say/do again*)

Pres. ind.: repito, repetes, etc.

Pres. subj.: repita, repitas, repita, repitamos, (repitais), repitam

Command: repita, repitam

dormir (*to sleep*)
Pres. ind.: durmo, dormes, etc.
Pres. subj.: durma, durmas, durma, durmamos, (durmais), durmam
Command: durma, durmam

subir (*to climb, to go/come up*)
Pres. ind.: subo, sobes, sobe, subimos, (subis), sobem
Command: sobe (tu)

Variations in the quality of the stem vowel are not always registered in spelling. (See the chart for vowel sounds in the Pronunciation section.)

– Falam português?	*Do you speak Portuguese?*
– Sim, falamos.	*Yes, we do.* (verb **falar**)
– Come carne?	*Do you eat meat?*
– Não, não como; sou vegetariano.	*No, I don't; I am a vegetarian.*

(verb **comer**)

There are cases in which an accent can be written over the vowel to prevent confusion with another form of the verb or indeed another word with a completely different meaning. This is the case with **pode**, for *you, s/he can*, and **pôde**, for *you, s/he could*, and with **pára** (*stop*) from verb **parar**, and **para**, a preposition translating *to* or *for*. However, native speakers do not need this help and often 'forget' to use the written accent.

Other changes

Verbs with infinitive in **a+ir** retain the **i** throughout their conjugation except in the 3rd person plural of the indicative present (*they* form). Also this **i** is given a written accent where it forms a stressed syllable.

sair (*to go/come out*)
Pres. ind: saio, sais, sai, saímos, (saís), saem

Verbs with infinitive in **e+ar** add an **i** after stressed **e**. Only the present indicative, present subjunctive and command forms are affected.

passear (*to go for a walk / ride*)
Pres. ind: passeio, passeias, passeia, passeamos, (passeais), passeiam

The verb **odiar** (*to hate*) is conjugated similarly.

Irregular verbs

Infinitive	Present Indicative	Preterite Indicative	Imperfect Indicative	Pluperfect Indicative	Future Indicative
crer to believe	creio crês crê cremos (credes) crêem	Regular	Regular	Regular	Regular
dar to give	dou dás dá damos (dais) dão	dei deste deu demos (destes) deram	Regular	dera deras dera déramos (déreis) deram	Regular
dizer to say	digo dizes diz dizemos (dizeis) dizem	disse disseste disse dissemos (dissestes) disseram	Regular	dissera disseras dissera disséramos (disséreis) disseram	direi dirás dirá diremos (direis) dirão
estar to be	estou estás está estamos (estais) estão	estive estiveste esteve estivemos (estivestes) estiveram	Regular	estivera estiveras estivera estivéramos (estivéreis) estiveram	Regular
fazer to do, make	faço fazes faz fazemos (fazeis) fazem	fiz fizeste fez fizemos (fizestes) fizeram	Regular	fizera fizeras fizera fizéramos (fizéreis) fizeram	farei farás fará faremos (fareis) farão
haver to exist, there to be, have	hei hás há havemos (haveis) hão	houve houveste houve houvemos (houvestes) houveram	Regular	houvera houveras houvera houvéramos (houvéreis) houveram	Regular

Note: the verbal forms corresponding to 'vós' are entered in brackets in view of their limited use.

Command forms	Present Subjunctive	Imperfect Subjunctive	Future Subjunctive	Conditional	Participles
— crê creia creiamos (crede) creiam	creia creias creia creiamos (creiais) creiam	*Regular*	*Regular*	*Regular*	*Pres.* crendo *Past* crido
— dá dê dêmos (dai) dêem	dê dês dê dêmos (deis) dêem	desse desses desse déssemos (désseis) dessem	der deres der dermos (derdes) derem	*Regular*	*Pres.* dando *Past* dado
— diz(e) diga digamos (dizei) digam	diga digas diga digamos (digais) digam	dissesse dissesses dissesse disséssemos (dissésseis) dissessem	disser disseres disser dissermos (disserdes) disserem	diria dirias diria diríamos (diríeis) diriam	*Pres.* dizendo *Past* dito
— está esteja estejamos (estai) estejam	esteja estejas esteja estejamos (estejais) estejam	estivesse estivesses estivesse estivéssemos (estivésseis) estivessem	estiver estiveres estiver estivermos (estiverdes) estiverem	*Regular*	*Pres.* estando *Past* estado
— faz(e) faça façamos (fazei) façam	faça faças faça façamos (façais) façam	fizesse fizesses fizesse fizéssemos (fizésseis) fizessem	fizer fizeres fizer fizermos (fizerdes) fizerem	faria farias faria faríamos (faríeis) fariam	*Pres.* fazendo *Past* feito
— há haja hajamos (havei) hajam	haja hajas haja hajamos (hajais) hajam	houvesse houvesses houvesse houvéssemos (houvésseis) houvessem	houver houveres houver houvermos (houverdes) houverem	*Regular*	*Pres.* havendo *Past* havido

Infinitive	Present Indicative	Preterite Indicative	Imperfect Indicative	Pluperfect Indicative	Future Indicative
ir to go	vou vais vai vamos (ides) vão	fui foste foi fomos (fostes) foram	*Regular* (ia, etc.)	fora foras fora fôramos (fôreis) foram	*Regular*
ler to read	leio lês lê lemos (ledes) lêem	*Regular*	*Regular*	*Regular*	*Regular*
ouvir to hear	ouço ouves ouve ouvimos (ouvis) ouvem	*Regular*	*Regular*	*Regular*	*Regular*
pedir to ask for	peço pedes pede pedimos (pedis) pedem	*Regular*	*Regular*	*Regular*	*Regular*
perder to lose	perco perdes perde perdemos (perdeis) perdem	*Regular*	*Regular*	*Regular*	*Regular*
poder can, may	posso podes pode podemos (podeis) podem	pude pudeste pôde pudemos (pudestes) puderam	*Regular*	pudera puderas pudera pudéramos (pudéreis) puderam	*Regular*
pôr to put	ponho pões põe pomos (pondes) põem	pus puseste pôs pusemos (pusestes) puseram	punha punhas punha púnhamos (púnheis) punham	pusera puseras pusera puséramos (puséreis) puseram	*Regular* (no accent ^)

Command forms	Present Subjunctive	Imperfect Subjunctive	Future Subjunctive	Conditional	Participles
—— vai vá vamos (ide) vão	vá vás vá vamos (vades) vão	fosse fosses fosse fôssemos (fôsseis) fossem	for fores for formos (fordes) forem	Regular	*Pres.* indo *Past* ido
—— lê leia leiamos (lede) leiam	leia leias leia leiamos (leiais) leiam	Regular	Regular	Regular	*Pres.* lendo *Past* lido
—— ouve ouça ouçamos (ouvi) ouçam	ouça ouças ouça ouçamos (ouçais) ouçam	Regular	Regular	Regular	*Pres.* ouvindo *Past* ouvido
—— pede peça peçamos (pedi) peçam	peça peças peça peçamos (peçais) peçam	Regular	Regular	Regular	*Pres.* pedindo *Past* pedido
—— perde perca percamos (perdei) percam	perca percas perca percamos (percais) percam	Regular	Regular	Regular	*Pres.* perdendo *Past* perdido
—— pode possa possamos (podei) possam	possa possas possa possamos (possais) possam	pudesse pudesses pudesse pudéssemos (pudésseis) pudessem	puder puderes puder pudermos (puderdes) puderem	Regular	*Pres.* podendo *Past* podido
—— põe ponha ponhamos (ponde) ponham	ponha ponhas ponha ponhamos (ponhais) ponham	pusesse pusesses pusesse puséssemos (pusésseis) pusessem	puser puseres puser pusermos (puserdes) puserem	Regular (no accent ^)	*Pres.* pondo *Past* posto

Infinitive	Present Indicative	Preterite Indicative	Imperfect Indicative	Pluperfect Indicative	Future Indicative
querer *to want*	quero queres quer queremos (quereis) querem	quis quiseste quis quisemos (quisestes) quiseram	Regular	quisera quiseras quisera quiséramos (quiséreis) quiseram	Regular
saber *to know*	sei sabes sabe sabemos (sabeis) sabem	soube soubeste soube soubemos (soubestes) souberam	Regular	soubera souberas soubera soubéramos (soubéreis) souberam	Regular
ser *to be*	sou és é somos (sois) são	fui foste foi fomos (fostes) foram	era eras era éramos (éreis) eram	fora foras fora fôramos (fôreis) foram	Regular
ter *to have*	tenho tens tem temos (tendes) têm	tive tiveste teve tivemos (tivestes) tiveram	tinha tinhas tinha tínhamos (tínheis) tinham	tivera tiveras tivera tivéramos (tivéreis) tiveram	Regular
trazer *to bring*	trago trazes traz trazemos (trazeis) trazem	trouxe trouxeste trouxe trouxemos (trouxestes) trouxeram	Regular	trouxera trouxeras trouxera trouxéramos (trouxéreis) trouxeram	trarei trarás trará traremos (trareis) trarão
ver *to see*	vejo vês vê vemos (vedes) vêem	vi viste viu vimos (vistes) viram	Regular	vira viras vira víramos (víreis) viram	Regular
vir *to come*	venho vens vem vimos (vindes) vêm	vim vieste veio viemos (viestes) vieram	vinha vinhas vinha vínhamos (vínheis) vinham	viera vieras viera viéramos (viéreis) vieram	Regular

Command forms	*Present Subjunctive*	*Imperfect Subjunctive*	*Future Subjunctive*	*Conditional*	*Participles*
—	queira	quisesse	quiser		*Pres.*
quer(e)	queiras	quisesses	quiseres		querendo
queira	queira	quisesse	quiser	*Regular*	*Past*
queiramos	queiramos	quiséssemos	quisermos		querido
(querei)	(queirais)	(quisésseis)	(quiserdes)		
queiram	queiram	quisessem	quiserem		
—	saiba	soubesse	souber		*Pres.*
sabe	saibas	soubesses	souberes		sabendo
saiba	saiba	soubesse	souber	*Regular*	*Past*
saibamos	saibamos	soubéssemos	soubermos		sabido
(sabei)	(saibais)	(soubésseis)	(souberdes)		
saibam	saibam	soubessem	souberem		
—	seja	fosse	for		*Pres.*
sê	sejas	fosses	fores		sendo
seja	seja	fosse	for	*Regular*	*Past*
sejamos	sejamos	fôssemos	formos		sido
(sede)	(sejais)	fôsseis	(fordes)		
sejam	sejam	fossem	forem		
—	tenha	tivesse	tiver		*Pres.*
tem	tenhas	tivesses	tiveres		tendo
tenha	tenha	tivesse	tiver	*Regular*	*Past*
tenhamos	tenhamos	tivéssemos	tivermos		tido
(tende)	(tenhais)	(tivésseis)	(tiverdes)		
tenham	tenham	tivessem	tiverem		
—	traga	trouxesse	trouxer	traria	*Pres.*
traz(e)	tragas	trouxesses	trouxeres	trarias	trazendo
traga	traga	trouxesse	trouxer	traria	*Past*
tragamos	tragamos	trouxéssemos	trouxermos	traríamos	trazido
(trazei)	(tragais)	(trouxésseis)	(trouxerdes)	(traríeis)	
tragam	tragam	trouxessem	trouxerem	trariam	
—	veja	visse	vir		*Pres.*
vê	vejas	visses	vires		vendo
veja	veja	visse	vir	*Regular*	*Past*
vejamos	vejamos	víssemos	virmos		visto
(vede)	(vejais)	(vísseis)	(virdes)		
vejam	vejam	vissem	virem		
—	venha	viesse	vier		*Pres.*
vem	venhas	viesses	vieres		vindo
venha	venha	viesse	vier	*Regular*	*Past*
venhamos	venhamos	viéssemos	viermos		vindo
(vinde)	(venhais)	(viésseis)	(vierdes)		
venham	venham	viessem	vierem		

Irregular past participles

abrir (*to open*)	– aberto	escrever (*to write*)	– escrito
aceitar (*to accept*)	– aceito *or* aceite	ganhar (*to earn, win*)	– ganho
acender (*to light*)	– aceso	gastar (*to spend*)	– gasto
entregar (*to deliver*)	– entregue	pagar (*to pay*)	– pago

Where both a regular and an irregular form are available, usually the former is used in compound perfect tenses and the latter is used as an adjective.

> Eu tinha **acendido** a luz. A luz estava **acesa**. *I had switched the light on. The light was on.*

Also, sometimes a past participle is used as a noun.

> Não tenho **trocado**. *I haven't got any change.*
> **Perdidos** e **Achados**. *'Lost and Found'*
> **Chegadas**. *Arrivals*

Compound verbs

Please remember that compounds of special verbs normally exhibit the same features as the single verbs.

		from
(i)	**Orthography-changing**	
	conseguir (*to achieve*)	seguir
	reconhecer (*to recognise*)	conhecer
(ii)	**Radical-changing**	
	conseguir (*to achieve*)	seguir
	consentir (to consent)	sentir
	descobrir (*to discover, to uncover*)	cobrir
	preferir (*to prefer*)	ferir
	referir (*to mention*)	ferir
(iii)	**Irregular**	
	compor (*to compose, to arrange together*)	pôr
	condizer (*to match*)	dizer
	conter (*to contain*)	ter
	contradizer (*to contradict*)	dizer
	convir (*to suit, to be convenient*)	vir
	desfazer (*to undo*)	fazer
	manter (*to maintain*)	ter
	satisfazer (*to satisfy*)	fazer
	supor (*to assume*)	pôr

Verbs, nouns and hyphens

The use of the hyphen can be subject to variation. For example in English, the abridged version of *electronic mail* occurs both as *e-mail* and *email*. The use, or omission, of a hyphen may reflect the stage of evolution of the compound word and the extent to which its constituent parts are seen as a unit in its own right, but there may also be other reasons. In Portuguese, please note the following cases.

(A) Nouns

(i) In **o depósito de bagagem** (*left luggage lockers / office*), perhaps no one will feel the need to hyphenate the three components. They are likely to be perceived as three distinct words.

(ii) In cases such as **segunda-feira** (*Monday*) and **guarda-chuva** (*umbrella*), the components have to some extent lost their independent meaning in favour of a new compound meaning. The hyphen shows this situation.

(iii) Words like **fim de semana** (*weekend*) and **pequeno almoço** (*breakfast*) (Eur.) appear to be in an intermediate position. You are likely to come across them in two different versions, i.e., as above or hyphenated, **fim-de-semana** and **pequeno-almoço**.

Please see also pp 19, 29, 39 and 50.

(B) Object pronouns (including reflexive pronouns)

With words such as those for *me, myself*, word order plays a role. As a general principle, a hyphen is used where the object pronoun follows the verb: **Pode dizer-me onde é a saída?** (*Can you tell me where the exit is?*) However, the following construction is more widely used: **Pode me dizer onde é a saída?**

In this construction, the object pronoun (**me**) comes before, not after, the verb to which it relates (**dizer**). Notwithstanding, there are those who defend that the object pronoun should be hyphenated to the verb that now precedes it (**Pode**): **Pode-me dizer onde é a saída?**

Please see also pp 89–90, 153, 219–20 and 232–3.

(C) The verb haver

For the one-syllable forms of this verb these two spellings occur:

hei-de, hás-de, há-de, hão-de   or   **hei de, hás de, há de, hão de**

Please see also pp 129–30.

PORTUGUESE–ENGLISH VOCABULARY

The words listed below can be used on both sides of the Atlantic. Where there is a difference, the word is followed by the sign (Eur.) or (Br.), which stand, respectively, for European and Brazilian.

a *the* (f); *you* (f); *her, it*; *at, to*
à (= a + a)
abaixo *below*
aberto *open*
abertura (f) *opening*; horas de abertura *opening hours*
abril, Abril *April*
abrir *to open*
abundar *to abound*
acabar *to finish, be over*; acabar de... *to have just...*
acampar *to camp*
aceitar *to accept*
acender *to light* (fire); *to switch / turn on*
acerca de *about*
aceso *on* (light)
achar *to find*; *to think*; que tal acha...? *what do you think of...?*
acidente (m) *accident*
acima *above*
acompanhar *to accompany*
aconselhável *advisable*
acontecer *to happen*
acordo (m) *agreement*; de acordo com *according to*
açoriano *from the Azores, Azorean*
acreditar *to believe*
actividade (Eur.), atividade (Br.) *activity*
actual (Eur.), atual (Br.) *present*
açúcar (m) *sugar*
adequado *appropriate*
adeus *goodbye*
adiantado *early*; *fast* (time)
adoecer *to fall ill*
adorar *to adore, love*
adquirir *to acquire*; *to obtain*
adulto (m) *adult*
aeromoço (m) (Br.) *air steward*
aeroporto (m) *airport*

afastar *to move away*
agência (f) *agency, office*; agência de viagens *travel agent*
agora *now*
agosto, Agosto (m) *August*
agradável *pleasing, pleasant*
agradecer *to thank*; desde já agradeço *thanking you in anticipation* (letter)
água (f) *water*; água mineral *mineral water*; água potável *drinking water*; água tónica (Eur.) / tônica (Br.) *tonic water*
aguardar *to await*
aí *there*
ainda *still*; ainda não *not yet*
ajudar *to help*
albergue (m) *hostel*
álcool (m) *alcohol*
aldeia (f) *village*
além de *beyond*; *besides*
alface (f) *lettuce*
alfândega (f) *Customs*
algodão (m) *cotton*
algum *some, any*
ali *there* (*see also* lá)
aliança (de casamento) (f) *wedding ring*
alimentação (f) *food*
alimento (m) *foodstuff*
almoçar *to have lunch*
almoço (m) *lunch*; pequeno almoço (Eur.) *breakfast*
almofada (f) *cushion*; *pillow* (Eur.)
alojamento (m) *accommodation*
altitude (f) *altitude*
alto *tall*; *high*; alto mar *deep sea*
alugar *to hire, rent, let*
aluguel (Br.), aluguer (Eur.) (m) *rental*
alvorada (f) *dawn*

amanhã *tomorrow*

amar *to love*

amarelo *yellow*

amável *kind, polite*

ambiente (m) *environment; atmosphere*

ambos *both*

ambulância (f) *ambulance*

americano *from America, American*

amigo (m) *friend*

amor (m) *love*

andar *to walk, move along*

andar (m) *floor* (level); andar térreo *ground floor*

anel (m) *ring*

angolano *from Angola, Angolan*

animal (m) *animal*

aniversário (m) *birthday*; aniversário de casamento *wedding anniversary*

ano (m) *year*; ter ... anos *to be ... years old*; fazer... anos *to become... years old*; Ano Novo *New Year*

antecedência (f): com antecedência *in advance*

anterior *former*

antes *before*

antigo *ancient, former, old*

anúncio (m) *advertisement*

ao (= a + o)

apagar *to put out* (fire); *to switch off* (light)*; to erase*

aparelho (m) *apparatus*; aparelho digestivo *digestive system*; aparelho de rádio *radio set*

apartamento (m) *apartment, flat; bed sitter; hotel room with ensuite facilities*

apelido (m) (Eur.) *surname*

apenas *only*

aperitivo (m) *aperitif ; appetizer*

apertado *tight*

apertar *to hold tight; to fasten*; apertar a mão *to shake hands*

apontar *to point*

após *after, upon*

aposentado *retired*

apreciar *to appreciate; to enjoy*

aprender *to learn*

apresentar *to present; to introduce*

aproveitar *take* (opportunity, advantage)

aproximadamente *approximately*

aproximar *to draw near*

aquático *aquatic, water* (sport)

aquecimento central (m) *central heating*

aquele *that, that one* (m); (*see also* esse)

aqui *here*

aquilo *that*; (*see also* isso)

ar (m) *air*; ar condicionado *air conditioning*; *look* (appearance)

área (f) *area*

armário (m) *cupboard; wardrobe*

armazém (m) *warehouse; grocery store*

arquitectura (Eur.), arquitetura (Br.) (f) *architecture*

arrumar *to tidy up; put in order*

arte (f) *art*

artesanal *craft* (product)

artificial *artificial; man-made*

artigo (m) *article; item*; artigos regionais *regional craft*

ascensor (m) *lift, elevator*

assim *like this*

assinalar *to mark*

assinar *to sign*

assinatura (f) *signature*

até *until, up to, as far as*

atender a *to see to, attend to*; *serve*

atracção (Eur.), atração (Br.) (f) *attraction*

atrás (de) *behind; at the back*

atrasado *late; slow* (time)

atravessar *to cross (over)*

atropelado *run over*

atum (m) *tuna fish*

aula (f) *class lesson*

auscultador (m) (Eur.) *receiver* (telephone)

australiano *from Australia, Australian*

auto-estrada (f) *motorway, expressway*

auto-serviço (m) *self-service*

autocarro (Eur.) (m) *bus, coach*

autodidacta (Eur.), autodidata (Br.) (m/f) *self-taught person*

autolocadora (f) *car rental agency*
automóvel (m) *automobile, car*
autonomia (f) *autonomy,*
independence
avariado *out of order, damaged*
ave (f) *bird*; ave(s) *poultry*
avenida (f) *boulevard*
aventura (f) *adventure*
avião (m) *aeroplane, aircraft*
avô (m) *grandfather*
azeitona (f) *olive*
azul *blue*

bacalhau (m) *cod, dried cod*
bacon (m) (Br.) *bacon*
bagagem (f) *baggage*
baile (m) *dance*; *ball*
baixo *low*; *short, small* (people)
baixo: em baixo *below*; lá/aqui em
baixo *downstairs, at the bottom*;
em baixo de (Eur.), embaixo de
(Br.) *underneath*
balcão (m) *counter*; *circle*
(theatre); *balcony* (Br.)
banca de jornais (f) *newspaper*
stand
bancada (f) *bench*
banco (m) *bank*; *stool*
banheira (f) *bathtub*
banheiro (m) (Br.) *bathroom*;
toilet
banho (m) *bath*; tomar banho *to*
have a bath (wash), *bathe, go*
into the water (beach)
bar (m) *bar*
barato *cheap, inexpensive*
barba (f) *beard*; fazer a barba *to*
have a shave
barbeiro (m) *barber*
barco (m) *boat*
barraca (f) *hut, tent*
barro (m) *earthenware*
barulhento *noisy*
barulho (m) *noise*
bastante *enough*
batata (f) *potato*; batata frita
chip; batatinha de pacote *crisp*
baunilha (f) *vanilla*
bebé (Eur.), bebê (Br.) (m/f) *baby*
beber *to drink*
bebida (f) *drink, beverage*

beijo (m) *kiss*
belo *beautiful*
bem *well*; *thoroughly*; *properly*,
quite; está bem! *that's all*
right!, okay!
biblioteca (f) *library*
bicha (f) (Eur.) *line, queue*; *row*
bife (m) *(beef) steak*
bilhete (m) *ticket*; bilhete de
identidade (Eur.) *identity card*
bilhete postal (m) (Eur.) *postcard*
(*see* postal)
bilheteira (Eur.), bilheteria (Br.)
(f) *ticket office*
biquíni (m) *bikini*
bisnaga (f) *tube*
blusa (f) *blouse*
boa *good* (f)
boate (Br.), buate (Eur.) (f) *night*
club
bocadinho (m) *small bit*
boião (m) (Eur.) *jar*
boletim meteorológico (m)
weather report, forecast
bolo (m) *cake*
bolsa (f) *handbag*; *purse*
bom *good* (m)
bombeiro (m) *fireman*
bonde (m) (Br.) *tram*
bonito *pretty*; *handsome*
botão (m) *button*
branco *white*
brasileiro *from Brazil, Brazilian*
breve: em breve *soon*
brinquedo (m) *toy*
britânico *from Britain, British*
buscar *to seek*; ir/vir buscar *to*
fetch, collect

cá *here*
cabeleireiro (m) *hairdresser*
cabelo (m) *hair*
cabo-verdiano *from Cape Verde,*
Cape Verdean
caça (f) *game*; *shooting*
cachorro (m) *puppy*; *dog* (Br.)
cadeira (f) *chair*
café (m) *coffee*; café da manhã
(Br.) *breakfast*
cair *to fall, fall over*
cais (m) *quay*; *platform* (Eur.)

caixa (f) *box*; *cashdesk*; *till*;
check-out; caixa de correio
letter box
calça/s (f) *trousers*
calçado (m) *footwear*
calção / calções de banho (m)
swimming trunks
calçar *to put on* (shoes, gloves)
calmo *calm*
calor (m) *heat*
cama (f) *bed*; cama de casal
double bed; cama de solteiro
single bed
câmara municipal (f) *town
council*; *town hall* (Eur.)
câmbio (m) *foreign exchange*
caminhar *to walk, progress*
caminho (m) *way, route*
camioneta (f) *coach* (Eur.); *van*
(Br.)
campeonato (m) *championship*
campismo (m) *camping*
campista (m/f) *camper*
campo (m) *field*; *countryside*;
ground, court (sport)
canadense, canadiano (Eur.) *from
Canada, Canadian*
canal (m) *channel*; *canal*
canção (f) *song*
candidato (m) *candidate* (exam,
job)
candidatura (f) *application*
caneta (f) *pen*
cansado *tired*
cantar *to sing*
canto (m) *corner* (inside of angle)
cão (m) *dog*
capital (f) *capital city*
cara (f) *face*
característica (f) *characteristic,
feature*
caravana (f) *caravan*
cardápio (m) (Br.) *menu card*
cargo (m) *post* (job)
carnaval (m) *carnival*
carne (f) *meat*
caro *dear, expensive*
carro (m) *car*; de carro *by car*
carta (f) *letter*; carta de condução
(Eur.) *driving licence*
cartão (m) *card*; cartão de crédito

credit card; cartão de visita
calling card
cartão postal (m) (Br.) *postcard*
(*see* postal)
carteira (f) *wallet*; carteira de
motorista (Br.) *driving licence*;
carteira de identidade (Br.)
identity card
casa (f) *house*; *home*; em casa
at home; para casa *home* (going
to); casa de banho (Eur.)
bathroom; toilet
casaco (m) *coat*
casado *married*
casal (m) *couple*
casamento (m) *marriage, wedding*
casar-se *to get married*
caso (m) *case*; (em) caso (de) *in
case of*
castanho *brown*
castelo (m) *castle*
católico *catholic*
catorze *fourteen*
causa (f) *cause*; por causa de
because
cavalheiro (m) *gentleman*
cebola(f) *onion*
cedo *early*
cem *a hundred*
centavo (m) *cent*
cento (m) *a hundred*; por cento
percent
central *central*
centro (m) *centre*; centro
comercial *shopping centre*
(Eur.)
cereal (m) *cereal*
certeza (f) *certainty*; ter (a) certeza
to be sure
certo *right*; certo! *okay!*
cerveja (f) *beer*
chá (m) *tea*
chamar *to call*; *to send for*
chamar-se *to be called*
chão (m) *floor, ground*
chave (f) *key*
chávena (f) *cup*
chegada (f) *arrival*
chegar *to arrive*
cheio *full, complete*
cheque (m) *cheque*; cheque de

viagem *traveller's cheque*
chorar *to cry, weep*
chumbo (m) *lead*
chuva (f) *rain*
chuveiro (m) *shower*
cidade (f) *town, city*; cidade natal *native town, home town*
cima: em cima *above*; lá/aqui em baixo *upstairs, at the top*; em cima de *on top of*; por cima de *over*
cimo (m) *top*
cinco *five*
cinema (m) *cinema*
cinquenta (Eur.), cinqüenta (Br.) *fifty*
cinto (m) *belt*
cinza (f) *ash*; *grey* (Br.)
cinzento *grey* (Eur.)
circundar *to surround*
clara (f) *egg-white*
claro *light* (luminosity)
classe (f) *class*
clima (m) *climate*
clube (m) *club*
cobertor (m) *blanket*
cobrar *to cash*
cobrir *to cover*
coco (m) *coconut*
coisa (f) *thing*; alguma coisa *something*
colcha (f) *bedspread*
colega (m/f) *colleague*; *classmate*
colégio (m) *school, college*
colher (f) *spoon*
colocar *to place, put*
com *with*
combinação (f) *combination*; *slip* (underwear)
combinar *to arrange, agree*
comboio (m) (Eur.) *train*
combustível (m) *fuel*
começar *to start, begin*
começo (m) *start, beginning*
comer *to eat*; dar de comer a *to feed*
comerciante (m/f) *business person*
comida (f) *food*
comigo *with me*
como *how*; *like*; *as*
companhia (f) *company*
comparecer *to attend* (function)

completamente *completely, totally*
completo *complete*
compra (f) *purchase*; fazer compras *to go shopping*
comprar *to buy*
compreender *to understand*
comprido *long*; ao comprido *lengthways*
comprimento (m) *length*
computador (m) *computer*
comunicar *communicate, inform*
conceder *to grant*; *to give*
concerto (m) *concert*
concordar *to agree*
conduzir (Eur.) *to drive* (vehicle)
conhecer *to know*; *to get to know*; *to meet for the first time*
conhecido (m) *acquaintance*
conhecimento (m) *knowledge*
conjunto (m) *collection*; *group*; *outfit* (clothes)
connosco (Eur.), conosco (Br.) *with us*
consertar *to repair, mend*
considerar *to consider*; *to regard*
consistir em *to consist of*
constipação (f) (Eur.) *cold* (health condition)
constipado: estar constipado (Eur.) *to have a cold*
construir *to build*
consulado (m) *consulate*
consulta (f) *consultation, appointment*
consultório (m) *surgery*
conta (f) *sum*; *bill*; *account*
contar *to count*; *to narrate, tell*; a contar de *counting from*
contente *happy, pleased*
contínuo *continuous*
conto (m) *story, tale*; *a thousand escudos* (Eur.)
contra *against*
controle (m) *controle*
conversa, conversação (f) *conversation*
conversar *to talk*
convidar *to invite*
convir *to suit*; *be convenient*
convite (m) *invitation*
copo (m) *glass, cup*

cor (f) *colour*
corredor (m) *corridor*; *passageway*
correio (m) *post office*; *mail*; pelo correio *by post*
correr *to run*
correspondência (f) *mail, correspondence*
corrigir *to correct*
cortar *to cut*
costa (f) *coast, coastline*
costumar *to use to*
couro (m) *leather*
couve (f) *cabbage*
cozer *to boil, cook*
cozinha (f) *kitchen*
creme de barbear (m) *shaving cream*
creme dental (m) (Br.) (*see* pasta de dentes)
crer *to believe*
criança (f) *child*
cruzamento (m) *crossroads, junction*
cuidado (m) *care*; cuidado! *watch out!*
cultivo (m) *cultivation*
cultura (f) *culture*
cumprimentos (m) *regards*
curso (m) *course, course of studies*
curto *short* (length or duration)
custar *to cost*

da (de + a)
dali (= de + ali)
daquele (= de + aquele)
daqui (= de + aqui)
daquilo (= de + aquilo)
dar *to give*; dar para *to look on to*
data (f) *date*
de *of*; *from*; *by*
décimo *tenth*
declarar *to declare, say*
defeito (m) *defect*; com defeito *out of order* (Br.)
deficiente (m) *handicapped person*
deitar-se *to lie down*; *to go to bed*
deixar *to leave* (abandon); *to allow*; deixar de... *to stop...*
dela (= de + ela)

dele (= de + ele)
demais *too, too much*
demorar *to take time*; *to delay*
dentista (m/f) *dentist*
dentro *in, inside*; dentro de *within* (time)
depois *after, afterwards, then*
depositar *to put in, deposit*
depressa *quickly*; depressa! *hurry!*
desafiador *challenging*
desaparecer *to disappear*
desarranjado *out of order* (Br.)
descalçar *to take off* (shoes, gloves)
descansar *to rest*
descascar *to remove shell or peel*
descer *to go/come down*
descobrir *to discover*
desconhecido *unknown*
descontar *to cash* (cheque)
desculpar *to excuse*; *to forgive*
desculpe *sorry*; *excuse me*
desde *since*; desde já *from now*
desejar *to desire, wish*
desfiar *to reduce to threads*
desfile (m) *parade*
desligar *to disconnect*
desodorante (Br.), desodorizante (Eur.) (m) *deodorant*
despir *to take off* (clothes)
despir-se *to get undressed*
desporto (m) (Eur) *sport*
desse (= de + esse) (*see also* dar)
deste (de + este)
destinatário (m) *addressee*
destino (m) *destination*
detestar *to dislike strongly, detest*
devagar *slowly*
dever *to owe*; *should, must, ought to*; *to be likely to*
dez *ten*
dezanove (Eur.), dezenove (Br.) *nineteen*
dezasseis (Eur), dezesseis (Br.) *sixteen*
dezassete (Eur), dezesete (Br.) *seventeen*
dezembro, Dezembro (m) *December*
dezoito *eighteen*
dia (m) *day*; bom dia *good*

morning; dia útil *working day*;
dia de anos (Eur.) *birthday*
dia-a-dia (m) *daily life*
diálogo (m) *dialogue*
diária (f) *daily cost*
diário *daily*
diarreia (Eur.), diarréia (Br.) (f)
diarrhoea
dicionário (m) *dictionary*
dieta (f) *diet*
diferente *different*
diga (*see* dizer)
dinheiro (m) *money*; (dinheiro)
trocado *small change*
diploma (m) *certificate, diploma*
direcção (Eur.), direção (Br.) (f)
direction
directo (Eur.), direto (Br.) *direct*
direita (f) *right*; à direita *on/to*
the right
direito *right*; *straight*
direito de importação (m) *import*
duty
dirigir *to direct*; *to drive* (vehicle)
(Br.)
discoteca (f) *discotheque, disco*
disse (*see* dizer)
disso (= de + isso)
distinção (f) *distinction*
disto (= de + isto)
divertir-se *to enjoy oneself*
divorciado *divorced*
diz (*see* dizer)
dizer *to say, inform, tell*; querer
dizer *to mean*
do (= de + o)
doce *sweet*
doce (m) *sweet, pudding*
documento (m) *document*
doente *ill*
doer *to hurt*
dois *two* (m)
dólar (m) *dollar*
domicílio (m) *home, residence*
domingo (m) *Sunday*
domínio (m) *command* (language)
dona de casa (f) *housewife*
dor (f) *pain, ache*
dormida (f) *sleep*; *sleeping*
accommodation
dormir *to sleep*

doze *twelve*
duas *two* (f)
ducha (f) (Br.), duche (m) (Eur.)
shower
duplo *double*
durante *for, during*
duzentos *two hundred*
dúzia (f) *dozen*; meia dúzia *half a*
dozen

e *and*
é (*see* ser)
edifício (m) *building*
efeito (m) *effect*
ela *she, it*
ele *he, it*
eléctrico (m) (Eur.) *tram*
elevado *high*
elevador (m) *lift, elevator*
em *in, on, at*
embarcar *to board*
embora *although* (*see also* ir)
embrulhar *to wrap up*
ementa (f) (Eur.) *menu card*
emergência (f) *emergency*
emitir *to issue*
empregado (m) *employee,*
assistant
emprego (m) *employment, job*
empurrar *to push*
encerrar *to close, shut*
encher *to fill*
encomenda (f) *parcel*
encontrar *to find, meet*
encontro (m) *meeting*; ponto de
encontro (m) *meeting point*
endereço (m) *address*
engenheiro (m) *engineer*
enorme *huge*
enquanto *while, whilst*
ensinar *to teach*
então *then*
entender *to understand*
entrada (f) *way in*; *entry*;
entrance; *hallway*;
admission ticket
entrar *to enter*; *go/come in*
entre *between, among* (*see also*
entrar)
entregar *to deliver*; *to hand*
in/over

entregue *delivered*
entrevista (f) *interview*
enumerar *to list*
envelope (m) *envelope*
enviar *to send*
equipado *equipped*
errado *wrong, incorrect*
erro (m) *error, mistake*
escada (f) *stairs*; escada rolante
 escalator
escocês *from Scotland, Scottish*
escola (f) *school*
escolher *to choose*
escova de dentes (f) *toothbrush*
escrever *to write*; como se
 escreve? *how do you spell it?*
escrito *written*
escritório (m) *office*
escudo (m) *unit of Portuguese
 currency*
escuro *dark*
escutar *to listen*
esforço (m) *effort*
esgotado *sold out*
espadim (m) *large sea fish*
especial *special*
espécie (f) *species; kind*
especialmente *particularly*
esperar *to wait, expect, hope*
esporte (m) (Br.) *sport*
esquecer(-se) *to forget*
esquerda (f) *left*; à esquerda *on/to
 the left*
esquina (f) *corner* (outside of
 angle)
esse *that, that one* (m); (*see also
 aquele*)
esta *this, this one* (f)
está (*see* estar)
estação (f) *station; season*
estacionamento (m) *parking*
estacionar *to park, wait*
estada, estadia (f) *stay*
estádio (m) *stadium*
estado (m) *state*
estado civil (m) *marital status*
estar *to be*; está bem *it's all right*
este *this, this one* (m)
este (m) *east* (*see also* leste)
estimar *to appreciate*; estimo as
 suas (rápidas) melhoras *I wish*

 you a speedy recovery
estômago (m) *stomach*
estrada (f) *open road*
estrangeiro *foreign*
estrangeiro (m) *abroad*
estreito *narrow*
estudante (m/f) *student*
estudar *to study*
eu *I*
europeu *European*
exactamente (Eur.), exatamente
 (Br.) *exactly*
exame (m) *examination*
excelente *excellent*
excepto (Eur.), exceto (Br.)
 except
excursão (f) *excursion*
exemplo (m) *example*; por
 exemplo *for instance*
exercício (m) *exercise*
êxito (m) *success*
experiência (f) *experience*
experimentar *to experiment, try*
expressão (f) *expression*
exterior (m) *outside, exterior*

faca (f) *knife*
faça (*see* fazer)
fácil *easy*
facilidade (f) *facility*
facto (Eur.), fato (Br.) (m) *fact*
factor (Eur.), fator (Br.) (m)
 factor
fadista (m/f) *'fado'-singer*
fado (m) *traditonal Portuguese
 song*; casa de fado(s) *'fado'-
 house*
falar *to speak*
falta (f) *lack*
faltar *to miss, be missing*
família (f) *family*
farmácia (f) *chemist's* (shop)
fatia (f) *slice*
fato (m) (Eur.) *suit*; (*see also
 facto*)
fato de banho (m) (Eur.) *bathing
 costume*
fauna (f) *fauna*
favor (m) *favour*; faça/faz/por
 favor *please, excuse me; please
 do*

favorito *favourite*
faz (*see* fazer)
fazer *to do; to make*
fechar *to close, shut*
federal *federal*
feito (*see* fazer)
felicidades (f) *all the best*
feliz *happy*
felizmente *fortunately*
feminino *female, feminine*
feriado (m) *holiday*
férias (f) *holidays, vacation*
ferir *to hurt, wound*
ferro (m) *iron*; estrada (Br.) /
  caminho (Eur.) de ferro *railways*
festa (f) *party, celebration*
fevereiro, Fevereiro (m) *February*
fiambre (m) (Eur.) *ham*
fica (*see* ficar)
ficar *to be; to be situated; to stay;*
  ficar com *to keep*
ficha (f) *form card; token*
fila (f) *line, queue; row*
filha (f) *daughter*
filho (m) *son*
fim (m) *end*; fim de semana
  weekend
finalidade (f) *purpose*
finalmente *finally, at last*
fingir *to pretend*
flexibilidade horária (f) *flexible
  time* (work)
flor (f) *flower*
flora (f) *flora*
fluentemente *fluently*
fogo (m) *fire*
foi (*see* ser *and* ir)
folheto (m) *leaflet*
fone (m) (Br.) *receiver*
  (telephone)
fora *out, outside*
forma (f) *shape;* em boa forma *fit*
formação (f) *studies, training*
formar-se *to graduate*
formulário (m) *form*
fotografia (f) *photograph;
  photography*
freguês (m) *customer*
frente (f) *front*; em frente de/a
  straight on/opposite
frequentar (Eur.), freqüentar (Br.)

attend (course)
frequente (Eur.), freqüente (Br.)
  frequent
frequentemente (Eur.),
  freqüentemente (Br.) *often*
frigorífico (m) (Eur.) *refrigerator*
frio *cold*
frio (m) *cold*
frito *fried*
fronteira (f) *frontier, border*
fruta (f) *fruit*
fui (*see* ser *and* ir)
fumador (Eur.), fumante (Br.)
  smoker
fumar *to smoke*
função (f) *function; role* (job)
funcionar *to work, function,
  operate*
fundo (m) *bottom; back* (room)
futebol (m) *soccer*
futuro (m) *future*

galeria (f) *gallery* (theatre);
  galeria de arte *art gallery*
galês *from Wales, Welsh*
ganhar *to earn, win*
garagem (f) *garage*
garantir *to guarantee*
garfo (m) *fork*
garrafa (f) *bottle* (beverage)
gás (m) *gas*; com gás *fizzy*; sem
  gás *still*
gasóleo (m) *diesel oil*
gasolina (f) *petrol*
gato (m) *cat*
geladeira (f) (Br.) *refrigerator*
gelado *frozen; ice-cold*
gelado (m) (Eur.) *ice lolly*
geleia (Eur.), geléia (Br.) (f) *fruit
  jelly/jam*
gema (f) *egg-yolk*
genro (m) *son-in-law*
gente (f) *people*; toda a gente
  every one
gentil *courteous, charming, kind*
geral *general*
gerente (m/f) *manager,
  manageress*
golfe (m) *golf*
gordo *fat*
gostar de *to like*; gostar muito de

... to like ... very much
governo (m) *government*
grama (m) *gram*
grande *large, big*
grátis, gratuito *free, without charge*
grau (m) *degree*
grave *serious*
grisalho *grey* (hair)
grupo (m) *group, party*
guarda (f) *guard, police*
guarda-chuva (m) *umbrella*
guarda-sol (m) *sunshade; parasol*
guardanapo (m) *napkin*
guichê (m) *service window* (bank, etc.)
guineense, guinéu *from Guinea-Bissau*
guitarra (f) *Portuguese lute*

há *for; ago; how long*; (*see also* haver)
habitante (m) *inhabitant*
habitualmente *usually*
haver *there to be; to exist; have* (auxiliary)
hei de *I will* (*see also* haver)
hipermercado (m) *hypermarket*
história (f) *history*
hoje *today*
homem (m) *man*
hora(s) (f) *hour(s); o'clock*; meia (hora) *half an hour, half past*; a que horas...? *at what time...?*; que horas são? *what time is it?*
horário (m) *timetable*
hospedeiro (de bordo) (m) (Eur.) *air steward*
hospital (m) *hospital*
hotel (m) *hotel*

ida (f) *going; one-way* (ticket)
ida e volta (f) *return, round-trip* (ticket)
idade (f) *age*
ideia (Eur.), idéia (Br.) (f) *idea*
identidade (f) *identity*
idioma (m) *language*
igreja (f) *church*
igual a *equal to; the same as*
igualmente *equally; likewise*

ilha (f) *island*
ímpar *odd* (number)
importância (f) *importance*; não tem importância *not to worry, it's all right*
importante *important; main*
imposto (m) *tax*
impressão digital (f) *fingerprint*
impresso (m) *printed paper; form*
incluir *to include; to enclose*
incomodar *to inconvenience, disturb*
incómodo (Eur.), incômodo (Br.) (m) *inconvenience*
indigestão (f) *indigestion*
individual *individual*
individualizar *to individualise*
indivíduo (m) *individual*
indústria (f) *industry*
inesquecível *unforgettable*
informação (f) *information*
informar *to inform; to report*
informática (f) *computing; computer science*
infracção (Eur.), infração (Br.) (f) *infringement*
inglês *from England, English*
inglês (m) *English* (language)
ingresso (m) (Br.) *admission ticket*
inicial *initial*
instalação (f) *facility*
instalar *to install*
instrução (f) *instruction; education*
insuficiente *insufficient*
integrado (em) *as part of*
interessado *interested*
interessante *interesting*
interesse (m) *interest*
interior *inner; inside*
internacional *international*
intérprete (m/f) *interpreter*
interurbano *long distance*
intervalo (m) *interval, break*
introdução (f) *introduction*
introduzir *to introduce, insert*
inverno, Inverno (m) *Winter*
iogurte (m) *yogurt*
ir *to go*; ir(-se) embora *to go away*; ir para casa *to go home*

irlandês *from Ireland, Irish*
irmã (f) *sister*
irmão (m) *brother*
irrigação (f) *irrigation*
isso *that*; (*see also* aquilo)
isto *this*

já *immediately*; *presently*;
 already; *ever*; já não (mais) *no
 longer*; já está! *done!*
janeiro, Janeiro (m) *January*
janela (f) *window*
jantar *to have dinner, the evening
 meal*; jantar fora *to eat out*
jantar (m) *dinner, evening meal*
jardim (m) *garden*
jogar *to play* (game)
jóia (f) *jewel*
jornal (m) *newspaper*
jovem *young*
julho, Julho (m) *July*
junho, Junho (m) *June*
juntamente *together*; *attached*
junto *next to, close by*

la *you, her, it*
lá *there* (*see also* ali)
lã (f) *wool*
lado (m) *side*; ao lado de *beside*;
 todo o lado *everywhere*
lanche (m) *snack*
laranja (f) *orange*
largo *wide*
largo (m) *square, precinct*; ao
 largo *off* (coast)
lata (f) *tin, can*
lavagem de roupa (f) *laundry
 service*
lavandaria (Eur.), lavanderia (Br.)
 (f) *launderette*
lavar *to wash*; lavar-se *to have a
 wash*
lazer (m) *leisure*
leitaria (Eur.), leiteria (Br.) (f) *dairy*
leite (m) *milk*
leito (m) *bed*
lembrança (f) *souvenir*
lembrar *to remind*; lembrar(-se)
 to remember
lençol (m) *sheet* (bcd)
lente de contacto (Eur.), contato

(Br.) (f) *contact lens*
ler *to read*
leste (m) *east* (*see also* este *and*
 ler)
levantar *to stand, pick up*;
 levantar-se *to stand up, get up*;
 to get up fom bed
levar *to take*; *to carry*; levar
 tempo *to require or take time*;
 to lead to
leve *light* (luminosity); *light*
 (weight) (*see also* levar)
lhe *(to) you, him*, her, *it*
libra (f) *pound*
lição (f) *lesson*
licença (f) *permission*
ligar *to connect*
limão (m) *lemon*
limpar *to clean, wipe clean*
limpeza (f) *cleaning*
limpo *clean*
lindo *beautiful*
língua (f) *tongue*; *language*
linha (f) *thread*; linha férrea
 railway
linho (m) *linen* (material)
liso *straight*; *plain* (pattern)
lista (f) *list*; lista dos telefones /
 telefónica (Eur.) / telefônica
 (Br.) *telephone directory*
literatura (f) *literature*
litoral (m) *coast, seaboard*
litro (m) *litre*
livraria (f) *bookshop*
livre *free, vacant*; *for hire*
livro (m) *book*
lixo (m) *rubbish, garbage*; *litter*
lo *you, him, it*
local (m) *site, place*
localização (f) *location*
logo *later*; *straightaway*
loja (f) *shop*
longe *far*
longo *long*; ao longo de *along*
louro *light brown*; *blond*
lua-de-mel (f) *honeymoon*
lugar (m) *place, space*; *seat*
luva (f) *glove*
luz (f) *light*

má *bad, evil* (f)

maçã (f) *apple*
maçaneta (f) *knob, handle*
madeira (f) *wood* (material)
madeirense *from Madeira, Madeiran*
madrugada (f) *early hours of the day, past midnight*
mãe (f) *mother*
magro *thin, slim*
maio, Maio (m) *May*
maiô (m) (Br.) *bathing costume*
maior *larger*; o maior *the largest*
mais *more*; o mais *the most*; mais (do) que *more than*
mal *badly*
mal (m) *harm*; não faz mal *never mind*; *it's all right* (in response to apology)
mala (de viagem) (f) *suitcase*
mandar *to be in charge*; *to order*; *send*; mandar consertar... *to have... repaired*
manhã (f) *morning*
manteiga (f) *butter*
manter-se *to remain, to stand/stay still*
manuscrito *handwritten*
mão (f) *hand*
mapa (m) *map*
máquina (f) *machine*; máquina fotográfica *photo camera*; máquina de filmar *movie / video camera*
mar (m) *sea*
maravilhoso *wonderful*
marcar *to mark*; *to book*
março, Março (m) *March*
marido (m) *husband*
marisco (m) *shellfish*
marmelada (f) *quince paste*
marrom (Br.) *brown*
mas *but*
masculino *male, masculine*
mau *bad, evil* (m)
máximo *maximum*
me *me, to me, for me*
medicamento (m) *medicine*
médico (m) *doctor*
meia (f) *sock, stocking*
meia-noite (f) *midnight*
meio (m) *half* ; ao meio *in half* ;

no meio *in the middle*
meio-dia (m) *midday*
melhor *better*; o melhor *the best*
menino (m) *young boy*
menor *smaller*; o menor *the smallest*
menos *less, fewer*; o menos *the least, fewest*
mensalmente *monthly*
mercearia (f) *grocer's* (shop)
mês (m) *month*
mesa (f) *table*
mesmo *same*; *really*; *right*; mesmo que *even if*
meter *to put (in)*; meter-se em *to get involved in*
metro (Eur.), metrô (Br.) (m) *underground train*
meu *my, mine* (m)
mil *thousand*
milhão *million*
mim *(to) me*
minha *my, mine* (f)
minuto (m) *minute*
misturar *to mix*
mobilado *furnished*
moçambicano *from Mozambique, Mozambican*
moço (m) *boy, young man*
moderno *modern*
moeda (f) *coin*
momento (m) *moment*
montanha (f) *mountain*
montra (f) (Eur.) *shop window*
morango (m) *strawberry*
morar *to live, be resident*
moreno *dark* (skin)
morrer *to die*
mostrar *to show*
motorista (m/f) *driver*
mudar *to change*; mudar-se *to move house*
muito *much*; *a lot of*; *very*
mulher (f) *woman*; *wife*
multa (f) *fine*
mundo (m) *world*; todo (o) mundo (Br.) *everyone*
museu (m) *museum*
música (f) *music*

na (= em + a)

nacional *national*
nacionalidade (f) *nationality*
nada *nothing* ; de nada *not at all*; não foi nada *not to worry, it's all right*
nadar *to swim*
não *no*; *not*; não mais *no longer*
nascer *to be born*
nascimento (m) *birth*
natal *native*
Natal (m) *Christmas*
natural *natural*; *native*
naturalmente *naturally*
natureza (f) *nature*
navegador (m) *navigator*
necessário *necessary*
negócio (m) *business*
negro *black*
nem *nor*; nem... nem... *neither... nor...*
nenhum *no, none*
neozelandês *from New Zealand, New Zealander*
neste (= em + este)
neto (m) *grandson*
ninguém *no-one*
nível (m) *level*
no (= em + o)
noite (f) *night*; boa noite *good night/evening*
noivado (m) *engagement*
noivo *engaged*; noivo (m) *fiancé*
nome (m) *name*; nome completo *full name*
nomeadamente *namely*
nono *ninth*
nora (f) *daughter-in-law*
normalmente *normally*; *usually*
norte (m) *north*
nós *we*
nos (= em + os); *(to/for) us, (to) ourselves*
nosso *our, ours*
nota (f) *note*
notar *to notice*
notícia (f) *news*
noticiário (m) *news bulletin*
novamente *anew, again*
nove *nine*
novecentos *nine hundred*
novembro, Novembro (m) *November*

noventa *ninety*
novo *new*; *young*
nublado *cloudy*
número (m) *number*
nunca *never*

o *the* (m); *you* (m); *him, it*
obrigada *thank you* (f), obrigado *thank you* (m)
obrigatório *obligatory*
observação (f) *observation*
obter *to obtain, get*
ocasionalmente *occasionally*
oceano (m) *ocean*
oculista (m/f) *optician*
óculos (m) *glasses, spectacles*; óculos de sol *sun glasses*
ocupação (f) *occupation*
ocupar *to occupy*
oeste (m) *west*
oferecer *to offer, to make a gift of*
oficial *official*
oi! (Br.) *hi!* (greeting)
oitavo *eighth*
oitenta *eighty*
oito *eight*
oitocentos *eight hundred*
olá! *hello!*; *hi!* (greeting)
óleo (m) *oil*
olhar *to look*; olhar por *to look after*
onde *where*
ônibus (m) (Br.) *bus, coach*
ontem *yesterday*
onze *eleven*
opcional *optional*
opinião (f) *opinion*
oportunidade (f) *opportunity*
óptimo (Eur.), ótimo (Br.) *excellent*
ora *now*; *well*
ordem (f) *order*; à ordem de *made out to* (cheque)
organização (f) *organisation*; *organising committee*
organizador (m) *organiser*
ou *or*; ou... ou... *either... or...*
ouro (m) *gold*
outono, Outono (m) *Autumn*
outro *other, another*
outubro, Outubro (m) *October*

ouvir *to hear*; ouvir com atenção
to listen to
ovo (m) *egg*

pacote (m) *packet*; *carton*
padaria (f) *bakery, baker's* (shop)
pagamento (m) *payment*
pagar *to pay*
pai (m) *father*
país (m) *country*
pais (m) *parents*
paisagem (f) *scenery*
palácio (m) *palace*
palavra (f) *word*
pane (f) *breakdown*
pão (m) *bread, loaf*
pãozinho (m) *roll* (bread)
papel (m) *paper*; papel higiénico
(Eur.), papel higiênico (Br.)
toilet paper
par *even* (number)
para *to, for*; (*see also* parar)
parabéns *congratulations*; *happy
birthday*
parada (f) (Br.) *stop*; parada de
ônibus *bus/coach stop*
paragem (f) (Eur.) *stop*; paragem de
autocarros *bus/coach stop*
paraíso (m) *paradise*
parar *to stop*
parcómetro (m) (Eur.) *parking
meter*
parecer *to appear, seem*
parede (f) *wall*
parente (m) *relative, relation*
parque (m) *park*; parque infantil
children's playground; parque
de campismo (Eur.) *camping /
caravanning site*
parquímetro (m) (Br.) *parking
meter*
parte (f) *part*; parte de trás *back*,
parte da frente *front*; outra parte
somewhere else; toda a parte
everywhere
participar *to take part*
partida (f) *departure*
partir *to leave, depart, set off*; *to
break*; a partir de *starting from*
Páscoa (f) *Easter*
passado *last, past*

passado: bem/mal passado *well
done / rare*
passageiro (m) *passenger*
passagem (f) *fare*
passaporte (m) *passport*
passar *to go past, by*; *to go
through*; *to spend* (time); *to pass*
(exam); *to iron* (clothes)
passatempo predilecto (Eur.),
passatempo predileto (Br.) (m)
hobby
passe (m) *pass*; fotografia tipo
passe *ID photograph*; (*see also*
passar)
passear *to go for a leisurely walk
or ride*; *to take for a walk*
passeio (m) *leisure walk or ride*
pasta de dentes (f) *toothpaste*
pastelaria (f) *cake shop*
património (Eur.), patrimônio
(Br.) (m) *heritage*
pé (m) *foot*; a pé *on foot*; de/em
pé *standing*
peão (Eur.), pedestre (Br.) (m)
pedestrian
pedaço (m) *piece*
pedir *to ask for*
pegar *to grab, pick up*; *to take
hold of*
peixe (f) *fish*
pele (f) *skin*
pelo (= por + o)
pena: ter pena *to feel sorry*
penalidade (f) *penalty*
pendurar *to hang*
pensão (f) *boarding house*
pensar *to think*; pensar em *to
think of / about*
penúltimo *penultimate*
pequeno *small*
perceber *to understand*; *to realize*
perder *to lose*; *to miss*
perfil (m) *profile*
pergunta (f) *question*; fazer uma
pergunta *to ask a question*
perguntar *to ask, enquire*
perigo (m) *danger*
permanent *permanent*
permitir *to allow*
pertencer a *to belong to*
perto *near*; perto daqui *or* aqui

perto *nearby*
pesca (f) *fishing*
pessoa (f) *person*; pessoas *people*
pessoal (m) *personnel, staff*
picolé (m) (Br.) *(ice) lolly*
pimenta (f) *pepper*
pior *worse*; o pior *the worst*
piorar *to get worse*
piscina (f) *swimming pool*
piso (m) *floor, level*
placa (f) *plate*; *signpost*; placa de
    matrícula (Eur.) / licença (Br.)
    car registration plate
plano (m) *plan*; primeiro plano
    forefront
plástico *plastic*; artes plásticas
    visual arts
plataforma (f) *platform*
pneu (m) *tyre*
pode *(see* poder)
poder *can*; *may*
pois não (Br.) *please do*
polícia (f) *police*
ponte (f) *bridge*
ponto (m) *point*; *dot*; ponto de
    táxi (Br.) *taxi rank*
popular *popular*; *pop*
por *for*; *per*; *a/an*; por causa de
    because; por que...? *why...?*; por
    quê? *why?*
pôr *to put*; *to put on* (clothes,
    shoes)
por aqui *hereabouts*; *this way*
porque *because*
porta (f) *door*
porto (m) *port, harbour*; *port*
    (drink)
português *from Portugal,*
    Portuguese
português (m) *Portuguese*
    (language)
possível *possible*
posso *(see* poder)
possuir *to possess, have*
postal (m) *postcard*
posto de abastecimento /
    combustível / gasolina (m)
    filling station
pouco *little, few*; um pouco *a little*
praça (f) *square*; *market place*;
    praça de táxis *taxi rank*

praia (f) *beach*; *seaside*
prata (f) *silver*
prateleira (f) *shelf*
praticamente *practically*
praticar *to practise*
prato (m) *plate*; *dish*
prazer (m) *pleasure*; muito prazer
    delighted to meet you
prazo (m) *period*; *time limit*
precisar (de) *to need*
preço (m) *price, cost*
preencher *to complete*
prefeitura municipal (f) (Br.) *town*
    hall
preferir *to prefer*
premer *to press*
preocupado *worried*
preocupar-se *to worry*
preparar *to prepare*
presente *present*
presente (m) *present, gift*
pressa (f) *hurry*; *haste*
pressionar *to put on pressure*; *to*
    press (button)
presunto (m) *bacon* (Eur.);
    presunto (cozido) (Br.) *ham*
pretender *to intend*; *to ask for*
    (requirement)
preto *black*
primavera, Primavera (f) *Spring*
primeiro *first*
principal *principal, main*
principalmente *mainly*
prioridade (f) *priority, right of*
    way
prisão de ventre (f) *constipation*
privado *private*
procurar *to look for*
produzir *to produce*
professor (m) *teacher*
profissão (f) *profession, job*
profissional *professional*
profissionalismo (m)
    professionalism
proibição (f) *prohibition*
proibir *to forbid*
pronto *ready*
propício *propitious, favourable*
próprio *own*; a mim próprio
    (to) myself
proteger *to protect*

prova (f) *proof*; prova de
    pagamento *proof of payment*;
    test (exam)
provar *to try, taste*; *to prove*
próximo *next*; *near*
publicação (f) *publication*
publicar *to publish*
puder (*see* poder)
puxar *to pull*

qual *which, what*
qualidade (f) *quality*
qualquer *any*
quando *when*
quantia (f) *amount, sum*
quantidade (f) *quantity*
quanto *how much*; quantos/as
    how many
quarenta *forty*
quarta-feira (f) *Wednesday*
quarto *fourth*
quarto (m) *quarter*
quarto (m) *room*; quarto (de
    dormir) *bedroom*; *hotel room*
quase *almost*
quatro *four*
quatrocentos *four hundred*
que *what, which, that, who; that*
    (conjunction)
quê *what*; para quê? *what for?*;
    não tem de quê *not at all*
quebrar *to break*
queijo (m) *cheese*
queimadura de sol (f) *sunburn*
queira (*see* querer)
quem *who*
quente *hot, warm*
querer *to want, will, wish*
queria (*see* querer)
quilo, quilograma (m) *kilogram*
quilómetro (Eur.), quilômetro
    (Br.) (m) *kilometer*
quinhentos *five hundred*
quinta-feira (f) *Thursday*
quinto *fifth*
quinze *fifteen*; quinze dias
    a fortnight

rádio (m) *radio*
rapaz (m) *boy, young man, lad*
rápido *rapid, quick*

raramente *seldom*
raro *rare*
razão (f) *reason*; ter razão *to be
    right*
real (m) *unit of Brazilian
    currency*
realizar-se *to take place*; *to come
    true* (dream)
receber *to receive*
receita (f) *recipe*; *prescription*
recepção (f) *reception*
recibo (m) *receipt*
recomendar *to recommend*
reconhecer *to recognise*; *to
    acknowledge*
refeição (f) *meal*
refogar *to sauté*
reformado (Eur.) *retired*
região (f) *region*
regra (f) *rule*
regularmente *regularly*
reinado (m) *reign*
relógio (m) *watch, clock*
remédio (m) *medicine*; *remedy*
remoto *remote, distant, far off*
remuneração (f) *remuneration*
repetir *to repeat*
repor *to put back*
repouso (m) *rest*
reputação (f) *reputation*
requisito (m) *requirement*
rés-do-chão (m) (Eur.) *ground
    floor*
reserva (f) *reservation, booking*
reserva natural (f) *nature reserve*
reservar *to reserve, book*
resfriado (m) (Br.) *cold* (health
    condition)
resfriado: estar resfriado (Br.)
    to have a cold
residência (f) *residence*
residencial *residence / home*
    (address)
resolver *to solve* (problem);
    to decide
respeitar *to respect, observe*
responder *to answer*; *to reply*
resposta (f) *answer*; *reply*
ressalva (f) *correction* (in
    document)
restaurante (m) *restaurant*

resultado (m) *result*
reunião (f) *meeting*
reunir *to bring together; to combine*
revista (f) *magazine*
rico *rich*
rio (m) *river*
rolha (f) *cork stopper*
rolo (m) *roll*
roubar *to steal*
roupa (f) *clothes*
roupão (m) *dressing gown*
rua (f) *street, urban road*
ruim *bad*

sábado (m) *Saturday*
saber *to know; to learn; can*
sabonete (m) *toilet soap*
sabor (m) *flavour*
saca-rolhas (m) *corkscrew*
saco (m) *bag, carrier bag*
saída (f) *way out, exit*
sair *to go/come out; to leave*
sal (m) *salt*
sala (f) *room* (house)
salada (f) *salad*
saldo (m) *balance* (account)
salsicha (f) *sausage*
sandes (f) *or* sande (Eur.) *sandwich*
sanduíche (f) (Eur.), (m) (Br.) *sandwich*
sanitário (m) *toilet*
são (*see* ser)
são-tomense, tomeense *from São Tomé and Príncipe*
sapato (m) *shoe*
satisfeito *pleased, satisfied*
saudade (f) *longing*
saúde (f) *health*; saúde! *cheers!*
se *one, oneself; if, whether*
secador de cabelo (m) *hairdryer*
século (m) *century*
sede (f) *thirst*; estar com *or* ter sede *to be thirsty*
seguinte *following*
seguir *to go, follow*
segunda-feira (f) *Monday*
segundo *second* (sequence)
segundo (m) *second* (clock)
segurança *security; safety*
seguro (m) *insurance*
sei (*see* saber)

seis *six*
seiscentos *six hundred*
selo (m) *stamp*
sem *without*
semáforo (m) *traffic lights*
semana (f) *week*
sempre *always*
senhor (m) *gentleman, sir; you*
senhora (f) *lady, madam; you*
sensível *sensitive*
sentar *to sit*; sentar-se *to sit down*
sentir *to feel*; sentir a falta *to miss*
ser *to be*
serviço (m) *service*; de serviço *on duty*
servir *to serve; to be fitting; to fit*
sessenta *sixty*
sete *seven*
setecentos *seven hundred*
setembro, Setembro (m) *September*
setenta *seventy*
sétimo *seventh*
seu *your, yours, his, her, hers, its, their, theirs* (m)
sexo (m) *sex*
sexta-feira (f) *Friday*
sexto *sixth*
significar *to mean*
sim *yes*
simpático *nice, friendly*
simples *single* (hotel room, etc.)
sinal (m) *sign; signal*
sinto (*see* sentir)
só, somente *only*; não só... mas também... *not only... but also...*
só, sozinho *alone, by oneself*
sob *under*
sobre *on; upon* (subject)
sobremesa (f) *dessert*
sobrenome (m) (Br.) *surname*
socorro! *help!*
sofrer *to suffer*
sofrido *long-suffering*
sogra (f) *mother-in-law*
sogro (m) *father-in-law*
sol (m) *sun; sunshine*
solteiro *single, unmarried*
sonho (m) *dream*
sopa (f) *soup*
sorriso (m) *smile*
sorte (f) *luck*; boa sorte! *good luck!*

sorvete (m) *ice-cream, sorbet*
sotaque (m) *accent* (speech)
sou (*see* ser)
sua *your, yours, his, her, hers, its, their, theirs* (f)
suave *gentle*
subir *to go/come up*
submeter-se a *take* (exam)
suco (m) (Br.) *juice*; suco de laranja *orange juice*
sugerir *to suggest*
sujo *dirty*
sul (m) *south*
sul-africano *from South Africa , South African*
sumo (m) (Eur.) *juice*; sumo de laranja *orange juice*
superfície (f) *area* (dimension)
supermercado (m) *supermarket*
suspensão (f) *suspension*

tal *such*
talvez *perhaps*
tamanho (m) *size*
também *also, too, as well*
tanto *so much*; tanto... quanto/como... *as/so much... as...*; tantos.. quanto/como... *as/so many... as...*; tanto... como... *both... and...*
tão *so*; tão... quanto/como... *as/so... as...*
tarde *late*
tarde (f) *afternoon/evening*; boa tarde *good afternoon/evening*
tarifa (f) *rate*
táxi (m) *taxi*
teatro (m) *theatre*; *drama*
tecla (f) *key* (pressing)
tecto (Eur.), teto (Br.) (m) *ceiling*
telefonar *to telephone*
telefone (m) *telephone*; telefone portátil *mobile phone*
telefonista (m/f) *telephone operator*
televisão (f) *television*
televisor (m) *TV set*
tem (*see* ter)
tema (m) *topic*
temperatura (f) *temperature*
tempo (m) *time*; *weather*

tencionar *to intend*
tenda (f) *tent*
tenho (*see* ter)
ter *to have*; ter de/que *to have to*
terça-feira (f) *Tuesday*
terceiro *third*
terço (m) *third (part)*
terno (m) (Br.) *suit*
terra (f) *earth*; *soil*; *land*; *(home) land*; terra natal *native/home land*
território (m) *territory*; *land*
tia (f) *aunt*
tio (m) *uncle*
típico *typical*
tira (f) *strip*; em tirinhas *shredded*
tirar *to take away/out/off*
toalete (Br.), toilete (Eur.) (m) *toilet*
toalha (f) *towel*; *table cloth*
tocar *to touch*; *to ring*; *to play* (instrument)
todo *the whole*; *all*; *every (one)*
toldo (m) *awning, shade*
tomada de corrente (f) *power point*
tomar *to take*; *to have* (drink, refreshment, medicine)
tomate (m) *tomato*
torcer *to twist*; *to sprain* (foot)
torre (f) *tower*
trabalhar *to work*
trabalho (m) *work*; *job*
tradição (f) *tradition*
tradutor (m) *translator*
traga (*see* trazer)
transbordo (m) *change, transfer* (passengers)
transeunte (m/f) *passer-by*
transportar *to carry*; *to transport*
transporte público (m) *public transport*
transversal *cross* (street, road)
tratar (de) *to treat*; *to deal with*; tratar por *to address as*
travessa (f) *serving dish*; *alley*
travesseiro (m) *bolster* (Eur.); *pillow* (Br.)
trazer *to bring, carry*
treino (m) *training*

trem (m) (Br.) *train*
três *three*
treze *thirteen*
trezentos *three hundred*
trilho (m) *path; track*
trinta *thirty*
trocar *to change*
troco (m) *change*
trouxe (*see* trazer)
tu *you*
tubo (m) *tube* (container)
tudo *all, everything*
turismo (m) *tourism; tourist office*
turista (m/f) *tourist*

uísque (m) *whisky*
ultimamente *lately*
último *last; latest*; nos últimos
dias *in the last few days*
ultrapassar *to overtake*
um *a, an; one* (m)
uma *a, an; one* (f)
universidade (f) *university*
urgência (f) *emergency*
urgente *urgent*
usar *to use; to wear*
útil *useful*

vacina (f) *vaccine*
vaga (f) *vacancy*
vago *vacant*
vai (*see* ir)
válido *valid*
valor (m) *value*
varanda (f) *balcony; verandah*
variedade (f) *variety*
vários *several*
vazio *empty*
vê (*see* ver)
vejo (*see* ver)
vela (f) *sailing* (sport); *sail*
velho *old*; (*see also* ano)
velocidade (f) *speed*; excesso de
velocidade (m) *speeding*
vem (*see* vir); que vem *coming,
next*
venda (f) *sale*
vendedor (m) *shop assistant;
seller*
vender *to sell*
venho (*see* vir)
vento (m) *wind*

ver *to see*
verão, Verão (m) *Summer*
verde *green; type of wine*
verificar *to check*
vermelho *red*
vestido (m) *dress, frock*
vestir *to put on* (clothes)
vestir-se *to get dressed*
vez (f) *time, occasion*; às vezes
sometimes; muitas vezes *often*;
outra vez *again*; poucas vezes
seldom
viagem (f) *journey*; boa viagem!
have a nice journey!
vida (f) *life*
vídeo (m) *video*
vidro (m) *glass; glass jar, bottle
(Br.)*
vigilância (f) *vigilance*
vinho (m) *wine*; lista / carta dos
vinhos *wine list*
vinte *twenty*
viola (f) *guitar*
violão (m) *guitar*
vir *to come*
virar *to turn; to turn over*
visita (f) *visit*; visita de negócio(s)
business visit; fazer uma visita
a... *to visit, pay a call to...*
visitar *to visit*
vista (f) *view*
visto (m) *visa*
vitrine (f) (Br.) *shop window*
viúva (f), viúvo (m) *widow,
widower*
viver *to live*
você *you*
volta (f) *turn*; estar de volta *to be
back*
voltar *to return, go/come back*;
voltar a... *to (do) again*
vontade (f) *will, wish*; à vontade *at
ease*
voo (Eur.), vôo (Br.) (m) *flight*
vou (*see* ir)

xerez (m) *sherry*
xícara (f) *cup*

zero *zero, nought*
zona (f) *zone*

ENGLISH–PORTUGUESE VOCABULARY

The Portuguese words given below can be used on both sides of the Atlantic. Where there is a difference, the word is followed by the sign (Eur.) or (Br.), which stand, respectively, for European and Brazilian.

a / an *um* (m), *uma* (f)
about *acerca de*
accident *acidente*
accommodation *alojamento* (m)
address *endereço* (m)
admission ticket *entrada* (f) /
  ingresso (m) (Br.)
adult *adulto* (m)
aeroplane *avião* (m)
Africa *África* (f)
after, afterwards *depois*
after-shave (lotion) *loção após-barba* (f)
again *outra vez, novamente*
age *idade* (f)
ago *há*
ahead (straight on) *em frente*
air *ar* (m); air conditioning *ar*
  condicionado (m)
all *todo*
allergic to *alérgico a*
almost *quase*
alone, by oneself *só, sozinho*
also *também*
always *sempre*
ambulance *ambulância* (f)
America *América* (f)
American *americano* (m), *americana* (f)
and *e*
Anglican *anglicano* (m), *anglicana* (f)
animal *animal* (m)
answer (to) *responder*
anticipation (thanking in)
  antecipadamente, desde já
any *qualquer*
apartment *apartamento* (m)
apple *maçã* (f)
apply (to) for (job, course) *apresentar*
  candidatura

appreciate (to) *estimar*
approximately *aproximadamente*
April *abril* (m)
Arab *árabe* (m/f)
arm (body) *braço* (m)
arrival *chegada* (f)
arrive (to) *chegar*
artist *artista* (m/f)
as far as *até*
Asia *Ásia* (f)
Asian *asiático* (m), *asiática* (f)
ask (to) for *pedir*
ask (to), enquire *perguntar*
at *a, em*
attacker *assaltante* (m/f)
August *agosto* (m)
aunt *tia* (f)
Australian *australiano* (m), *australiana* (f)
away: to go away *ir(-se) embora*

baby *bebé* (Eur.)/ *bebê* (Br.) (m/f)
back (body) *costas* (f)
back: to be back *estar de volta*
bad *mau* (m), *má* (f) (Eur.) / *ruim* (m/f) (Br.)
bad(ly) *mal*
baggage *bagagem* (f)
baker's (shop), bakery *padaria* (f)
banana *banana* (f)
bank *banco* (m)
bar *bar* (m)
bath *banho* (m); to have a bath *tomar*
  banho
bathroom *casa de banho* (f) (Eur.) /
  banheiro (m) (Br.)
be (to) *estar; ser; ficar*
beach *praia* (f)
beachwear *roupa de praia* (f)
beard *barba* (f)

beautiful *belo, lindo*
because *porque, por causa de*
bed *cama* (f); double bed *cama de casal* (f)
beer *cerveja* (f)
before *antes*
begin (to) *começar*
behind *atrás*
believe (to) *acreditar*
belt *cinto* (m); safety belt *cinto de segurança* (m)
bill *conta* (f)
bird *ave* (f), *pássaro* (m)
black *preto*
blanket *cobertor* (m)
blue *azul*
boat *barco* (m)
boiled *cozido*
book (to) *marcar, reservar*
both *ambos*
Brazilian *brasileiro* (m), *brasileira* (f)
bread *pão* (m); wholemeal bread *pão integral* (m)
break *intervalo* (m)
break (to) *quebrar*
breakdown *pane* (f)
breakfast *pequeno almoço* (m) (Eur.) / *café da manhã* (m) (Br.)
bring (to) *trazer*
British *britânico* (m), *britânica* (f)
brother *irmão* (m)
brown *castanho* (Eur.) / *marrom* (Br.)
Buddhist *budista* (m/f)
building *edifício* (m)
bus stop *paragem de autocarros* (f) (Eur.) / *parada de ônibus* (f) (Br.)
bus, coach *autocarro* (m) (Eur.) *camioneta* (f) (Eur.) / *ônibus* (m) (Br.)
business *negócio* (m)
businessman *homem de negócios, comerciante* (m)
businesswoman *mulher de negócios, comerciante* (f)
but *mas*
butter *manteiga* (f)
buy (to) *comprar*

cake *bolo* (m)
camera (photo) *máquina fotográfica* (f); (video) *máquina de filmar* (f)
camper *campista* (m/f)
campsite *parque de campismo* (m) (Eur.) /

camping (m) (Br.)
can *poder, saber*
can, tin *lata* (f)
Canadian *canadense* (m/f) / *canadiano* (m), *canadiana* (f) (Eur.)
capital (city) *capital* (f)
car *carro* (m); by car *de carro*
card, form *ficha* (f)
carnival *carnaval* (m)
carrier bag *saco* (m) / *sacola* (f) (Br.)
cashdesk, check-out *caixa* (f)
castle *castelo* (m)
Catholic *católico* (m), *católica* (f)
cent *centavo* (m)
central heating *aquecimento central* (m)
centre *centro* (m)
cereal *cereal* (m)
change (small change) *(dinheiro) trocado* (m), *troco* (m)
change (to) *mudar*
cheap, inexpensive *barato*
check (to) *verificar*
cheese *queijo* (m)
chemist's (shop) *farmácia* (f)
cheque *cheque* (m); traveller's cheque *cheque de viagem* (m)
chest (body) *peito* (m)
child *criança* (f)
children's playground *parque infantil* (m)
Chinese *chinês* (m), *chinesa* (f)
chips *batata(s) frita(s)* (f)
choose (to) *escolher*
Christian *cristão* (m), *cristã* (f)
church *igreja* (f)
city *cidade* (f)
clean *limpo*
clean (to) *limpar*
clock: o'clock *hora(s)*
closed *fechado, encerrado*
clothes *roupa* (f)
club *clube* (m)
coat *casaco* (m)
coconut *coco* (m)
coffee *café* (m)
coin *moeda* (f)
cold *frio*
cold (have a) *estar constipado* (Eur.) / *resfriado* (Br.)
come (to) *vir*; come (to) in *entrar;* come (to) out *sair*
come (to) from (originally) *ser de*

computer *computador* (m)
connect (to) *ligar*
constipation *prisão de ventre* (f)
consulate *consulado* (m)
contact lens *lente de contacto* (Eur.),
   contato (Br.) (f)
cost (to) *custar*
country *país* (m)
couple *casal* (m)
course (of studies) *curso* (m)
credit card *cartão de crédito* (m)
crisps *batatinha(s) de pacote* (f)
cross (to) over *atravessar*
crossroads, junction *cruzamento* (m)
cupboard *armário* (m)
customs *alfândega* (f)

daily cost *diária* (f)
dairy shop *leitaria* (Eur.), *leiteria* (Br.) (f)
dark *escuro*
date *data* (f)
daughter *filha* (f)
daughter-in-law *nora* (f)
day *dia* (m)
dear, expensive *caro*
December *dezembro* (m)
dentist *dentista* (m/f)
deodorant *desodorizante* (m)(Eur.) /
   desodorante (m) (Br.)
departure *partida* (f)
diarrhoea *diarreia* (Eur.) / *diarréia* (Br.) (f)
dictionary *dicionário* (m)
diet *dieta* (f)
different *diferente*
difficult *difícil*
dinner *jantar* (m)
direct *directo* (Eur.)/ *direto* (Br.)
dirty *sujo*
disabled *deficiente*
disappear (to) *desaparecer*
disco, discotheque *discoteca* (f)
disembark (to) *desembarcar*
do (to) *fazer*
doctor *médico* (m), *médica* (f)
document *documento* (m)
dog *cão* (m) / *cachorro* (m) (Br.)
dollar *dólar* (m)
door *porta* (f)
double *duplo*
downstairs *lá em baixo* (Eur.) / *embaixo*
   (Br.)

dozen *dúzia* (f) half a dozen *meia dúzia*
dressed, get (to) *vestir-se*
drink (beverage) *bebida* (f)
drink (to) *beber*
drive (to) *conduzir* (Eur.) / *dirigir* (Br.)
driving licence *carta de condução* (f)
   (Eur.) / *carteira de motorista* (f) (Br.)
duty: on duty *de serviço*

early *adiantado*
earn (to) *ganhar*
east *este, leste* (m)
easy *fácil*
eat (to) *comer*
egg *ovo* (m)
eight *oito*
eighteen *dezoito*
eighty *oitenta*
either... or... *ou... ou...*
elderly person *pessoa de idade* (f)
electronic *electrónico* (Eur.) / *eletrônico*
   (Br.)
eleven *onze*
embark (to) *embarcar*
embassy *embaixada* (f)
emergency *emergência* (f)
empty *vazio*
end (to), finish *acabar, terminar*
engineer *engenheiro* (m), *engenheira* (f)
English *inglês* (m), *inglesa* (f)
enjoy (to) *apreciar, desfrutar (de)*; (like)
   gostar de
escalator *escada rolante* (f)
Europe *Europa* (f)
European *europeu* (m), *europeia* (Eur.) /
   européia (Br.) (f)
everyone *toda a gente* / *todo (o) mundo*
   (Br.)
everything, all *tudo*
except *excepto* (Eur.)/ *exceto* (Br.)
exchange (foreign currency) *câmbio* (m)

facility *facilidade* (f); *instalação* (f)
fall (to) *cair*
family *família* (f)
far *longe*
fare (ticket) *passagem* (f)
father *pai* (m)
father-in-law *sogro* (m)
February *fevereiro* (m)
feed *dar de comer*

fiancé, fiancée *noivo* (m), *noiva* (f)
fifteen *quinze*
fifty *cinquenta* (Eur.)/ *cinqüenta* (Br.)
fill (to) *encher*
filling station *posto de abastecimento /
    combustível / gasolina* (m)
find (to) *achar, encontrar*
fine (penalty) *multa* (f)
finger (body) *dedo* (m)
finish (to), end *terminar, acabar*
fire *fogo* (m)
first *primeiro*
fish *peixe* (m)
five *cinco*
flight *voo* (Eur.)/ *vôo* (Br.) (m)
floor *andar* (m)
flower *flor* (f)
food *comida* (f)
foot (body) *pé* (m)
for *para; to*
for (time) *há*
for, during *durante*
foreign *estrangeiro*
forget (to) *esquecer(-se)*
fork *garfo* (m)
forty *quarenta*
four *quatro*
fourteen *catorze, quatorze*
free *livre*; (gratis) *gratuito*
French *francês* (m), *francesa* (f)
Friday *sexta-feira* (f)
fried *frito*
friend *amigo* (m), *amiga* (f)
from *de*
front: in front of *em frente de*
frozen *gelado*
fruit *fruta* (f)
fuel *combustível* (m)
full *cheio*

garage *garagem* (f)
garden *jardim* (m)
gate *portão* (m)
German *alemão* (m), *alemã* (f)
get (to) up *levantar-se*
give (to) *dar*
glass (drinking) *copo* (m)
glasses, spectacles *óculos* (m); sun glasses
    óculos de sol (m)
go (to) *ir*; go (to) in *entrar;* go (to) out
    sair

gold *ouro* (m)
good *bom* (m), *boa* (f)
granddaughter *neta* (f)
grandfather *avô* (m)
grandmother *avó* (f)
grandson *neto* (m)
grant (to) *conceder*
grape *uva* (f)
green *verde*
grey *cinzento* (Eur.) / *cinza* (Br.)
group, party *grupo* (m)

hair *cabelo* (m)
hair spray *laca* (f) (Eur.) / *laquê* (m) (Br.)
hairdresser *cabeleireiro* (m)
hairdryer *secador de cabelo* (m)
half *meio*
ham *fiambre* (m) (Eur.) / *presunto* (m) (Br.)
hand *mão* (f)
handbag, purse *bolsa* (f)
happy *feliz, contente*
have (to) (drink, medicine) *tomar*
have (to) to *ter de / que*
he *ele*
head (body) *cabeça* (f); headache *dor de
    cabeça* (f)
hear (to) *ouvir*
heart (body) *coração* (m)
heat *calor* (m)
heavy *pesado*
help (to) *ajudar*
help! *socorro!*
here *aqui*
Hindu *hindu* (m/f)
hire (to) *alugar*
holiday (public) *feriado* (m)
holiday(s), vacation *férias* (f)
home *casa* (f) (going to) *para casa*; at
    home *em casa*
hope (to) *esperar*
hospital *hospital* (m)
hot *quente*
hotel *hotel* (m); hotel room *quarto* (m),
    apartamento (m)
housewife *dona de casa* (f)
how long? *há*
how much *quanto*
how? *como?*
hundred *cem, cento*
hurt (to) *doer*
husband *esposo* (m)/ *marido* (m)

hut *barraca* (f)
hypermarket *hipermercado* (m)

I *eu*
ice cold *gelado*
ice lolly *gelado* (m) (Eur.) / *picolé* (m)
   (Br.)
ice-cream, sorbet *sorvete* (m)
ID *documento de identidade* (m)
idea *ideia* (Eur.) / *idéia* (Br.) (f)
if, whether *se*
ill *doente* (m/f)
import duty *direito de importação* (m)
important *importante*
in *em*
in, inside *dentro*
inconvenience *incómodo* (Eur.)/
   incômodo (Br.) (m)
Indian (from India) *indiano* (m), *indiana*
   (f); (from America) *índio* (m), *índia* (f)
indigestion *indigestão* (f)
individual *individual*
industry *indústria* (f)
information *informação* (f)
insert (to) *introduzir*
inspection *fiscalização* (f)
instance, for *por exemplo*
insufficient *insuficiente*
insurance *seguro* (m)
intend (to) *tencionar*
interested *interessado*
interesting *interessante*
international *internacional*
introduction *introdução* (f)
introductory *de introdução a*
Irish *irlandês* (m), *irlandesa* (f)
island *ilha* (f)
Italian *italiano* (m), *italiana* (f)

January *janeiro* (m)
Japanese *japonês* (m), *japonesa* (f)
jewel *jóia* (f)
Jewish *judeu* (m), *judia* (f)
job *emprego* (m)
journalist *jornalista* (m/f)
journey *viagem* (f)
juice (fruit) *sumo de fruta* (m) (Eur.) /
   suco de fruta (m) (Br.)
July *julho* (m)
June *junho* (m)

key *chave* (f)
knife *faca* (f)
know (to) *saber, conhecer*

language *língua* (f)
large *grande*
last *último*
late (slow) *atrasado*
later *logo*; see you later *até logo*
laundry service *lavagem de roupa* (f)
lawyer *advogado* (m), *advogada* (f)
learn (to) *aprender*
leave (to) *partir, sair*
leave (to) behind *deixar*
left: on / to the left *à esquerda*
leg (body) *perna* (f)
leisure *lazer* (m)
lemon *limão* (m)
less *menos*
letter (message) *carta* (f)
lie (to) down *deitar-se*
lift (elevator) *ascensor* (m)/*elevador* (m)
light *claro*; (weight) *leve*
like *como*
like (to) *gostar de*
like this *assim*
likewise *igualmente*
list *lista* (f)
listen (to) *escutar*
litter *lixo* (m)
little *pouco*; a little *um pouco*
live (to) be resident *morar*
look (to) *olhar*; look after *olhar por*; look
   for *procurar*
lose (to) *perder*
lot: a lot of *muito*
love (to) *gostar muito de, amar* (person)
lunch *almoço* (m)

mainly *principalmente*
make (to) *fazer*
make-up *maquilhagem* (Eur.) /
   maquilagem (Br.) (f)
man *homem* (m)
mango *manga* (f)
map *mapa* (m)
March *março* (m)
margarine *margarine* (f)
married *casado* (m), *casada* (f)
May *maio* (m)
me *me*; to/for me *para mim*

mean (to) *significar, querer dizer*
meat *carne* (f)
medicine *medicamento* (m), *remédio* (m)
meet (to) *encontrar*
menu card *ementa* (f) (Eur.) / *cardápio* (m) (Br.)
milk *leite* (m)
million *milhão*
minute *minuto* (m)
miss (to) (transport) *perder*; (be missing) *faltar*
Monday *segunda-feira* (f)
money *dinheiro* (m)
month *mês* (m)
more *mais*
morning *manhã* (f); good morning *bom dia*
mother *mãe* (f)
mother-in-law *sogra* (f)
motorway *auto-estrada* (f)/*rodovia* (f) (Br.)
much *muito*
music *música* (f)
Muslim *muçulmano* (m), *muçulmana* (f)
must *dever*
my, mine *meu* (m), *minha* (f)

name *nome* (m)
napkin *guardanapo* (m)
nappy *fralda* (f)
nationality *nacionalidade* (f)
native town / city *cidade natal* (f)
near *perto;* nearby *perto daqui, aqui perto*
necessary *necessário*
neck (body) *pescoço* (m)
need (to) *precisar*
nephew *sobrinho* (m)
never *nunca*
New Zealander *neozelandês* (m), *neozelandesa* (f)
news *notícia* (f)
newspaper *jornal* (m)
next, near *próximo;* (time) *próximo, que vem*
nice, friendly *simpático*
niece *sobrinha* (f)
night *noite* (f); good night *boa noite*
nine *nove*
nineteen *dezanove* (Eur.) / *dezenove* (Br.)
ninety *noventa*
no, not *não*

no-one *ninguém*
noise *barulho* (m)
north *norte* (m)
nothing *nada*
November *novembro* (m)
now *agora*
number *número* (m)
nurse *enfermeiro* (m), *enfermeira* (f)

October *outubro* (m)
of *de*
office (public service) *secretaria* (f); (room) *escritório* (m)
often *muitas vezes*
oil *óleo* (m)
okay! *certo!, está bem!*
old *velho;* I am ... years old *tenho ... anos*
on *em*
one *um* (m), *uma* (f)
only *somente, apenas*
open *aberto*
open (to) *abrir*
or *ou*
orange *laranja* (f)
order (out of), damaged *avariado / com defeito* (Br.), *desarranjado* (Br.)
other, another *outro*
out, outside *fora*

pain, ache *dor* (f)
papaya *mamão* (m)
paper *papel* (m)
parasol *guarda-sol* (m)
pardon? *como (disse)?*
parents *pais* (m)
park *parque* (m)
parking *estacionamento* (m)
part: take part in *participar em*
party *festa* (f)
passenger *passageiro* (m), *passageira* (f)
passport *passaporte* (m)
pay (to) *pagar*
payment *pagamento* (m)
peach *pêssego* (m)
pear *pera* (f)
pen *caneta* (f)
pepper *pimenta* (f)
percent *por cento*
perhaps *talvez*
person, people *pessoa, pessoas* (f)

petrol *gasolina* (f)
photograph *fotografia* (f)
physically impaired *deficiente físico* (m/f)
pink *cor-de-rosa*
place *lugar* (m)
place (to), put *colocar*
plaster: sticking plaster *penso adesivo* (m)
(Eur.) / *esparadrapo* (m) (Br.)
plate (eating from) *prato* (m)
platform *plataforma* (f) / *cais* (m) (Eur.)
play (to) (game) *jogar*
please *por favor*
police (police force) *polícia* (f); policeman
/ woman *agente de polícia* (m/f)
Portuguese *português* (m), *portuguesa* (f)
possible *possível*
post office *correio* (m)
postcard *postal* (m)
poultry *ave(s)* (f)
pound *libra* (f)
prefer (to) *preferir*
present, gift *presente* (m)
price *preço* (m)
Protestant *protestante* (m/f)
pull (to) *puxar*
push (to) *empurrar*

question *pergunta* (f)
quickly! *depressa!*
quiet *calmo*

ready *pronto*
receipt *recibo* (m)
red *vermelho*
refrigerator *frigorífico* (m) (Eur.) /
geladeira (f) (Br.)
remember (to) *lembrar(-se)*
remind (to) *lembrar*
repair (to) *consertar*
report (to) *informar*
rest (to) *descansar*
restaurant *restaurante* (m)
retired *aposentado/reformado* (Eur.)
return (to) *voltar*; return (ticket) *ida e
volta* (f)
right: on / to the right *à direita*
ring *anel* (m)
road *estrada* (f)
route *caminho* (m)
run (to) *correr*

salt *sal* (m)

salty *salgado*
same: the same as *igual a*
sandwich *sande(s)* (f) (Eur.), *sanduíche* (f)
(Eur.) / *sanduíche* (m) (Br.)
sanitary towel *penso higiénico* (m) (Eur.) /
toalha higiênica (f) (Br.)
Saturday *sábado* (m)
say (to) *dizer*; how do you say ... in
Portuguese? *como se diz ... em
português?*
school, college *escola* (f), *colégio* (m)
Scottish *escocês* (m), *escocesa* (f)
sea *mar* (m)
secretary *secretário* (m), *secretária* (f)
seldom *raramente*
self-service *auto-serviço* (m)
sell (to) *vender*; sold out *esgotado*
send (to) *enviar*
send for (to) *chamar*
September *setembro* (m)
serious *grave*
seven *sete*
seventeen *dezassete* (Eur.) / *dezessete* (Br.)
seventy *setenta*
several *vários*
shampoo *champô* (m) (Eur.) / *xampu* (m)
(Br.)
shave (to) *fazer a barba*
shaving cream *creme de barbear* (m)
she *ela*
shellfish *frutos do mar* (m), *marisco(s)*
(m)
shoe *sapato* (m)
shop *loja* (f)
shopping *compras* (f); to go shopping
fazer compras
shopping centre *centro comercial* (Eur.) /
shopping (m) (Br.)
show (to) *mostrar*
shower *chuveiro* (m); *duche* (m) (Eur.) /
ducha (f) (Br.)
side *lado* (m)
signature *assinatura* (f)
silver *prata* (f)
since *desde*
single (hotel room, etc.) *simples*
single (ticket) *ida/simples*
single, unmarried *solteiro* (m), *solteira* (f)
sister *irmã* (f)
six *seis*
sixteen *dezasseis* (Eur.) / *dezesseis* (Br.)
sixty *sessenta*

sleep (to) *dormir*
slowly *devagar*
small *pequeno*
snack *lanche* (m)
some *algum*
something *alguma coisa*
sometimes *às vezes*
son *filho* (m)
son-in-law *genro* (m)
sorry! *desculpe!*
south *sul* (m)
South-african *sul-africano* (m),
  sul-africana (f)
souvenir *lembrança* (f)
Spanish *espanhol* (m), *espanhola* (f)
speak (to) *falar*
speed *velocidade* (f)
spell: how do you spell it? *como se
  escreve?*
spend (to) (money) *gastar*; (time) *passar*
spoon *colher* (f)
sport *desporto* (m) (Eur.) / *esporte* (m)
  (Br.)
square, precinct *praça* (f), *largo* (m)
stairs *escada* (f)
stamp *selo* (m)
start (to) *começar*
station *estação* (f)
stay (to) *ficar*
stomach *estômago* (m)
stop (to) *parar*
strawberry *morango* (m)
street, urban road *rua* (f)
student *estudante* (m/f)
study (to) *estudar*
sugar *açúcar* (m)
suit (to), be convenient *convir*
suitcase *mala (de viagem)* (f)
sunburn *queimadura de sol* (f)
Sunday *domingo* (m)
supermarket *supermercado* (m)
sweet *doce*

take (to), carry *levar*
talk (to) *conversar*
tax *imposto* (m)
taxi rank *praça de táxis* (f) / *ponto de táxi*
  (m) (Br.)
tea *chá* (m)
teach (to) *ensinar*
teacher *professor* (m), *professora* (f)

telephone *telefone* (m); mobile phone
  telefone portátil (m)
telephone (to) *telefonar*
telephone directory *lista dos telefones* /
  telefónica (Eur.) / *telefônica* (Br.) (f)
telephone operator *telefonista* (m/f)
television set *televisor/aparelho de
  televisão* (m)
tell (to) *dizer, contar*
ten *dez*
thank (to) *agradecer*; thank-you *obrigado*
  (m), *obrigada* (f)
that (one) *aquele, esse* (m), *aquela, essa* (f)
that (thing) *aquilo, isso*
that, which *que*
the *o* (m), *a* (f)
then *então*
there *aí; ali; lá*
there is / are *há*
think (to) *pensar*
thirteen *treze*
thirty *trinta*
this (one) *este* (m), *esta* (f)
this (thing) *isto*
thousand *mil*
three *três*
Thursday *quinta-feira* (f)
ticket *bilhete* (m); (fare) *passagem* (f)
time *tempo* (m); what time...? *que horas ...?*;
  take time *levar tempo*
time, occasion *vez* (f)
timetable *horário* (m); *tabela de horário*
  (f) (Br.)
tired *cansado*
to *a, para*
today *hoje*
toe *dedo (do pé)* (m)
together *juntamente*
toilet *sanitário* (m)
toilet paper *papel higiénico* (Eur.) / *papel
  higiênico* (Br.) (m)
toilet soap *sabonete* (m)
token *ficha* (f)
tomorrow *amanhã*
too much *demais*
toothpaste *pasta de dentes* (f) / *creme
  dental* (m) (Br.)
tourist office *agência de turismo* (f)
tourist spot *ponto turístico* (m)
town council *município* (m), *câmara
  municipal* (f)

town hall *câmara municipal* (f) or *paços do cancelho* (m) (Eur.)/*prefeitura* (f) (Br.)
toy *brinquedo* (m)
traffic lights *semáforo* (m)
train *comboio* (m) (Eur.) / *trem* (m) (Br.)
tram *eléctrico* (m) (Eur.) / *bonde* (m) (Br.)
transfer (passengers) *transbordo* (m)
try (to) *experimentar*
Tuesday *terça-feira* (f)
twelve *doze*
twenty *vinte*
two *dois* (m), *duas* (f); two-way ticket *ida e volta* (f)
tyre *pneu* (m)

umbrella *guarda-chuva* (m)
uncle *tio* (m)
underground train *metro* (Eur.)/ *metrô* (Br.) (m)
understand (to) *compreender, entender*
undressed, get (to) *despir-se*
until *até*
upstairs *lá em cima*
urgent *urgente*
useful *útil*
usually *habitualmente, normalmente*

vacant *vago*
vaccine *vacina* (f)
valid *válido*
vegetarian *vegetariano (m), vegetariana* (f)
very *muito*
view *vista* (f)
visa *visto* (m)
visit *visita* (f); business visit *visita de negócio(s)* (f)
visit (to) *visitar*

wait (to) *esperar*
wallet *carteira* (f)
want (to), will *querer*
wash (to) *lavar*
watch out! *cuidado!*
watch, clock *relógio* (m)
water *água* (f); drinking water *água potável* (f)
way *caminho* (m); way in, entry *entrada* (f), way out, exit *saída* (f)
we *nós*
weapon *arma* (f)

weather *tempo* (m); fine weather *bom tempo*, bad weather *mau tempo*
weather forecast *previsão do tempo* (f)
Wednesday *quarta-feira* (f)
week *semana* (f)
weekend *fim de semana* (m); at the weekend *no/ao fim de semana*
well *bem*
Welsh *galês* (m), *galesa* (f)
west *oeste* (m)
what...? *(o) que...?*
when *quando*
where *onde*
which? *qual?*
while, whilst *enquanto*
white *branco*
who? *quem?*
why? *por quê?*
wife *esposa* (f) / *mulher* (f)
window *janela* (f)
wine *vinho*; red *tinto*; branco *white*
wish (to) *desejar*
with *com*
with me *comigo*
without *sem*
woman *mulher* (f)
work (to) *trabalhar*; I work *estou empregado* (m), *empregada* (f)
work (to), function *funcionar*
worried *preocupado*
wounded *ferido* (m),
wrap (to) up *embrulhar*
write (to) *escrever*
wrong, incorrect *errado*

year *ano* (m)
yellow *amarelo*
yes *sim*
yesterday *ontem*
yoghurt *iogurte* (m)
you *você*; *tu*
young *jovem*

zero *zero*
zone *zona* (f)

INDEX TO GRAMMAR AND PROBLEM WORDS

LIST OF TOPICS